Analysing the Boundaries of the Ancient Roman Garden

Ancient Environments

Series Editors

Anna Collar, Esther Eidinow and Katharina Lorenz

The Ancient Environments series explores the worlds of living and non-living things, examining how they have shaped, and been shaped by, ancient human societies and cultures. Ranging across the Mediterranean from 3500 BCE to 750 CE, and grounded in case studies and relevant evidence, its volumes use interdisciplinary theories and methods to investigate ancient ecological experiences and illuminate the development and reception of environmental concepts. The series provides a deeper understanding of how and why, over time and place, people have understood and lived in their environments. Through this approach, we can reflect on our responses to contemporary ecological challenges.

Also available in the series

Mountain Dialogues from Antiquity to Modernity,
edited by Dawn Hollis and Jason König
Seafaring and Mobility in the Late Antique Mediterranean,
edited by Antti Lampinen and Emilia Mataix Ferrándiz
The Spirited Horse: Equid–Human Relations in the Bronze Age Near East,
by Laerke Recht

Analysing the Boundaries of the Ancient Roman Garden

(Re)Framing the Hortus

Victoria Austen

BLOOMSBURY ACADEMIC
LONDON • NEW YORK • OXFORD • NEW DELHI • SYDNEY

BLOOMSBURY ACADEMIC
Bloomsbury Publishing Plc
50 Bedford Square, London, WC1B 3DP, UK
1385 Broadway, New York, NY 10018, USA
29 Earlsfort Terrace, Dublin 2, Ireland

BLOOMSBURY, BLOOMSBURY ACADEMIC and the Diana logo are trademarks of
Bloomsbury Publishing Plc

First published in Great Britain 2023
Paperback edition published 2024

Copyright © Victoria Austen, 2023

Victoria Austen has asserted her right under the Copyright, Designs and
Patents Act, 1988, to be identified as Author of this work.

For legal purposes the Acknowledgements on p. viii constitute an extension
of this copyright page.

Cover design: Terry Woodley
Cover image © The villa of Poppea situated in the ancient Roman town of
Oplontis near Naples. Maria Luisa Corapi/Getty

All rights reserved. No part of this publication may be reproduced or transmitted
in any form or by any means, electronic or mechanical, including photocopying,
recording, or any information storage or retrieval system, without prior
permission in writing from the publishers.

Bloomsbury Publishing Plc does not have any control over, or responsibility
for, any third-party websites referred to or in this book. All internet addresses given
in this book were correct at the time of going to press. The author and publisher
regret any inconvenience caused if addresses have changed or sites have ceased
to exist, but can accept no responsibility for any such changes.

A catalogue record for this book is available from the British Library.

Library of Congress Control Number: 2022946914

ISBN: HB: 978-1-3502-6518-9
PB: 978-1-3502-6522-6
ePDF: 978-1-3502-6519-6
eBook: 978-1-3502-6520-2

Series: Ancient Environments

Typeset by RefineCatch Limited, Bungay, Suffolk

To find out more about our authors and books visit www.bloomsbury.com
and sign up for our newsletters

Contents

List of Figures	vi
Acknowledgements	viii
Preface	xi
Introduction: Defining Garden Space	1
1 Setting the Framework	11
2 Who Has the Time? Virgil, Columella and *Hortus* Poetry	29
3 Augustus' Garden Room? Re-Framing the *Ara Pacis Augustae*	61
4 *Distinguit et Miscet*: Framing Roman Villa Gardens	103
Conclusion: Seneca's *Thyestes* and the Anti-Garden	141
Notes	151
Bibliography	185
Index Locorum	207
Index	209

Figures

Unless otherwise stated, all images are the author's own.

1	Map of the Campus Martius (from Pollini 2012, University of Oklahoma Press)	63
2	3-D model of the *Ara Pacis* (from Pollini 2012, University of Oklahoma Press)	68
3	Interior wall decoration of *Ara Pacis* complex; representation of hanging garlands and wooden panelling	69
4	Plan of *Ara Pacis*, with identification of upper register panels (from Pollini 2012, University of Oklahoma Press)	73
5	Lower-register frieze panel, *Ara Pacis*	74
6	Livia's Garden Room, Museo Nazionale Romano (© ArchaiOptix 2015)	77
7	Niche painting featuring garden scene, 'Auditorium of Maecenas' (© Troels Myrup 2008)	79
8	'Red Room', Villa of Agrippa Postumus, Museo Archeologico Nazionale Napoli (© ArchaiOptix 2018)	80
9	Panel II, featuring central oak tree, Livia's Garden Room	82
10	Panel V, featuring central pine tree, Livia's Garden Room	83
11	Acanthus detail, *Ara Pacis*	84
12	Spiralling vine tendril, transforming into oak leaves, *Ara Pacis*	85
13	Pruned fruit trees, Panel I, Livia's Garden Room	92
14	Multiple perimeters at work, Panel V, Livia's Garden Room	95
15	Garden fresco, *oecus* 32, east wall, House of the Golden Bracelet (© S. Bolognini 2009)	104
16	Plan of Villa A at Oplontis (produced by Victoria I and James Stanton-Abbott)	108
17	Framing features, garden room 20, Villa A at Oplontis	118
18	West wall, garden room 20, Villa A at Oplontis	118
19	View from room 69, looking north into room 70, Villa A at Oplontis	121
20	View from room 74, looking south, Villa A at Oplontis	122

21	Rear (south) wall painting, room 61, Villa A at Oplontis (© S. Jashemski)	123
22	Painted column detail, south-east side of garden room 20, Villa A at Oplontis (© S. Jashemski)	126
23	Garden painting, north-west wall of room 70, Villa A at Oplontis	133
24	Garden paintings, south-west corner and west wall of room 68, Villa A at Oplontis	134
25	West wall panel with engaged columns featuring painted ivy detail, garden room 20, Villa A at Oplontis (© S. Jashemski)	135
26	Inside room 68, looking through in room 65, with room 61 in the distance, Villa A at Oplontis (© S. Jashemski)	137
27	Painted detail under window, exterior wall of room 78 facing on to large swimming pool garden, Villa A at Oplontis	138

Acknowledgements

This book is inextricably tied to my pandemic experience in Winnipeg. It began life in April 2020 as a product of my just-completed PhD, was accepted for publication at the beginning of 2021, and finally submitted in 2022 – the majority of the writing took place sitting at the desk in the corner of my living room, on an IKEA kitchen chair that was definitely not designed for extended periods of sitting, in spare moments found between Zoom classes. For better or worse, I will always associate the words written in these pages with the various stages of lockdowns and the added personal challenges that I experienced during this time. The past three years have been a time of immense transformation for me, on both a professional and personal level, and I am incredibly grateful for the support I have received that has allowed me to reach this point. There were many times I thought I would not make it, but here we are – and, although it is impossible to name everyone who helped me reach this point, I would like to acknowledge those individuals who have been integral to helping me throughout this journey.

Firstly, I would like to thank my colleagues and my students, past and present, in the Classics department at the University of Winnipeg – I simply could not have asked for a better department to begin my academic career. You welcomed me with open arms and have given me every opportunity to thrive and grow as a scholar and a teacher. At the time of writing this, I am just finishing my final semester at UofW, before moving to Carleton College, and I will be forever thankful for the friendships I have formed here and the lessons learned. Special thanks to Matt Gibbs, for taking a leap of faith on an unknown fellow Brit and giving me my first job; to Melissa Funke, for the confidence-boosting pep talks about my pedagogy projects, and for the outstanding Zoom trivia nights; to Conor Whately, for always indulging my interests in obscure agricultural texts and sharing so many of your teaching resources with me over the years; and to Alyson Brickey (an honorary member of the department thanks to Thursday or Friday drinks), for being the one person I can always rely on to get as excited about literary theory, Foucault and Derrida as I do.

The chair of the Classics department, Peter Miller, in conjunction with his wife, Carla Manfredi deserve a paragraph of their own. As a single person, living alone during a global pandemic, in a new city that I only moved to five months prior to Covid-19 times, my lockdown experience could have been extremely isolating. Peter and Carla (along with baby A!) never allowed that to happen, constantly checking in on me and offering me every type of support, both professional and personal, as part of the Miller-Manfredi family bubble. In fact, there were large blocks of time when Carla was the only other person I saw in the flesh. There were several months, during the strictest lockdowns, when I was only permitted to meet one person from a designated 'bubble', and only outside – Carla would meet me, religiously, twice a week to run together, even during the depths of the Winnipeg winter (a true sign of friendship!). These runs were like therapy for me, and a truly energizing experience.

Speaking of running, I would also like to take a moment to give a shout-out to the Winnipeg running community. I have run with many different groups within the city, each with their own vibe and their own special place in my heart. Again, there were many months when all our 'group' activities were virtual, but you were a constant source of support and that all-important mental break from my academic life. So, to the members of BridgeForks Run Club, FunRunCrew204, Winnipeg Run Club and Squad, thank you for inspiring me every day with your infectious positivity and inspiration; and to the OG Sufferun Crew, you are my heroes.

Outside of my Winnipeg pandemic bubble, there are several other individuals and groups who deserve a special mention. Thank you to William Fitzgerald, Michael Squire, Catharine Edwards, Diana Spencer, Lisa Hughes, Amy Russell, Phillip Thibodeau, and the members of the Columethods reading group, who have all acted as readers or interlocutors for part or all of the material in this final manuscript – the feedback and guidance I have received from these individuals contributed significantly to the ideas expressed in the book. Thank you to the Classics department at King's College London, for providing me with financial support to visit Italy during my PhD; this trip enabled me to visit and photograph the majority of the sites discussed in this book. Over the past couple of years, I have also been fortunate to receive pandemic-relief financial support from both the Women's Classical Caucus and the Classical Association of Canada. To #ClassicsTwitter, the team at Peopling the Past, and my fellow executive committee members at the Women's Network of the Classical Association of Canada, thank you for the memes, the gifs, the laughs, the support, and the solidarity. To my family and the High School OGs (Becky, Hannah and Sophie), thank you for your unwavering support from across the pond and also for the

UK care-packages (it is almost impossible to source Galaxy chocolate in Canada – a travesty).

Finally, this past year has been infinitely more enjoyable as a result of one person entering my life. Wilton, thank you for believing in me even when I did not believe in myself – and for all the Sunday pancakes. *Te quiero mucho.*

Preface

While our intention in writing this preface was to provide a neutral introduction that could stand for the whole series, recent events are too dramatic and relevant to ignore. As we launch the series, and write this text, we are (hopefully) emerging from the ravages of the Covid-19 pandemic. Along with the climate crisis, this experience has increased awareness of human reliance and impact on the environments we occupy, dramatically emphasized human inability to control nature, and reinforced perceptions that the environment is the most pressing political and social issue of our time. It confirms our belief that the time is right to situate our current (abnormal?) relationship with nature within an examination of human interactions with the environment over the *longue durée* – a belief that has given rise to this series.

Ancient Environments sets out to explore (from a variety of perspectives) different constructions of the 'environment' and understandings of humankind's place within it, across and around the Mediterranean from 3500 BCE to 750 CE. By 'environment' we mean the worlds of living and non-living things in which human societies and cultures exist and with which they interact. The series focuses on the *co-construction* of humans and the natural world. It examines not only human-led interactions with the environment (e.g. the implications of trade or diet), but also those that foreground earth systems and specific environmental phenomena; it investigates both physical entities and events and ancient, imagined environments and alternate realities. The initial and primary focus of this series is the ancient world, but by explicitly exploring, evaluating and contextualizing past human societies and cultures in dialogue with their environments, it also aims to illuminate the development and reception of environmental ideas and concepts, and to provoke a deeper understanding of more long-term and widespread environmental dynamics.

The geographical remit of this series includes not only the cultures of the Mediterranean and Near East, but also those of southern Europe, North Africa including Egypt, northern Europe, the Balkans and the shores of the Black Sea. We believe that encompassing this broader geographical extent supports a more dynamic, cross-disciplinary and comparative approach – enabling the series to transcend traditional boundaries in scholarship. Its temporal range is also far-reaching: it begins with the Neolithic (a dynamic date range, depending on location in the Near East/Europe) because it marks a distinct change in the ways in which human beings interacted with their environment. We have chosen c. 750 CE as our end date because it captures the broadest understanding of the end of Late Antiquity in the Central Mediterranean area, marking the rise of the Carolingians in the West, and the fall of the Ummayyad Caliphate in the East.

Our series coincides with, and is inspired by, a particular focus on 'the environmental turn' in studies of the ancient world, as well as across humanities more generally. This focus is currently provoking a reassessment of approaches that have tended to focus solely on people and their actions, prompting scholars to reflect instead (or alongside) on the key role of the environments in which their historical subjects lived, and which shaped and were shaped by them. By extending beyond the chronological and geographical boundaries that often define – and limit – understanding of the meaning of 'antiquity', we intend that this series should encourage and enable broader participation from within and beyond relevant academic disciplines. This series will, we hope, not only advance the investigation of ancient ecological experiences, but also stimulate reflection on responses to contemporary ecological challenges.

The editors would like to express heartfelt thanks to Alice Wright at Bloomsbury Press who first conceived of the idea and suggested it to Esther, and who has done so much to develop it, and to Georgina Leighton, in particular for her work in launching the series. We are extremely grateful to the members of the Series Board, who have provided such wonderful encouragement and support, and to our authors (current and future) who have entrusted their work to this 'home'. We have chosen the 'Mistress of Animals' or *Potnia Theron*, a figure found in Near Eastern, Minoan, Mycenean, Greek and Etruscan art over thousands of years, as the motif for the series.

Anna Collar
Esther Eidinow
Katharina Lorenz

Introduction: Defining Garden Space

Let us, then, begin by defining what a garden is, and what it ought to be . . .[1]

I begin this study by posing a seemingly straightforward question: what is a garden? Since gardens and the act of gardening are a feature of practically every human culture, our familiarity with 'the garden' as a concept suggests that we can easily recognize them as entities. However, *recognizing* gardens and actually *defining* them are two very different things; and the more we try to seek a definition for this type of space, the more our implicit knowledge of them becomes a hindrance to providing any sort of definitive set of necessary and sufficient conditions for all their potential features, appearances and purposes.

Providing a definition, though, is still a worthwhile exercise – as John Dixon Hunt has argued, if a subject is to be fully and usefully considered, it is useful to know its parameters and essential constituents.[2] It seems useful, then, before we embark on our journey down the *Roman* garden path, to seek to establish a definition of a garden that, first, captures reasonably well our current everyday understanding of the term; second, allows enough specificity to determine key characteristics; but also, third, allows enough flexibility to account for the variety of forms and functions that the garden space can take.

The garden as a bounded space

When scholars have attempted definitions of 'the garden' in the past, they continually assign two core principles to the space, albeit to various degrees – boundedness and cultivation. Miller, for example, hints at these principles when she states that a garden is a 'purposeful arrangement of natural objects'.[3] Pagán, meanwhile, lays them out explicitly:[4]

> A garden is a three-dimensional space within a clearly defined boundary, whose foundation is soil, in which plants are deliberately cultivated for the purpose of providing food or aesthetic pleasure.

Despite the many possible manifestations of what can constitute a garden, it seems that the majority of scholars always return to these same fundamental characteristics, defining the garden as a space segregated from its surroundings and one that is developed into something different from these surroundings through a process of cultivation.

The particular emphasis on boundedness is, in fact, so dominant that it is even reflected in the etymological origins of the word 'garden'. The Old Persian *pairidaeza*, formed of *pairi* (around) and *daeza* (fence), was the basis for the Hellenized *paradeisos* (a reserve containing wild animals to hunt and a garden for produce);[5] which, in turn, became 'paradise', a term deeply embedded in the Christian understanding of the Garden of Eden.[6] Similarly, other European and proto-European words for 'garden' all appear to share the same root association with enclosure: Old English *geard* (fence) developed into the modern English 'yard'; Indo-European *gher* (fence) and *ghort* (enclosure) are parents to the Greek *chortos* (an enclosed space used for growing food) and its Latin derivation *hortus* (garden);[7] and the modern Italian (*giardino*), Spanish (*jardin*) and French (*jardin*) terms for garden are all derived from the Vulgar Latin *gardinum* (enclosure). This shared etymological concern with boundaries and enclosure led van Erp-Houtepen, in her investigation of the European terminology for gardens, to conclude that 'put simply, the fence or wall is a basic and characteristic feature' of garden space, and that 'a garden without a fence is no longer a proper garden'.[8]

The notion of a boundary, however, does not have to entail the obvious physicality of a fence, nor does it just have to encompass spatial control. It can also be a way of concretely articulating the more complex conceptual separation of the garden from its surroundings. The garden, as we shall see, is different to other elements of the natural world, and what distinguishes these chunks of land is not just a physical boundary, but, also, the way in which we understand, connect to and interact with them. Returning to Miller's and Pagán's definitions, it is clear that to create a garden is not just to set a space apart from its surroundings, but also to cultivate that separated space to the point that it represents something 'different' compared to those surroundings. The 'purposeful arrangement' or 'deliberate cultivation' involved in creating a garden is representative of the gardener's ultimate aim of controlling nature enough in order to satisfy their needs, whether that be the physical need for food, the aesthetic need for pleasure, or the kinaesthetic need to move in, out or through space. This level of control represents something ideologically distinct compared to, say, a piece of farmland (which is also an enclosed 'natural' space), or an aesthetically pleasing, yet wild and un-tame forest.[9]

It is this combination of many different practical and aesthetic concerns within the garden that creates its unique conceptual identity, an identity that is physically reflected by the separation and control implemented by its boundary. This unique identity enables a variety of activities, which, in turn, endow the garden with a whole range of mythological, religious, socio-economic and even intellectual meanings.[10] In doing so, garden spaces invite us to think about the boundaries separating other literal and metaphorical dichotomies (beyond garden/not-garden), and to question how we might mediate between those categoric opposites. Therefore, although this is perhaps only hinted at by a simple definition, it is important to remember that the garden is much more than just a physical entity. To define it purely in spatial or physical terms would be to simplify its significance and limit its potential manifestations. The garden is both practical and ideological, physical and metaphysical, 'at once part of the real world – actual pieces of land – and also virtual worlds – coherent sets of possible sensory stimuli'.[11]

The garden as a microcosm of the ideal landscape

As such, gardens operate within the broader remit of 'landscape'. According to Spencer, landscapes are spaces demarcated by walls or boundaries, and, therefore, semiotically framed; they affect those who visit or inhabit them in ways more or less determined by culture and design; and they do not suggest raw or unmediated space, but rather, a collaboration between nature, humankind and the inhabited world.[12] There are several elements of this reading of landscape that are worth unpacking in relation to our definition of garden space. First, Spencer makes clear that 'landscape' is set aside, both physically and conceptually, from its surroundings, and it is therefore marked out as different in some way.[13] In this way, by designating an area as a landscape, we transform raw 'space' into a specific 'place', asserting discursive control so that 'what was previously unmarked and unseparated is now a site quilted into a fabric of meaning'.[14]

However, as Spencer's definition of landscape highlights, this fabric of meaning, this set of values that marks the landscape out as different, is not necessarily fixed, but, rather, determined culturally – so, although a place may be marked out physically in an objectively fixed way, that does not mean that every individual person interprets it subjectively in the same way.[15] By foregrounding cultural context and pointing to the subjectivity of the individual's experience within any given fixed 'place', Spencer's notion of landscape aligns with other sophisticated approaches to space, many of which have arisen in response to the seminal work of Lefebvre on *The Production of Space*.[16] In light of this work and other subsequent scholarship, space is now understood to play an active role in the constitution and reproduction of social identities, and social identities and relations are recognized as producing material and symbolic or metaphorical spaces — space and society do not merely interact with or reflect one another, but, rather, are mutually constituted.[17] For Lefebvre, space is a product of social relations, and precisely because it is a product of *active* practices, it should no longer be conceived as a static geographical entity; and it thus follows that landscape, as a subjective cultural product intrinsically linked to time and memory, can similarly provide a medium for the analysis of social identities.[18] Landscapes, then, although objectively marked out as individual places, still operate at the level of space in that they 'reflect and articulate practices of social behaviour', producing meanings that are 'dynamic and multiple thanks to the unpredictable ways in which they interact with their users over time'.[19]

It is in this context that garden space, as a form of landscape, has come to be understood as a powerful setting in which societies embed beliefs, myths and fictions.[20] A garden may well be a physical place, but it also has the power to transcend its physicality through the actions that take place there and the meanings those actions produce. Understanding landscapes requires understanding the 'forms of actions out of which they arise, to which they give expression, and to which they contribute';[21] and so, as Francis and Hester have argued, we cannot examine a garden as a physical place without probing the ideas that are generated within it and understanding the actions that created those ideas – the 'power of the garden' lies in its 'simultaneous existence as an idea, a place, and an action'.[22]

What is in general true of landscapes, then, is equally true of gardens – both are set aside as different, whether that be physically or conceptually, and both transform objectively defined locations into culturally informed sites imbued with specific, but ultimately subjective, meanings and frames of reference. Gardens, however, more than any other landscape, appear to be especially associated with a sense of physical boundedness, to the point where the very roots of the word 'garden' are tied to notions of enclosure; and it is this pointed association with the boundary that has led scholars to perceive the garden as a 'microcosm of the ideal landscape as it is understood by the culture that creates it'.[23]

Ambiguous edges?

Thinking about the garden as a landscape, then, and establishing *how* it is marked out as 'different' also forces us to interrogate the relationship between the garden space and its surroundings more closely, and to question how the notion of 'enclosure' can be understood as part of this relationship. One section of the *Lugale*, a Sumerian hymn and perhaps the oldest literary evidence of spatial segregation within the landscape, is an excellent demonstration of these issues.[24]

In one episode of this hymn, which recounts the deeds of the hero Ninurta, the fresh water of the earth, instead of flowing into the Tigris and watering the fields, flows uselessly into the *kur* ('wilderness').[25] Ninurta's dealings with the *kur* signify a transition from wilderness to civilization: he enters the *kur*, defeats the enemy Asag and piles stones of the *kur* into mountains that enclose Sumer and create a dam that returns the waters to the Tigris. Ninurta's blessing upon this new artificial landscape is significant:[26]

> Its valleys shall be verdant with vegetation for you,
> Its slopes shall produce wine and honey for you,
> Shall produce for you cedar, cypress, zabulum trees, and boxwood on
>   its terraces,
> Shall be adorned with fruit for you like a garden ['kiri'].

The root of this Sumerian story is that, from its origin as a wild and inimical space, the *kur* is transformed into a 'garden' (*kiri*) through an act of separation, which, in turn, leads to a protected safe space for cultivation and habitation.[27] The crucial point here is that, although the garden is 'other', it has been formed from the *kur* – it is both different to the *kur* but also related to it, made from it but no longer fully integrated within it, familiar and yet also alien. In creating his garden, Ninurta founds a proto-Eden for his people 'defined by its fundamental opposition to what was there before', yet what remains is a 'dynamic tension between the past and the present', between the *kur* and the *kiri*.[28]

Gardens, then, may well be experienced by the subject as a 'particular place ... enclosed by a clear boundary' and 'separated from a qualitatively differentiated outside world', but their situation remains 'ambiguous'.[29] The idea of a garden is often relative, 'based on perception and attitudes rather than any objective reality';[30] and, as is the case in the Sumerian hymn, when we actually go to analyse individual garden sites, we find that part of the issue in determining the limits of these sites, both physical and metaphorical, is the slipperiness of the seemingly obvious distinction between 'garden' and 'not garden'. Indeed, it is often easier to say what the garden *is not*, rather than what it actually *is*. We define the space explicitly through the notion of separation and division, but if we cannot actually make sense of the most basic divide, what use is it to characterize gardens by that notion?

In response to this question, I seek to interrogate the notion of 'the boundary' as an essential characteristic of the Roman garden and to explore the perception of Roman garden space in response to its limits and context. As already discussed, the basic Latin term for the garden – *hortus* – continues the etymological pattern of garden terminology as emphasizing enclosure; and the importance of delineating the garden in the Roman imagination is also reflected by the fact that garden boundaries are deemed worthy enough of protection by a specific god, Priapus.[31] As a rustic 'scarecrow' figure, defending the garden from would-be thieves and potential transgressors, Priapus' presence in the space is both a productive and prohibitive symbol; and literary depictions make it clear that the fertile god's often-exposed phallus is designed to act as crude warning against potential perpetrators:[32]

> *sed truncum forte dolatum*
> *arboris antiquae numen venerare Priapi*
> *terribilis membri, medio qui semper in horto*
> *inguinibus puero, praedoni falce minetur.*
>
> [seek] ... the rugged trunk
> of some ancient tree god which you may venerate
> in the midst of your garden as the god Priapus,
> who with his mighty member scares the boys
> and with his reaping-hook the looter.

The image of Priapic statues put forward here is further reflected in the use of real statues and paintings in houses in ancient Pompeii (such as the House of the Vettii), where Priapus' phallus is used as a way to monitor the threshold between different spaces and ward off the Evil Eye;[33] and, as a literary trope, the god has also been used as an invitation to think about other, more metaphorical, boundaries and the various dichotomies that play out within the Roman garden.[34]

It is important to make clear at this stage, though, that there is no singular form of 'Roman garden', and it is therefore crucial to set out the parameters of my study in order to make clear its specific aims and limitations. Using six case studies from across literature and material and visual culture, this book explores a series of individual garden sites all 'located' in either the city of Rome or the wider Italian peninsula, through a series of framing questions: what purpose do boundaries serve in each example? Why are they constructed in the way they are? How do they affect the relationship between the garden and the not-garden, the garden and the visitor, the garden and the viewer? And how does the notion of a garden boundary translate across real, represented and textual forms? My chosen case studies are formulated as three sets of comparative pairs, each representing a different 'type' of garden from one of the three broader categories of garden space of the Late Republican and Early Empire periods I identify in chapter one – utilitarian, sacred and ornamental.

In chapter two, I examine the 'original' Roman garden space (the *hortus*) and its relationship to the agricultural network it belongs to through an analysis of two literary treatments of the space – Virgil's *Georgics* 4.116–48 and the preface to Columella's *De Re Rustica* Book 10. Here, I consider whether the garden's bounded status constitutes an actual separation from the rest of the agricultural world it is situated within; and I explore the ways in which both poets articulate the ambiguous garden-agriculture relationship through the deliberate ways in which they structure and frame their garden texts. Chapter three, meanwhile, focuses on the shared botanical imagery of the *Ara Pacis Augustae* and Livia's Garden Room, reframing the *Ara Pacis* as a sacred grove purposefully constructed as part of an Augustan green landscape. My discussion here argues that the ways in which boundaries are constructed, represented and contested within the two artistic compositions creates an intersection between garden space and sacred space, an intersection that, in turn, reflects some of the ideological structures of the Augustan regime. Finally, in chapter four, I explore the garden spaces and paintings of Villa A at Oplontis in conjunction with the descriptions of ornamental villa gardens in Pliny the Younger's *Ep.* 2.17 and 5.6. My analysis in this chapter examines the extent to which the Romans regarded ornamental villa gardens as objects of artificially constructed viewpoints; and will demonstrate how the garden boundary operates as a porous membrane within the villa that challenges our sense of perspective and mediates between a series of oppositions.

By examining the ambiguities of Roman garden space across a number of different registers, this book highlights the importance of an intermedial approach to garden space, while still maintaining nuanced and critical analysis of individual garden sites. Despite an increase in examinations of Roman gardens, the study of these sites is still relatively new, and so it is perhaps unsurprising that the survey format of edited volumes has dominated the field thus far.[35] This has certainly been a positive approach for a developing field, since it provides both a recognition of the broad range of evidence available to us across different media sources, and also a foundational analysis of individual garden sites that can be used to identify and highlight potential avenues for further investigation. However, despite drawing on diverse sets of evidence, each individual contribution to these volumes tends to focus either on garden space solely from within the bounds of separate disciplines (art, archaeology, literature, botanical analysis, etc.), or they focus exclusively on one of the sub-categories of garden space without any cross comparison.[36] This division within the edited volumes, in turn, reflects a broader two-strand approach in the traditional study of Roman gardens, with scholars focusing on either material evidence (art historical or archaeological) to reach conclusions about what gardens *looked* like, or on literary treatments to reach conclusions on what gardens *meant* for the society that created them.

More recently, however, there have been increased examples of cross-media or cross-category analysis within the study of Roman gardens – a trend that reflects a broader application of sophisticated approaches to space by scholars of the ancient world following the 'spatial turn' post-Lefebvre.[37] Pagán, for example, has looked to literature to examine not only how the Romans thought about gardens, but, also, how they used the garden to think about and define themselves;[38] and Spencer has used specific garden sites and texts to explore how the Romans conceived of and responded to landscape.[39] von Stackelberg, meanwhile, is closest to a true intermedial analysis in her study of 'space, sense, and society' in the Roman garden, and she is correct in her claim that she is the first to examine Roman gardens using a combination of literary and archaeological evidence in conjunction with contemporary space theory.[40]

This book, then, builds on these more complex and nuanced approaches to garden space, but also responds to a particular weakness in scholarship by maintaining an intermedial focus *and* concentrating specifically on boundaries. My analysis within chapters two, three and four not only sheds light on familiar objects and texts from the fresh perspective of garden space, but it also expands current scholarship on more traditionally accepted Roman garden spaces through its focus on boundaries. This focus is critical since, despite broad acknowledgement of its integral role in delineating the space, the garden boundary has been largely neglected as a point of exclusive study.[41] By exploring the status of the six chosen gardens as they relate to, or are framed by, their individual contexts, my analysis across the three chapters will also demonstrate how the Romans of the Late Republic and Early Empire constructed garden boundaries specifically in order to open up or undermine the division between a number of oppositions, such as inside/outside, practical/aesthetic, sacred/profane, art/nature and real/imagined. Although the extent of this deconstruction, and the ways in which it is accomplished, varies across the individual garden sites and across different media, my analysis will highlight how the garden boundary does not simply police access and control, but, rather, acts as a porous membrane that mediates between a series of dichotomies.

Throughout my analysis, I seek to avoid one of the main difficulties of such an intermedial approach. When attempting to incorporate different media under one overarching category of 'garden space', it is all too tempting to try and unearth the 'true essence' of all the individual places. Logically, we want to find a meeting point between the different types of evidence and question what it is that brings them all together; and this introduction has indeed shown that 'the boundary' could well be that one essential characteristic that we attach to all gardens. However, as we examine the individual case studies, it will become clear that what is important is not so much a matter of what the different gardens have in common – in that they have a form of boundary – but, rather, how we use that notion of a boundary as a specific standpoint from which to analyse them;[42] and I will demonstrate that what is significant is not so much the boundary itself, but, rather, the delight in playing with concepts of boundedness and separation in order to deconstruct traditional dichotomies. The resultant liminal and interstitial nature of the garden will lead me to conceptualize its boundaries as more akin to frames, in that they not only delineate the space, but also load that space with meaning.

In this way, we will come to understand that, although Roman gardens of the Late Republic and Early Empire all demonstrate a basic adherence to the understanding of the garden as a marked-off and 'separate' space, they also all operate within broader spatial networks; and it is the relationship with these networks that creates such intriguing ambiguity and paradox within each individual garden site. Through an exploration of these ambiguities, this book contributes to the growing number of intermedial studies of Roman garden space by moving away from the traditional tendency of to 'consider objects, texts and sites in isolation from the networks in which they exist and which they help constitute';[43] and it establishes a series of theoretical frameworks, introduced in chapter one, that can be applied to the future study of individual garden sites from other periods and other regions.

So, let's dig in. . .

1

Setting the Framework

When Pliny the Elder, writing in the latter half of the first century CE, introduces his discussion of gardens, he claims that the subject is worth treating because of the intrinsic value of horticulture and because antiquity had admired and recorded famous gardens.[1] The diversity and volume of evidence for gardens in the Late Republic and Early Empire, ranging across the archaeological, art historical and literary registers, certainly seems to reflect Pliny's suggestion that garden culture held a particularly special place in the Roman imagination. However, as I have already noted, there is no singular form of Roman garden: we may use the term *hortus* as an equivalent to 'garden', but this was only one of many different terms used in the Latin language to denote a wide variety of spaces, all of which fall under a single overarching spatial categorization. Furthermore, there is plenty of flexibility in the designations used to describe individual garden sites, something which Roman writers seem all too happy to play with: Pliny, for example, uses the same phrase (*pensilos . . . hortos*) to describe both the cucumber beds of the emperor Tiberius and the famous Hanging Gardens of Babylon![2]

To begin this chapter, then, I will provide an overview of the sub-categorizations of Roman gardens, and highlight how, across the board, each category shows a basic adherence to the notion of a garden as a marked-off or bounded space. My discussion of these terms will reveal the three broader groups of garden types that informed my choice of case studies – utilitarian, sacred and ornamental villa – and it will also point to the fluidity of these groups, a fluidity that will be important to keep in mind as we approach the more specific analyses. There are many different ways one could choose to organize such sub-categories (design, location, function, ideological significance, etc.), but I have chosen to be guided by the terminology used for the various spaces and their semantic associations.[3]

The terminology of Roman gardens

In scholarship on Roman gardens, there is often a somewhat crude division between the 'practical' and 'aesthetic' garden forms, created by the difference in interpretation between the singular *hortus* and the plural *horti*. The singular form tends to refer to the 'traditional' vegetable or kitchen garden, governed primarily by practical needs and the requirement of *labor*.[4] Ideally, as Pliny the Elder describes, maintaining this type of garden was a job for the women of the household, who were responsible for cultivating enough produce and flowers for the house to be self-sufficient:[5]

> *hinc primum agricolas aestumabant prisci, et sic statim faciebant iudicium, necquam esse in domo matrem familias – etenim haec cura feminae dicebatur – ubi indeligens esset hortus, quippe e carnario aut macello vivendum esse.*

> People in the old days used to rate farmers by their garden produce, and thus at once gave a verdict that there was a bad mistress in the house when the garden outside (which used to be called the woman's responsibility) was neglected, as it meant having to rely on the butcher or the market.

In line with this utilitarian and productive perception of the *hortus*, Cato names this type of garden as one of the subdivisions of the larger rustic farm:[6]

> *Praedium quod primum siet, si me rogabis, sic dicam: de omnibus agris optimoque loco iugera agri centum, vinea est prima, si vino bono et multo est, secundo loco hortus inriguus, tertio salictum, quarto oletum, quinto pratum, sexto campus frumentarius, septimo silva caedua, octavo arbustum, nono glandaria silva.*

> If you ask me what is the best kind of farm, I should say: a hundred iugera of land, comprising all sorts of soil, and in a good location: a vineyard is first priority, if it produces a lot of wine of a good quality; second, a watered garden; third, an osier bed; fourth, an oliveyard; fifth, a meadow; sixth, grain land; seventh, a wood lot; eight, an arbustum; ninth a vast grove.

Pliny the Elder, meanwhile, re-affirms that it is 'proper' to have a garden 'adjoining' the farmhouse (*hortos villae iugendos non est dubium*).[7] Within this agricultural setting, Columella, a contemporary of Pliny the Elder, emphasizes the need to set up functional physical barriers around such garden spaces in order to control the access of both animals and humans. For example, he states that 'before you set the bounds [for a garden] … [you should] surround the bounds with a wall or a fence or a ditch' to 'deny a passage not only to cattle but to man'.[8] Later on, he reiterates that, once a site has been determined for a garden, it should be 'enclosed by walls or rough hedges';[9] and he also sets out a method for 'wall[ing] off a garden, from trespass by people or livestock, without major input'.[10]

This particular manifestation of the garden, as a paradigm of ancient rusticity, should be understood in conjunction with the 'myth of the peasant patriarch' in Roman thought, and can therefore be seen as a reflection of their deep-seated belief in the archaic agricultural origins of the national and civic identity.[11] Indeed, the Roman view of agriculture (and, thus, by extension, of the garden), so deeply rooted in tradition, contributed to a specific and targeted ideological construction for the land-owning elite.[12] Agriculture was considered the source of income *par excellence* for Roman senators – it was generally judged to be safe and secure as an economic pursuit and, perhaps more importantly, it was deemed socially acceptable as a form of commerce.[13]

On the opposing side of the supposed 'practical' vs. 'aesthetic' binary, we find the space of the *horti* – peri-urban 'ornamental' estates owned by the Roman elite, situated on the fringes of the city of Rome and beyond.[14] Of course, the 'original' *hortus* did not simply cease to exist, but sources do indicate that there was a gradual shift in focus from production to pleasure starting in the first century BCE, and this was accompanied by a lexical shift from the singular *hortus* to the plural *horti*.[15] Pliny the Elder credits the Greek philosopher Epicurus as 'inventing' the concept of *horti*, particularly emphasizing the inclusion of these green spaces within an *urban*, as opposed to a more agricultural, landscape:[16]

> *iam quidem hortorum nomine in ipsa urbe delicias agros villasque possident. Primus hoc instituit Athenis Epicurus otii magister; usque ad eum moris non fuerat in oppidis habitari rura.*

> Nowadays, under the name of gardens, people possess the luxury of farms and villas actually within the city. This practice was first introduced at Athens by Epicurus, that master of leisure; before this, the custom had not existed to have country dwellings in towns.

The earliest well-known examples of these neither truly 'urban' nor fully 'rural' *horti* belonged to some of the key political figures of the Late Republic;[17] and references to these spaces align with many of the political rivalries and activities of this period.[18] Pompey, for example, used his gardens on the Campus Martius to hand out lavish donations to Rome's votes as bribery;[19] the Gardens of Lucullus are historically viewed negatively as a symbol of the owner's apolitical withdrawal into frivolity and excess;[20] and Caesar's gardens are known predominantly through his final political acts, in which he left the space in his will to the Roman people, cementing his popularity with the plebs.[21]

However, although we know about *horti* from inscriptions and texts, limited physical evidence survives;[22] and, as result of our reliance on (ideologically charged) literature, these spaces are unfortunately 'apt to be misappropriated by scholarly investigators' and pitted against the simplicity and self-sufficiency of the *hortus* as just another 'set of topoi in the repertoire of Roman luxury'.[23] Indeed, commentators, both ancient and modern, have often viewed the reported shift in taste towards pleasure and aesthetic beauty as a reflection of Roman moralizing discourse, where the growth of Rome's territory is blamed for the decline in simple virtues in favour of a system of personal wealth and a desire for luxury. Myers, for example, has documented the range of associations between the new ornamental gardens and morally unacceptable luxury and excess:[24] in the moralistic writings of authors such as Horace, both Senecas and Pliny the Elder, garden features were frequently condemned as a luxurious and unnatural perversion of nature;[25] in Tacitus' accounts of Messalina and Agrippina in the *Annals*, he represents gardens as places of perverse power plays;[26] and, finally, building on the associations between gardens and Late Republican leaders, gardens are also frequently used in invective against Roman emperors as a sign of luxury and perverse behaviour.[27]

Such passages have led to an echoing of the Roman sentiment in modern scholarship. Lawson, for example, states that 'the vitalizing energy of the Republic found an outlet in the productive vegetable plot [while] the elaborate but sterile gardens of the Empire were symbolic of incipient decay';[28] and, similarly, Pagán argues that 'the difference between *hortus* and *horti* can also be measured in terms of fertility and sterility . . . the less usable the produce the garden yields, the more morally suspect it becomes.[29] Coincidence or not, the temporal alignment of the increase in *horti*, the supposed shift away from productivity and the gradual collapse of the Republic certainly make all of these associations appealing. However, as Purcell has suggested, we must approach such associations with caution, since it could be argued that the *horti* of Rome were not really gardens at all, but, rather, 'select *suburbana* . . . lavish residences first, and landscape fantasies next' that merely played with the paradox of urban and rural further than ever before.[30]

Although the *horti* of the Late Republic are particularly hard to categorize, there were green spaces within the city of Rome that we can more easily call 'pleasure parks' or 'gardens' – *porticus*.[31] Essentially enclosed public parks, this type of garden quickly became a prominent feature within the city; and, unlike many *horti*, we are able to confidently reconstruct some of these spaces – such as the *Porticus Pompeiana* and the *Porticus Liviae* – based on literary and archaeological evidence.³² These porticoed gardens were designed to imitate the Greek *gymnasia*, with large green areas featuring covered walkways (hence 'porticus') designed to give shade and seclusion. Interestingly, Farrar suggests that this adoption of Hellenistic porticoes to enclose these public garden spaces may have been partially motivated by the need to distinguish the greenery from the surrounding streets, since maps locating the ancient portico gardens of Rome reveal their close proximity to other structures; and this suggestion fits once again with our understanding of the garden space as being deliberately set-aside and bounded.³³

As we shall see in chapter three, many of these public parks also had sacred or religious connotations. The *Porticus Pompeiana*, for example, was a space for public entertainment and leisure, but the inclusion of the Temple of Venus Victrix within the green space suggested that 'the garden was [also] a sacred *kēpos*, a planted enclosure dedicated to the service of a god and a temple';³⁴ and, similarly, Caesar's gardens were part of a building programme that promoted Venus as the mother of the *gens Julia*.³⁵ Roman religion was deeply connected to agricultural and vegetal deities, so it comes as no surprise that *religio*, the sense of divine reverence, also extended to garden spaces.³⁶ Indeed, according to Neudecker, only in mythical retrospective did religious experiences of nature ever take place in entirely untouched environments, whereas, in reality, they always happened in more or less ordered spaces, in nature treated or tamed by human hands.³⁷ As part of, in addition to, or alongside a *horti* or *porticus*, such 'sacred groves' thus fulfil our basic definition of garden space in that they are a form of constructed nature, based on the fundamental action of 'cutting out' a specific area of land and designating it as 'other'.³⁸

The connection between religious practice and garden space can also be seen through the presence of garden altars or shrines (*lararia*) in many houses.³⁹ These cultic sites were prominent features in Pompeian households, and, significantly, approximately one-fifth of all these household shrines were located within garden spaces.⁴⁰ The shrine or altar could be constructed in the form of a niche, an *aedicula* or simply a wall painting, and they featured two common elements: first, a representation of the god to be worshipped; and, second, some provision for sacrifice. Most of these shrines tended to be dedicated to the worship of the *Lares* or the *Penates*, but there is also evidence for the worship of other gods such as Diana (House VII.6.3) or Hercules (House II.8.6).⁴¹

The religious or sacred connotations of Roman garden space also extended to the funerary context in the form of tomb gardens (*cepotaphium*).⁴² Unfortunately, evidence for plantings, in the form of root cavities, is seldom encountered at actual tomb sites, but there are many texts and inscriptions that can account for their existence and design, as well as examples of tombs decorated with garden paintings.[43] An inscription from a tomb in Rome, for example, describes the site as being planted with vines, fruits, flowers and greenery;[44] further afield, an inscription in Gaul provides a detailed description of a large tomb garden that would require the assistance of three landscapers for its upkeep;[45] and there are also two surviving plans of garden tombs on marble plaques.[46] What is particularly interesting about many of the inscriptions still available to us is that they include the phrase '*hortus cinctus maceria*', thus emphasizing that the tomb garden in question was surrounded by a wall or enclosure.[47] In this sense, then, tomb gardens appear no different to other gardens, but, as with other religious or sacred garden spaces, it appears that it is particularly easy to incorporate gardens into funerary sites because of their shared emphasis on well-defined perimeters.[48] As Bodel has noted, the site of a Roman tomb was a *locus religiosus*, a place bound by *religio* and therefore not liable to any other use, and inscriptions showcase how Roman tomb owners tried to protect the cultivated lands attached to their monuments by declaring them inalienable from the tomb itself.[49]

Finally, in this brief survey of Roman gardens, let us consider the more 'ornamental' types found in a domestic context. We have already noted that garden shrines were a prominent feature within Roman households, but this was certainly not the only type of garden space found in the *domus* or the *villa*. The earliest known evidence for domestic gardens in Pompeii reflects the characteristics of the traditional *hortus*: in the House of the Pansa, for example, one of the most significant examples of the old Samnite-style houses, the rear garden reveals a perfectly preserved planting pattern design for produce, the layout of which reflects the horticultural advice given by Pliny the Elder.[50] However, in line with the development of the so-called *horti* and *porticus* structures in the city of Rome, a more ornamental focus and shift to aesthetic pleasure quickly disseminated throughout domestic gardens from the second century BCE.[51] This was not just a trend enjoyed by the upper echelons of Roman society in their sprawling villas; but, rather, it appears to be a cultural shift that filtered down into even the most modest of homes.[52] It should, of course, be noted, though, that even with the distinct shift from a focus on production to aesthetic pleasure, this was by no means a linear progression – 'productive' gardens did still exist in a domestic context, and archaeological evidence demonstrates that some 'ornamental' gardens also produced food.[53]

The introduction of the so-called 'peristyle' garden design, in particular, dramatically changed the style, layout and ideological significance of Roman domestic gardens, and, in a similar way to the *porticus*, these more ornamental garden types within the home are predominantly labelled by scholars in reference to the main architectural structure that surrounds them.[54] Originally imprinted on to the old *hortus*, wherever that be located, later examples show an evolution towards a more consistent and intentional central location within the building;[55] and, in line with the design of the *porticus*, these new peristyles were ideally surrounded by four covered walkways supported by a series of columns (although sometimes fewer walkways, if space did not allow it). The material record of the gardens of Pompeii makes clear that fences or other partitions were an important aspect in the design of the peristyle, despite there no longer being any functional requirement to keep cattle or people out (as was the case for Columella).[56] Although occasionally enclosed by a low masonry wall, more often than not it was a wooden fence that created the boundary between the centralized green space and the surrounding walkways:[57] the two holes found in many columns surrounding garden spaces, often with pieces of heavy nail still inside them, indicate that a fence had once been attached.[58] Sometimes a vertical cut was made in the columns to accommodate the end of a piece of fence;[59] or, alternatively, the fence was attached to the end of the columns, thus enclosing them.[60]

However, although the term 'peristyle' has become a byword for all domestic gardens that are not a *hortus*, it is actually only one of many terms used by ancient authors to signify garden spaces of the more 'ornamental' or 'aesthetic' variety. Vitruvius, for example, in *de Architectura*, employs a range of terminology to denote cultivated garden landscapes:[61] not just *hortus*, or *porticus*, or *peristyle*, but also *silvae*, a luxury plantation;[62] *topia* or *ars topiara*, the art of arranging plants into shapes to evoke certain associations;[63] *viridia*, a novel display of well-arranged plants;[64] and also *xystus*, garden walkways.[65] Furthermore, in her examination of the Vitruvian terminology, Leach notes that 'peristyle' appears interchangeable with other labels, such as *gymnasium* and *palaestra*, which emphasize the columned design; and also less technical terms, such as *ambulacrum*, which emphasize the space's function.[66] Whether or not the term 'peristyle' is specifically used, though, and whether or not the garden space is actually surrounded by a true peristyle structure, what we can say about this group of domestic gardens is that they all represent the same ideological shift away from production that we saw in the *horti* and *porticus*-spaces of Rome.

The peristyle structure itself also crystallizes an important aspect of the way boundaries function in many of the garden spaces we will encounter – namely, the way in which physical boundaries often act as manifestations of more conceptual or metaphorical frameworks. Zarmakoupi, for example, argues that the peristyle structure acts as an architectural framework for ornamental garden space that mediated between associations of discipline and excess to create a space of aesthetic pleasure that was specifically acceptable to the Romans of the Late Republic and Early Empire periods.[67] Although ornamental green spaces had previously evoked the 'excessive *luxuria* of the Hellenistic East', by 'subordinating' this potentially excessive pleasure element to the disciplined architectural form of the Greek *gymnasia*, the Roman peristyle garden design created an enclosed green space wherein the 'unruly nature of the corrupting Eastern influence' could be tamed.[68] Thus, 'by framing the architecture of pleasure within the architecture of discipline ... [in the form of the peristyle] ... Roman designers domesticated the threatening *luxuria* of the Hellenistic East and used architectural design in the construction of their identity'.[69]

This architectural framing of green space here, and the ideological mediation between discipline and excess, also points to another layer of mediation at work, this time between 'closed' (interior) and 'open' (exterior/outdoor) space – the typical location of the peristyle often leads to it being a focal point in the flow of space throughout the *domus* or *villa*, and this, in turn, gives the space the feel of a transitional zone. Leach, for example, describes the peristyle garden's function as 'giving an elegant route of access to other privileged rooms in the house'; and she suggests that 'with the orderly files of columns, the physical appearance of the peristyle signals passage', and 'its function as a walkway' is 'usually highlighted by repetitive patterns of wall design with strong vertical orientation to reinforce that of the columns'.[70] In this way, the peristyle quite obviously acts as a space of mediation and transition between different domestic spaces; and, as I will demonstrate in my case study analysis, mediation between oppositions is key to how boundaries function across the many manifestations of garden space.

Issues with categorization

What can we take away, then, from this short summary of garden types within the Roman imagination of the Late Republic and Early Empire? For the Romans, the garden was, just as it is today, a recognizable and defined space within their environment that could entail a variety of designs and format, each providing a setting for, or a backdrop to, a whole range of horticultural, artistic, social, theological and even political activities and practices. Furthermore, despite the range of cultivated spaces that fall under the category of gardens, we can identify three broad sub-categories of the space – utilitarian, sacred (or religious) and ornamental – and each of the spaces within these sub-categories demonstrates a basic adherence to the transcultural understanding of the garden as a marked-off or segregated space – whether that be in the form of fences to keep cattle out, walls to designate the sanctity of a specific zone, or columns and partitions that mark the transition into a 'different' part of the domestic space.

However, despite the ubiquity of boundary elements, the ways in which the Romans used their garden terminology reveals underlying tensions within the categorization of their garden spaces. Indeed, although modern scholars have used the term *hortus* to signify a whole range of garden spaces, it is clear that between the term and its translation as 'garden' lies an 'ambiguity of meaning that stands as an obstacle' to understanding the full breadth of its potential manifestations.[71] This ambiguity is highlighted by the broad range of other terms also used by the Romans to denote the different sub-categories within their overall notion of 'the garden', and the ways in which they appeared to struggle to definitively distinguish, label and identify different spatial areas. In particular, we noted how the lexical shift from *hortus* to *horti* does not necessarily denote a linear progression from production to pleasure; and how architectural terms, such as *porticus* and *peristyle*, could be used both to denote a specific area or an architectural structure within the *horti* or a *domus* or *villa*, and also as interchangeable terms for the garden space as a whole. Finally, it is also clear that all these garden sub-categories operate, to varying degrees, within broader spatial networks or categories – whether that be a large agricultural complex, a public park, a vast villa, a modest house or a sacred site – and despite the emphasis on the garden's 'otherness', quite how each garden site is separate from its networks is something that is not always obvious.

If we reflect back on the Sumerian hymn outlined in my introduction, it appears that, in the Roman imagination, there is a similar tension between defining the garden through physical segregation and struggling to conceptualize the basic divide between garden and not-garden space. Although the garden may be thought of as 'other', it is not always exclusively 'separate' – gardens remains intimately connected to the rest of their surroundings to the extent that the boundary between garden and not-garden, and also the distinction between different types of gardens, at times involves little distinction at all.[72] Furthermore, the emphasis on physical boundaries, which automatically suggest a division between two categories, also points to the garden's role in mediating between these categories, and all of their accompanying (and often problematic) tensions. Roman garden space cannot, and perhaps should not, be categorized in the black and white sense that its boundaries suggest. It is a grey, fuzzy, interstitial space open to many possible interpretations.

Approaching ancient Roman garden space

How, then, should we approach an analysis of these ambiguous, and potentially problematic, spaces, presented to us through a wide range of evidence? Is it possible to further our understanding of individual Roman gardens by combining critical and nuanced analysis of each site's boundaries with an overall theoretical framework that also allows for intermedial analysis?

von Stackelberg proposes Soja's concept of 'Thirdspace' as a 'critical framework' through which we can approach the garden space and its 'interplay of multiple associations'.[73] Soja's framework seeks to demonstrate an important intersection between real world perspectives ('Firstspace') and imagined representations of that same world ('Secondspace').[74] Within this tripartite formulation of space, Thirdspace is understood as a space of extraordinary openness and critical exchange; and, most significantly, the concept seeks to reject traditional binaries or dichotomies and, instead, establish a space wherein perspectives previously considered incompatible can be encompassed to create postmodern 'both/and also' analyses, rather than simple 'either/or' conclusions.[75]

For von Stackelberg, then, Firstspace is formed of the material garden and its constituent parts (trees, lawns, flowerbeds, ornaments, etc.), Secondspace consists of representations (pictorial and literary) of this material reality, and Thirdspace is the lived and practice reality of the garden or, to put it another way, the cultural value of the activities and events that are located there. In her application of Soja's framework, the author uses Thirdspace to comprehend how potentially alternate physical realities and literary conceptions of garden space can be perceived as a 'palimpsest, with one overlying the other';[76] and she argues that the true essence of what constitutes the garden space cannot be fully embodied in either Firstspace or Secondspace but, rather, it exists in a Thirdspace between the two. von Stackelberg thus demonstrates how Thirdspace can be a useful platform from which to approach Roman gardens, since it allows us to step back from individual sites, texts or representations by 'relocating the garden within the wider framework of conceptual space'.[77]

Her approach is therefore important in pointing to a way of understanding my intermedial case studies, and it will be useful for considering the interaction between the different types of gardens I discuss (agricultural vs. sacred vs. ornamental villa), and also the different types of media (literary vs. artistic vs. archaeological) – the Thirdspace model allows us to locate the 'essence' of the garden space *between* these categories without naively forcing them together. This shift away from an insistence on traditional binary oppositions, a central tenet of

Thirdspace, also points to the heart of my own argument. My analysis will highlight how traditional binaries (such as inside/outside, practical/aesthetic, sacred/profane, real/imagined) still exist – the underlying structures are still there – but they are also consistently undermined, reworked or played with. Thus, by rejecting a strictly dialectic approach to the space, in which all oppositions create contestations, my alignment with a tripartite framework will allow the so-called oppositions on display within each garden site to 'operate *around* one another in a less direct way'.[78]

In my adherence to a Thirdspace-type framework, my approach also recognizes the emergence of so-called 'heterotopias', a category of space proposed by Michel Foucault in which 'the nature of the spaces of the world is debated and also produced', and a category within which we can include garden space.[79] According to Foucault, the space in which we live, the space that 'claws and gnaws at us' should not be interpreted as a void 'in which we place individual and things', but rather as a 'set of relations' irreducible to simple distinctions.[80] Within this set of relations, Foucault is interested in looking at a category of sites that have the 'curious property of being in relation' to all other sites, but in such a way as to 'suspect, neutralize, or invert the set of relations that they happen to designate, mirror, or reflect' – such spaces, such 'heterotopias', are linked to all other sites, while also contradicting them, outside of all place, and yet also possible to locate in reality.[81]

Foucault attaches a set of six principles to the concept of heterotopia, with a diverse range of examples:[82] 1) they are a constant of every human culture, but can arise in diverse forms; 2) just as any given society can evolve through time, so too can any given heterotopia function in a different fashion according to the demands of this evolution; 3) they are capable of juxtaposing several seemingly incompatible spaces within a single space; 4) they are intrinsically linked to time, encapsulating either temporal discontinuity or accumulation; 5) they presuppose a system of opening and closing that both isolations them and makes them penetrable; and 6) they have the ability to function in relation to all the space that remains, either as a space of illusion or compensation.[83] Foucault's description of heterotopia thus suggests that these spaces are sites of difference, simultaneously central to a culture, yet also designated as areas where the 'normal' rules of that culture are suspended, neutralized or reversed.

Most significantly, Foucault identifies the garden as 'perhaps the oldest example' of these 'contradictory sites', in that they are both 'the smallest parcel of the world' and also the 'totality of the world'.[84] His brief, but intriguing, suggestion that the garden should be understood as a heterotopia has subsequently found its way into the analysis of Roman garden space. Pagán, for example, takes the categorization seemingly at face value, merely noting that the term is a useful way of describing the garden space: constructed by society (first principle), but varying in design and function (second principle), the garden represents a microcosm of the world (third principle), maintained through seasonal activity (fourth principle), that is both separate from, and related to, the rest of space (fifth/sixth principle).[85] von Stackelberg also identifies the ancient Roman garden as a heterotopia, particularly picking up on the 'persistent association' between the concept and notions of resistance and/or transgressions;[86] and, since we know the garden is so frequently associated with boundaries, it is unsurprising that such a space would invite transgression through the crossing of those boundaries.

This, more specific, application of Foucault's term has been put forward by scholars from other disciplines, such as Hetherington, who argues that heterotopias are 'sites of marginality that act as postmodern spaces for resistance and transgression – treating them in many way as liminal spaces';[87] and Genocchio, who applies the term to 'counter-sites embodying a form of resistance to our increasingly surveyed, segregated and simulated socio-spatial order'.[88] It is in this context, then, that von Stackelberg repositions the ancient Roman garden, arguing that the liminality of the space encourages 'encounters that diverge from the social norm'.[89] Pagán, meanwhile, also explores the notion of transgression in the garden in response to the frameworks imposed by the satiric genre. Although she does not use the term heterotopia specifically in her discussion, her earlier acknowledgement of the ancient garden as an example of this type of space surely informs her conclusion that the garden is a 'logical symbol' for satire, a genre 'obsessed with social hierarchy and the distasteful transgressions of strictly imposed boundaries'.[90]

Rather than focusing on Roman gardens as 'heterotopias of deviation', though, my study is most concerned with the 'relational disruption between space and time' that forms part of the heterotopic discourse, and how this can help us understand and analyse the construction, and potential deconstruction, of the boundaries of space and time within each of my garden settings.[91] As detailed above, according to Foucault's fourth principle, a heterotopia is a space often linked to time – they are 'heterochronias' that 'function at full capacity' when we arrive at 'an absolute break' with 'traditional' time[92] – and it is within this context that I too will consider the 'temporal discontinuities' of the Roman garden.[93] Each of the garden sites I explore engages with a combination of different, and potentially conflicting, temporal frameworks, and we will find that the way in which these frameworks work in conjunction with one another is what leads to the each garden's specific and unique identity.

In chapter two, for example, I explore how the temporal structures at play in Virgil's garden *excursus* (*G.* 4.116–48) are able to inform us on the connection between the garden space and the agricultural network it is situated within; and I will demonstrate how the inclusion of opposing and alternative dimensions of time within the passage is a direct reflection of two different, yet, simultaneous relationships between gardens and agriculture. Similarly, in chapter three, I reflect on how the representations of garden space within the compositions of the *Ara Pacis* and Livia's Garden Room demonstrate a resistance to conventional temporal structures; and how this resistance creates an intersection between garden space and sacred space that becomes a key part of the construction of ideological and political frameworks.

The disruption of time within heterotopic space is also often matched by the disruption of space itself, something explicitly illustrated in Foucault's example of the mirror. Although the mirror itself is a 'placeless place', it is also an actual site that disrupts our spatial position – 'the space occupied is at the same time completely real and unreal, forming an utter dislocation of place'.[94] Indeed, the positioning of the heterotopia at the intersection of theoretical axes of imaginary/real and normal/other effectively renders it a mirroring space imbued with inversionary possibilities.[95] Foucault sees heterotopia as 'counter-sites' in which 'all the other real sites that can be found within culture are simultaneously represented, contested and inverted';[96] and this mirroring or inversionary function is then complemented by the overarching ambivalence of heterotopia where boundaries and binary thinking are held in 'productive suspension'.[97]

My analysis in the following chapters will thus demonstrate that the garden, as both a physical artefact and a palimpsest of multiple other dimensions, has the potential to become a space of illusion – a heterotopic placeless place – that utilizes literal and metaphorical constructs in order to contest binaries of space and time. In fact, the dislocation of space will be a key feature across the individual garden sites, as we will be repeatedly forced to question where we are in relation to the garden space. This is particularly the case in chapter four, where I explore the garden spaces of luxury villas, both in the material remains of Villa A at Oplontis and through the eyes of Pliny the Younger in his villa letters (*Ep.* 2.17 and 5.6). At Oplontis, for example, it becomes clear that the boundaries of the garden spaces are carefully constructed in such a way that they constantly challenge our sense of orientation and realign our focus again and again; and we are thus left unable to make a clear division between what is 'inside' or 'outside' any particular garden space. Such a 'diffusion of perspective' also pervades Pliny's letters, with attempts to reconstruct the 'plan' of his villas proving fruitless.[98] As we approach each of the garden sites, we must be aware of how supposed binaries (such as inside/outside) are simultaneously constructed and contested, and how the resulting dislocation of time and space impacts our perception of that particular site and also, potentially, other garden sites. In this way, my analysis across chapters two, three and four will move beyond a reading of garden boundaries as simply policing access and control, and I will demonstrate how conceiving of a garden boundary as purely an act of spatial division limits our understanding of what a garden boundary is and how it functions.

Garden boundaries – or frames?

Gardens and their boundaries have often been included in studies influenced by Hillier and Hanson's social theory of space, within which the notion of the boundary features prominently.[99] Within this system of social organization, the boundary is viewed as enclosing a 'definite region of space', segregating it 'from what would otherwise be undifferentiated space'; and this segregation 'affects the level of presence-availability within the space, in that the probability that an encounter will occur by chance alone is significantly reduced'.[100] To apply this in more practical terms, for Hillier and Hanson, architecture is understood as an act of spatial division and, by extension, the art of social organization as expressed through buildings. Talking about boundaries within architecture in this way, then, is inherently linked to thinking about power and control, and the primary concern of many scholars has been to question how certain dimensions (such as publicity/privacy, segregation/access, identity/difference) manifest themselves materially in the remains of structures.[101]

In a Roman setting, such questions have particularly guided the study of Pompeian households, which, as we know, often included a garden space of some form. Grahame, for example, has produced a number of studies that use Hillier and Hanson's 'access analysis' (presenting the house as a series of open and closed cells linked by access routes) to analyse social structures and behaviours within the Roman household.[102] In this context, it is unsurprising that the presence and importance of boundaries within the garden, and their initial implication of spatial segregation has led scholars to align garden space with other building 'interiors', and interpret them in the same way as architectural space. Anguissola, for example, is concerned with defining 'privacy' in the context of the peristyle gardens of the House of the Labyrinth (VI.11) and the House of the Golden Cupids (VI.16.7); and her analysis focuses on the 'role of peristyles in shaping the private dimensions of a house through the skilled management of circulation, access, and visibility'.[103] von Stackelberg, too, specifically uses Hillier and Hanson's access analysis to examine the Pompeian houses of Octavius Quartio (II.2.2) and Menander (I.10.4) in order to highlight the different functions of their peristyle gardens within their respective floor plans.[104] In fact, she explicitly aligns her approach towards encounters within domestic garden spaces with architectural analysis, arguing that:

> For society to function, architecture must also weaken boundaries by enabling continuity between exterior and interior. Weakened boundaries generate encounters with the 'other', and it is encounters, not segregation, that generate social stability ... This effect of weakened boundaries and encounter generation is usually considered wholly in architectural terms [but] it can also be present in the liminal space of the garden.

The problem, though, with analysing the garden boundary in these architectural terms is that it privileges a reading of garden boundaries centred on access and control, which, although important, are not exclusive. Thus, although insights can be gained from approaches like access analysis, these quantitative models are too restrictive as a model to consider both the physical *and* the conceptual boundaries of space and time at work in individual heterotopic garden sites, and they are also not flexible enough to account for both the real *and* the representational garden spaces that I will be exploring.

In response, and through the exploration of my six chosen case studies, I propose that conceiving the garden boundary as a 'frame' is a more useful way of opening up possibilities of interpretation for how the garden boundary 'works' and our understanding of garden space more generally.[105] A 'frame' can, of course, be understood as a demarcating or dividing line, but, unlike a boundary, it also has the potential for increased ideological significance – a frame can be a set of ideas or facts, a system of support or even a way of thinking – and so, although a frame is still predominantly a physical entity, it also has broader conceptual implications.[106] Platt and Squire have articulated this subtle but crucial difference between the two concepts and, although the authors are discussing the frame here in the specific context of art theory, there are useful parallels between the ways in which they discuss frames and the ways in which we will see garden boundaries operating across my case studies.[107] Here, the authors state that 'at the most fundamental level, frames serve to articulate boundaries' – like a boundary, frames zone or delimit the field of representation, and, therefore, define the physical and conceptual space of that representation.[108] Frames, however, also 'order the space of an image', categorizing that space internally, and thus loading the field of view with 'different ideas about how it should be seen and understood'.[109]

This reading of 'the frame' should be understood in the context of Derrida's dismantling of the Kantian *parergon*.[110] For Derrida, the *parergon* should not be understood in hierarchical terms as a subservient or secondary category. Instead, he defines it as neither work (*ergon*) nor outside the work (*hors d'oeuvre*), neither inside nor outside, a frame that stands out against two grounds but, with respect to each of these grounds, merges in to one another;[111] and, as such, it follows that frames 'do not just circumscribe their contents, but actively mediate' between the so-called inside and outside as 'permeable sites of communications' that 'establish the conditions according which the work is experienced'.[112] Like a frame to a piece of art, then, the garden boundary, at its most basic level, marks out a space; but, in doing so, it also loads that space with potential meanings. As set out in the introduction to this book, to create a garden is not just to set a space apart, but also it is to cultivate that space to the point that it represents something 'different', something 'other', compared to its surroundings; and, yet, the garden also remains intimately connected to those surroundings in the way it mediates between traditional binaries positioned either side of its dividing line. Understanding the garden boundary in this same way, then, underscores the garden's status as a heterotopic site. I do not claim that the concepts of 'boundary' and 'frame' are mutually exclusive, but, rather, my analysis will demonstrate that including 'framing' in our thinking about gardens space provides a useful analytical tool for examining how the games of destabilization and deconstruction are put to use in each individual garden site.

The notion of 'cultural framing', in which categorizations are 'bound within ideological frameworks', is particularly brought to the forefront of my discussion in chapter three, where I analyse the shared imagery of the garden-inspired lower friezes of the *Ara Pacis*, and the composition of Livia's Garden Room.[113] Here, my discussion argues that the way in which boundaries are constructed, represented and contested within the two artistic displays can be read as both as a reflection and also an undermining of some of the ideological principles promoted by the Augustan regime. Their shared characteristics of hyperfertile abundance and contained profusion reveal a complex balancing act, or perhaps even a deliberate collision, of supposes antitheses, with two types of co-existing temporal frameworks bound together in spaces that negotiate the boundary between discipline and excess. In this way, the two compositions amount to 'tangible reifications of a host of less overt social practices and expectations'; and thus showcase how acts of framing can 'throw into relief' political and cultural factors, and 'make visible the larger organisational principles governing visual display', as well as the 'complex, ever-shifting, and ideological manoeuvres' that inform the creation, display and reception of artefacts.[114] Furthermore, I will also demonstrate how the structural principles embedded in the representation of boundaries within the two examples also extends to the organization of the physical spaces they inhabit – we should not view these images statically, but, rather, understand them as part of carefully constructed physical and spatial relationships that also rely on the negotiation of various boundaries.

Thinking about the garden boundary in terms of framing – and its connection to art theory – is also useful because it naturally emphasizes the *representational* aspect of gardens and the importance of the gaze or view in establishing and conceptualizing these spaces (something that the 'architectural' approach to boundaries lacked).[115] My final chapter, then, questions the extent to which Romans regarded ornamental villa gardens as artificially constructed viewpoints through its exploration of the villa spaces represented in Pliny's villa letters and those that feature in the remains of Villa A at Oplontis. Here, I will demonstrate how both Pliny and the designers of Villa A were guided by a central desire to partition the natural world into a series of perfectly framed vistas; and yet, despite an insistence on the apparent proliferation of framing devices, the boundaries set up do not operate as finite divisions, but, rather, as porous membranes that mediate between a series of oppositions. This blurring of boundaries creates a situation where the garden boundary seems to draw attention to itself, while also deconstructing itself, to the point where the 'garden' element can simultaneously be framed space and the frame itself.

To begin my analysis, though, I must first return to the very roots of Roman garden space by analysing the garden texts of Virgil and Columella – both of which focus on the Roman garden as *hortus*. As examples of this 'original' garden type, these two texts provide the perfect starting point for a detailed examination of individual garden sites, since this analysis will enable us to establish important foundational principles in the Roman conception of garden space. Earlier, I noted how the *hortus* was often located as part of a broader agricultural network; and so, if Virgil and Columella position their garden passages within agricultural texts, does this mean they buy into the 'cultural framing' of the *hortus* as 'inside' of agriculture? Or do they categorize it in contrast to agriculture, even 'below' it, and therefore 'outside' of their textual remit? Perhaps the *hortus* sits neither inside nor outside of the agricultural world, but has a more complex, perhaps *parergonal*, relationship to it? It is with these questions in mind, that we can now cross the threshold and begin our exploration.

2

Who Has the Time? Virgil, Columella and *Hortus* Poetry

Like so many 'natural' spaces of the ancient Roman world, the gardens described in the agricultural texts of Virgil and Columella do not exist for us to visit. The garden as a place may well occupy two spatial categories – the physical space inhabited by the actual garden ('Firstspace') and the representational space of painting or literature ('Secondspace') – but, in the absence of material evidence, it is often the latter representational evidence, already an interpretation of the artist or poet, that emerges as our first point of entry into the garden. This is especially the case when it comes to the most traditional of Roman gardens, the *hortus*, which we perceive today almost entirely from a literary perspective.

The aim of this chapter, then, is to unpack the representation of the *hortus* as described by Virgil and Columella, in order to explore the Roman understanding of garden space in relation to agriculture at large. Although I am concerned with how each author describes their *hortus*, my primary focus is to consider how the garden *as text* is situated within each work as a whole: do Virgil and Columella situate their gardens in a similar way to each other? Does the placement of the garden text reflect how gardens are spatially situated in reality? And what are the implications of viewing garden texts in the same way as physical garden spaces? In order to explore the issues raised by these questions, I will first focus on Virgil's garden *excursus* at *Georgics* 4.116–48, and the temporal structures at play within the passage through an examination of three key elements of his narrative: 1) his awareness of the timely nature of his poetic task; 2) the significance of the old man; and 3) the cycles of activity associated with the garden space. This examination will demonstrate how the alternate versions of time represented in the garden text are a symptom of the way the garden is perceived in relation to the rest of the agricultural world. The distinctive temporal frameworks that Virgil employs within and around his passage point to a relationship between gardens and agriculture; but, as we shall see, the nature of this relationship appears to oscillate between potentially conflicting interpretations.

Building on the implications of this analysis, I will then examine the status and positioning of Columella's gardening verse book within the context of his own agricultural text *and* in relation to Virgil's earlier work. Through an analysis of the prose preface to Book 10 of *De Re Rustica* as a 'paratext' to the verse book proper, I will question the impact of this framing strategy on our perception of the garden-as-text within the realm of agronomic literature.[1] My analysis in this second half of the chapter will consider Columella's stated motivations for writing the book, as well as his comments on the garden text's position in relation to the other eleven books; and this, in turn, will reveal the two distinct but interrelated, ways in which Columella frames Book 10: first, as a direct and important response to Virgil's *Georgics* (4.116–48), and, second, as a small part-payment towards the completion of his own agricultural treatise. On the surface, Columella appears to be breaking with tradition with his 436-hexameter garden poem; but, despite the stand out nature of Book 10, and his desire to fill in the missing part of the *Georgics*, the language of the preface highlights how he continues to be bound by a framework of terminology that emphasizes the garden text's meagreness compared to the other parts of the agricultural world. My analysis will thus demonstrate that neither Virgil nor Columella discount gardening as part of agriculture entirely, but they also clearly grapple with how to incorporate that part; and so, in order to articulate the garden-agriculture relationship expressed in their texts, I will propose the use of Derrida's supplement as a critical concept through which we can begin to unpack and understand these representations of the *hortus*.

Entering the garden space in Virgil, *Georgics* 4.116–48

When Virgil recounts his memory of the Old Corycian in his garden as part of his didactic poem on agricultural practice, he frames his brief *excursus* explicitly in terms of two factors: space and time. He *would* sing of how to tend gardens if his labours were not near the end (116); but he must pass the subject by, shut out by space's unfair constraints (147), leaving the subject matter for later poets to discuss (148). We, as readers, must be content with this short story of the old man in Tarentum:

> *Atque equidem, extremo ni iam sub fine laborum*
> *vela traham et terris festinem advertere proram,*

forsitan et, pinguis hortos quae cura colendi
ornaret, canerem, biferique rosaria Paesti,
quoque modo potis gauderent intiba rivis
et virides apio ripae, tortusque per herbam
cresceret in ventrem cucumis; nec sera comantem
narcissum aut flexi tacuissem vimen acanthi
pallentisque hederas et amantes litora myrtos.
Namque sub Oebaliae memini me turribus arcis,
qua niger umectat flaventia culta Galaesus,
Corycium vidisse senem, cui pauca relicti
iugera ruris erant, nec fertilis illa iuvencis
nec pecori opportuna seges nec commoda Baccho.
Hic rarum tamen in dumis olus albaque circum
lilia verbenasque premens vescumque papaver
regum aequabat opes animis, seraque revertens
nocte domum dapibus mensas onerabat inemptis.
Primus vere rosam atque autumno carpere poma,
et cum tristis hiems etiamnum frigore saxa
rumperet et glacie cursus frenaret aquarum,
ille comam mollis iam tondebat hyacinthi
aestatem increpitans seram Zephyrosque morantis.
Ergo apibus fetis idem atque examine multo
primus abundare et spumantia cogere pressis
mella favis; illi tiliae atque uberrima tinus,
quotque in flore novo pomis se fertilis arbos
induerat, totidem autumno matura tenebat.
Ille etiam seras in versum distulit ulmos
eduramque pirum et spinos iam pruna ferentis
iamque ministrantem platanum potantibus umbras.
Verum haec ipse equidem spatiis exclusus iniquis
praetereo atque aliis post me memoranda relinquo.

And maybe, for my own part, if my labours were not near their end, and if I were not drawing in my sails and steering my prow in haste to land, I would sing of how to tend lush gardens to make them beautiful, and of the twice-flowering rose beds of Paestum, and of how the endive rejoices in watery banks while verdant banks rejoice in wild celery, and of how the gourd, snaking through the grass, swells into paunch; nor would I be silent about late-flowering narcissus, or the willowy acanthus, pallid ivy, or myrtle, which adore to be near water. For I remember once, beneath the walls of hill-top Tarentum, where black Galaesus waters golden crops, I saw an old Cilician, who had a little plot of land, not rich enough for cattle, no use for sheep, unsuitable for vines. Yet here he dotted cabbage-plants among the brambles, with white lilies and verbena and slender poppies in between. To his mind, such wealth was equal to a king's; and when he came home late at night, he piled his table high with unbought feasts. He was the first in spring to pick the roses, and in autumn fruit, and, when bitter winter still made rocks explode with cold and rivers' flow was frozen up with ice, there he was already trimming dainty hyacinths' locks, and cursing summer and its zephyrs for being late in coming. Yes, he was first to overflow with families of bees and bounteous swarms and force the spurting liquid from squeezed honeycombs. His lime trees and his pines were all abundant, and all the fruit these fertile trees gave promise of from early blossom came to ripeness in the autumn. Elms he planted out, full-grown, in lines, along with hardy pear, thorn trees full of plums, and planes already serving shade to drinking parties. All this I pass by with regret, shut out by space's unfair constraints, and leave for others after me to recollect.[2]

Virgil's preoccupation with time in this passage is hardly surprising. Gardening is inherently a temporal activity due to its necessary engagement with cycles of maintenance and change occurring as daily, seasonal or annual rates. The concept of time, however, is notoriously difficult to define and intimately connected with the society that experiences it – although the progression of time from past to present to future may seem 'natural', societies rarely fashion their experience of time in linear form.[3] As for the garden specifically, these are spaces that are always experienced first in 'real time', that is time as it is moved through physically and coordinated socially; but they also thematize time by bringing together into the same framework things that 'take place' on completely different timescales.[4] All the various cycles of time represented in the garden, therefore, and their implied contrast with the linear progression of human life, are available to be juxtaposed and contrasted for effect. This is, in turn, important for our understanding of Virgil's garden text, since how he chooses to represent garden *time* can provide insights into how he also understands the cultural meaning of garden *space*.

Thinking, then, in terms of cultural framings, prior to reading this passage one might (quite rightly) assume that the inclusion of a rustic *hortus* – a paradigm of ancient rusticity governed primarily by practical needs and the requirement of *labor* – would be a natural fit within the similarly rustic and laborious agricultural world of the *Georgics*.[5] Indeed, as noted in chapter one, earlier agricultural writers, such as Cato (*Agr.* 1.7) and Varro (*R.* 1.7.10), name the *hortus* as one of the subdivisions of the large rustic farm-estate, the *villa rustica*.[6]

Interpreters, however, have been consistently intrigued and challenged by Virgil's passage because, rather than a full description of the garden space and its associated practice, integrated seamlessly in to the broader agricultural text, it is merely a short account of the poet's personal memory (*memini . . . vidisse*, 125/7) of an old man tending his plot – an 'unnatural' *excursus* that interrupts a set of instructions concerning bee keeping. As Harrison rightly asks, can any specific function be attached to this digressive narrative about a mysterious and unnamed old man?[7] After all, Virgil could have easily incorporated a more in-depth discussion of gardens into his discussion on bees:[8] earlier in Book 4, he mentions the bees' need for a garden (109), and he even describes the old man as tending his bees (139–40). Instead, though, he changes the location and time of the episode completely, making the garden setting doubly remote.[9]

The garden passage, then, is 'pointedly detached' from its surroundings through a number of devices, which, together, suggest that Virgil went 'to great lengths' to set off the old man from his main theme and 'label it an *excursus*'.[10] First, the passage itself is cast in the form of a *praeteritio*, the device that purports to minimize but in fact creates emphasis.[11] Second, *namque* is used (125) at the beginning of the garden description proper, in order to indicate that what will follow is an independent episode.[12] Finally, it is during this description of the old man that Virgil reaches an almost 'unparalleled intensity of involvement' in the text, since this is the only part of the *Georgics* framed as the poet's own personal memory;[13] and, by framing the passage in this way, Virgil 'creates an effect whereby we almost struggle with him to conjure the details'.[14] Thus, although this personal touch certainly adds intimacy to the description, it also forms the crux of Virgil's apparent strategy to throw his gardening episode into relief, and it invites us to question the passage's meaning far more than if it had been seamlessly integrated into the broader narrative on bees.

The challenges of interpreting the passage are then further compounded by our necessary reliance on Virgil as a starting point for the analysis of textual evidence on Roman gardens.[15] Not only is the pre-Virgilian evidence for gardening extremely limited, but the passage itself is one of very few in Latin literature to represent the garden in this *hortus* form – intentionally or not, Virgil sets the framework for what we expect from a garden text, which, in turn, has an impact on how we view later garden texts and the very space of the garden itself. Questions therefore remain as to what function or meaning we can attach to this digressive narrative – perhaps the garden is *not* such a natural fit within the agricultural world after all?

Virgil's preoccupation with time

If we begin by analysing the temporal structures employed within the passage, Virgil's preoccupation with time is stated from the outset. He is nearing the end of his metaphorical journey: approaching the shore (*terris*, 117), he can sense that he is reaching the end of his labours (*extremo . . . sub fine laborum*, 116);[16] and so, he *would* sing (*canerem*, 119) about gardens if he had the time, but he does not. Virgil, as narrator, presents himself as turning his prow in the present tense (*trahem . . . festinem*, 117); but, when it comes to imagining singing about gardens, the time of the song is in the imperfect (*canerem*), and so the time taken to narrate 117–19 is all that it has taken to make that missed chance part of the past. This is further emphasized by the pluperfect subjunctive (*nec . . . tacuissem*, 122), since the hypothetical occasion of 'not being silent' is now set firmly in the past, with no continuation in the future.[17] The change of tenses here makes clear that all Virgil has time for is the story of the old man, and this lack of time is reiterated at the close of the passage, when he confirms that he must pass the subject by and leave it (*praetereo atque . . . relinquo*, 148).

We could, of course interpret these statements in a fairly straightforward way – the time left on his 'journey' (i.e. his poetic task) is limited, and he cannot possibly write about everything within these constraints, so some things will just have to be left out – and such an interpretation is supported by statements elsewhere in the *Georgics*. At *G.* 1.40, for example, as he contemplates the poetic task ahead, Virgil hopes to be granted 'a calm voyage' (*da facilem cursum*). The choice of *cursum* here is noteworthy because it can be used as a metaphor for navigation, but also for chariot racing;[18] and at the close of Books 1 and 2, Virgil uses the metaphor of chariot racing to denote his own work and the poetic journey.[19] At *G.* 2.541–2, he then represents the poet as resting his weary horses before setting out on the second half of his journey:[20]

> *sed nos immensum spatiis confecimus aequor,*
> *et iam tempus equum fumantia soluere colla.*
>
> But in our course we have traversed a mighty plain,
> and now it is time to unyoke the necks of our smoking steeds.

Once we enter Book 3, however, there is an indication that Virgil seems to have felt, or at the very least gives the impression that he felt, pressures of time to complete this journey. At *G.* 3.284–5, he says that time is flying away from him and he fears he lingers too long:

> *sed fugit interea, fugit inreparabile tempus,*
> *singula dum capti circumvectamur amore.*

> But time meanwhile is flying, flying beyond recall,
> while we, charmed with love of our theme, linger around each detail.

The issue of time is reinforced here by the anaphora of *fugit* in the line *sed fugit interea, fugit inreparabile tempus*; and this reminds us of Jupiter's speech at *Aeneid* 10.467–8, which combines the *topoi* of the brevity of life with the idea that life, once gone, cannot be recovered:

> *stat sua cuique dies, breve et inreparabile tempus*
> *omnibus est vitae.*

> Each has his day appointed: short and irretrievable
> is the span of life for all.

Collectively, these passages suggest that time in the *Georgics* is essentially goal-directed.[21] Virgil has set himself a poetic/agricultural task, with a set time (and space) attached to it, and anything outside of that task is a distraction or a digression from the end goal.

Why though, are gardens singled out as a digression? If we look at other agricultural texts, the authors do point to a potential reason as to why, out of all of the topics that could potentially be covered in the *Georgics*, it is the *hortus* that Virgil claims he must bypass. Despite Cato's suggestion that the garden is second in importance in terms of areas of the farm, in the pseudo-Virgilian *Moretum* it is noted that time spent in the garden can only be achieved after all other agricultural work has been completed or, alternatively, during the holidays:[22]

> *si quando vacuum casula pluviaeve tenebant*
> *festave lux, si forte labor cessebat aratri,*
> *horti opus illud erat.*

> If ever rain or holiday kept him unoccupied at home,
> if by chance there was respite from ploughing,
> that time was spent in the garden.

This sentiment is actually shared by Cato elsewhere in his own treatise (*Agr.* 2.4):

> *per ferias potuisse fossas veteres tergeri, viam publicam muniri, vepres recidi,*
> *hortum fodiri . . .*

> Remind him also that on feast days old ditches might be cleaned, road works
> done, brambles cut, the garden spaded . . .

and also Columella (2.21.1, 4):[23]

> *sed cum tam otii quam negotii rationem reddere maiores nostri censuerunt, nos quoque monendos esse agricolas existimamus, quae feriis facere quaeque non facere debeant...*
> *...in horto quicquid holerum causa facias, omne licet.*

> But inasmuch as our ancestors saw fit to render an account of their leisure hours as well as of their times of non-leisure, I also believe that farmers should be advised of what they should do on holidays and what they should leave undone...
> ...Anything you may do in your garden for the good of your vegetables is lawful.

Broadly speaking, then, the passages above suggest that the Romans defined their agricultural activities within a temporal context – a foreseeable conclusion, perhaps, since we know that such activities are intrinsically linked to temporal cycles, but especially noteworthy when we consider how Virgil wrote the *Georgics* following the implementation of the new Julian calendrical framework (instituted in 46 BCE), which finally synchronized the celestial and the civil year. As Gee has noted, prior to this implementation, the 'arbitrary intercalculation' required to synchronize calendrical and solar years had 'rendered the Republican calendar useless as a guide to seasonal agricultural tasks'; and so, Virgil, publishing his work in 29 BCE, had the benefit of plenty of time to implement this new synchronized time-keeping framework into his didactic poem. Yet there is not a single date in the *Georgics* – Virgil names no months, nor any specific festival days, instead sticking to the more 'Hesiodic tradition' of astronomical guidance for seasonal tasks.[24] Why?

Feeney's introductory comments on the study of the implementation of Caesar's calendar, which are worth quoting in full here, offer some insight into Virgil's apparent hesitancy to adopt new calendrical forms in to the *Georgics*:[25]

> Rome was as highly developed in terms of social and technological organization as a premodern society could possibly be, with an accompanying battery of elaborate calendars, astronomical knowledge, and records and monuments of the past. At the same time, in its lack of clock regulation for synchronizing mass labor and travel, or of particular divisions of daily time beyond the fluctuating hour, it was a society that remained profoundly premodern and preindustrial in terms of the impact of time structures on the individual's lived experience. Further, one may observe without undue romanticizing that even urban Romans were aware of their society's agrarian basis and of the patterns of recurrent life in the country, in a way that few modern city-dwellers are.

Feeney's observations point to some key issues pertinent to my study. Firstly, although as a society, the Romans did have intricate devices for measuring time ('clock' time), it appears that they adhered to what modern historians have termed 'task time':[26] within the structure of time, certain activities are defined and available at set times, which in turn leads to patterns of movement, and thus creates a spatial environment.[27] This idea has been explored and examined in specific Roman contexts before. Ray Laurence's study on the space and society in Pompeii examines the activities of the elites within the city to present the temporal logic that structured city space;[28] and, similarly, Riggsby has looked at how space and time work together in Pliny's *Letters* to show the 'routine' of elite *otium*.[29] There have also been several studies on 'ritual time' in the Roman imagination, with a particular focus on the perceived connections between the Roman ritual calendar and the 'traditional' peasant society of archaic Rome.[30]

However, the issue of how to specifically define *agricultural* activities in a temporal context has not attracted the same level of analysis as the ritual calendar or the world of elite work and leisure;[31] and yet Feeney's insistence on the Romans' awareness of rural time structures, coupled with the evidence from the aforementioned agricultural texts, does suggests that there was a temporal dimension to the use of space in the agricultural world. We know that agricultural *activities* are intrinsically linked to temporal seasonal cycles, but I would argue that the importance of time can also be extended to include how we categorize agricultural *space* itself, with the time allocated to agricultural tasks reflecting back on how we view the space associated with those tasks. In fact, the adherence to task time (and thus its spatial consequences) is especially strong in a rural and agricultural context that appears somewhat exempt from Caesar's new *fasti*. This exemption can perhaps be linked to 'the conservative illusion that nothing fundamental has really changed' in the repetitive process of working the land;[32] or it might quite simply be because, as Pliny states, one 'cannot expect the weather to change on dates fixed in advance'![33]

In this context, the garden, although potentially productive, appears to be viewed as a side-line, an inessential off-shoot maybe, of whatever constitutes the 'essential' agricultural sphere. As the agricultural writers suggest, the time allotted to agricultural tasks has created a space-time framework that leads us to question the garden space's position within the agricultural world – the idea that you should only work on the garden during 'spare' time suggests that the activity is of low priority and, therefore, can easily be marginalized.[34] This attitude to the garden is then directly reflected in the small allocation of space for (or, alternatively, the short amount of time spent writing on) the topic of gardening within the *Georgics*.[35] Although it is still included in the *Georgics* as an agricultural topic, it is also sub-*Georgic* in that it is not, or perhaps cannot be, treated properly within the space and time constraints that Virgil has imposed on his agricultural task. By claiming that he must bypass the garden, Virgil thus points to two issues: first, he reaffirms the sub-standard status of the garden within the space-time framework; and, second, he suggests that he does not have the spare time required for gardening, and so to garden 'properly' would be a digression from the correct course of his journey. There is to be no lingering here!

Pliny the Elder's comments on the *hortus* and on Virgil's garden passage also point to this issue of a potential link between time (to write) and the garden's status. Not only does he refer to the *hortus* as a 'poor man's farm' (*hortus ager pauperis erat*, 19.52), but he also notes that the garden as a topic may well be considered 'mundane' (*nec deterrebit rerum humilitas*, 14.7). Furthermore, in reference to his own writing on gardens, he says that 'some gratitude' should be attached to his labour 'on the grounds that Virgil also confessed how difficult (*difficile*) it was to provide small (*parvis*) matters with dignified appellations (*verborum honorem*).[36] He then goes on to state that, in the garden topics Virgil chose *not* to shun, the *Georgics* demonstrates only the 'choicest of flowers (*et in his quae rettulit flores modo rerum decerpsisse*, 14.7).[37] So what does it say when the 'choicest of flowers' is the story of the old man? How does this relate to our space-time framework? It is time now to turn to the figure of the *senex Corycius*.

The significance of the old man

One of the very first things we learn about the man in his garden is that he is old (*memini . . . Corycium vidisse senem*, 125–7). Like Virgil, this figure is also sailing towards the end of his journey, in this instance, the journey of his life.[38] It is not unusual to find a portrayal of an old man tending to his garden;[39] and Virgil certainly reinforces the issue of the man's age by locating him in Tarentum, a 'secluded corner of the world' (*terrarium . . . angulus*) that, according to Horace, is synonymous with retreat or retirement.[40] The old man in Virgil's passage, then, having retired, does not have to wait for the holidays, nor is he burdened by having to prioritize the 'more important' or 'more pressing' agricultural work as described in the rest of the *Georgics*.[41] He is the only figure in this world that can devote any substantial time to the garden, which is perhaps a little ironic as he is also clearly limited in terms of his own lifespan.

Both Perkell and Clay have pointed to the significance of old age specifically within the *Georgic* world that the man occupies.[42] At *G*. 3.95–100, for example, Virgil describes an old stallion:

hunc quoque, ubi aut morbo grauis aut iam segnior annis
deficit, abde domo, nec turpi ignosce senectae.
frigidus in Venerem senior, frustraque laborem
ingratum trahit, et, si quando ad proelia uentum est,
ut quondam in stipulis magnus sine uiribus ignis,
incassum furit.

Yet, you even shut up such a steed in the stalls when he begins to fail, worn with disease and burdened with years; and do not pity his inglorious old age, though he has often driven the foe in flight and claims Epirus or valiant Mycenae for his birthplace, and traces his line to Neptune himself for founder. The aged stallion is cold to passion, and he vainly struggles with a thankless task; when he comes to the fray his ardour is futile – as when a great fire rages in the stubble, but there is not strength in it.

In this passage, the stallion is to be harshly dismissed from the farmer's care and attention when he is no longer able to procreate or to make war. The old age of the stallion is described as dishonourable (*nec turpi ignosce senectae*, 3.96) and a condition that should be dealt with ruthlessly.[43] As Perkell points out, although this approach may seem harsh, the advice given here by Virgil mirrors that of other agricultural writers who also prescribe the elimination of old or sick animals in favour of those that will bring profit.[44] Cato, for example, emphasizes old age when describing superfluous aspects of the farm that should be put on sale.[45] So, in an agricultural (or *Georgic*) context, so often synonymous with *labor* and toil, old age seems to suggest a sort of uselessness — the attributes of old age do not belong 'inside' the agricultural world, and should thus be cast 'out'.

This, in turn, links directly to Virgil's description of the actual plot of the old man's garden:[46]

pauca relicti
iugera ruris erant, nec fertilis illa iuvencis
nec pecori opportuna seges nec commoda Baccho.

a little plot of unwanted land,
not rich enough for cattle,
no use for sheep, unsuitable for vines.

It is particularly interesting to me that Virgil chooses to describe the plot through negation, with the tricolon repetition of *nec ... nec ... nec*, and, even more specifically, in relation to agricultural concepts. In setting up a common trope and then utterly rejecting it, Virgil makes clear to us that the old man uses this land for his garden precisely because it cannot be used for any of the 'regular' agricultural activities:[47] Virgil singles out ploughing, pasturing and growing vines here because crops, cattle and vines are the three divisions of agriculture that form the overriding themes of the three previous books of the *Georgics*.[48]

The use of *relicti* is also noteworthy here. '*Loci relicti*' is used in the *Corpus Agrimensorum* (a collection of writings from Roman land surveyors) to denote land left unallocated outside the boundaries of *coloniae*.[49] The connection between establishing colonies and agricultural practice can be seen in the common symbolic practice of ploughing a sacred furrow to mark the establishment of a new territory – a practice that Virgil himself links back to the time of the proto-founder of Rome, Aeneas.[50] Augustan legislation, too, reaffirms and presupposes arable cultivation as integral to territorial expansion, stating that land should be granted 'as far as the scythe and plough go'.[51] Within this legal framework, *loci relicti* are specifically noted to be outside of the organizational framework of the *limites* (*quod extra limitum ordinationem sint*) – the defining marker of all Roman conquest and land acquisition.[52] Virgil's use of *relicti* in this gardening passage thus surely suggests, once again, that the old man's plot is somehow 'outside' of the rest of the agricultural landscape, and by, implication, perhaps even outside the scope of the agricultural writer.

Overall, both the poetic task of Virgil and the age of the old man point to a teleological framework of time that has a direct impact on the way we perceive the garden space. We know that the garden, and thus the garden text, is viewed as a distraction from the agricultural task/text at hand. The difference between Virgil and the old man, then, and their ability and desire to 'garden' (metaphorically and literally) is an issue of time: Virgil is still actively participating in his agricultural task and, therefore, cannot afford to digress, whereas the old man is able to garden precisely because he is useless in terms of 'proper' agricultural work. This reinforces the idea that the garden, as a space, can be perceived as outside of the georgic world, perhaps even sub-*Georgic* and 'below' agriculture in the space-time hierarchy. However, just because the old man and his garden are useless in this specific context, does that mean that they are useless altogether?

Cyclical patterns of time in Virgil's garden

So far, the general temporal framework that we have come across is that time can create limitations, which creates a framework through we perceive space: the act of gardening is low-priority compared to other agricultural tasks, relegated to 'spare' time, thus creating the potential for the garden space to be marginalized. However, this framework is not the only pattern of time on display. The activities of the old man present us with a number of paradoxes. Firstly, his activities within the garden, as described in lines 130–46, are specifically aligned with the seasons – he picks roses in the spring (*vere*, 134) and fruit in the autumn (*autumno*, 134), trims hyacinths in the winter (*hiems*, 135) and curses the summer (*aestatem*, 138) for being late. This section of the garden passage makes clear that certain tasks must be done at certain times in order to be successful (another example of 'task time'), but that these tasks also combine to form a collective continuous cycle of planting, cultivation and decay.

In fact, Thibodeau has argued convincingly that, despite the short passage length, what Virgil describes to us is actually 'unquestionably' the gardener's works over a period of three to four years;[53] and it is worth summarizing his argument here. Virgil opens the passage by detailing the status of the land when the old man first came to it, unused and largely covered in brush (*in dumis*, 130); next comes the planting of necessities and the old man's first harvest (the activities of the first year, 130–3); this is followed by the pruning of dead foliage (*comam*) from his hyacinths, which must belong to the start of the second year. In the lines (and years) that follow, plants appear progressively more mature, and the old man starts to collect honey from his bees (140–1) and acquire trees (141) that develop into an orchard (142–3); and, finally, (144–6) having transplanted them into rows as saplings, the trees are now fully mature and able to provide shade.[54] Thibodeau's argument points to how, although individual activities in the garden are supposedly fixed in terms of their seasonal appropriateness, the garden space as a whole is anything but static. The garden is a dynamic space with an ever-changing appearance – something is always growing, even when other elements are withering away.

Such a dynamic process is thus potentially at odds with the limitations imposed on the garden space by Virgil: he wants to frame the garden *excursus* as a digression from the 'essential' course of his didactic teleology and box it in as separate from the rest of the text, but the description of the cyclical growth patterns within his snapshot of the old man promotes a vision of growth and abundance within the garden that cannot necessarily be confined. This potential conflict, between the imposed limitations on the time to garden and the unlimited natural cycles within that garden, is evident in the description of the old man's activities cited above. What is particularly interesting in this section of the *excursus* is that, within the continual process of gardening, the old man is actually characterized as being ahead of time. Virgil conveys the old man's ability to anticipate the seasons through the repetition of *primus, primus* (first, 134/140), and *iam, iamque* (now, 137–46); he is consistently described as cramming in his productivity, through phrases such as *premens* (squeezing in, 131), *onerabat* (he used to pile high, 133) and *spumantia cogere pressis* (to overflow and force squirting [liquid] from squeezed [honeycombs], 132); and he is shown to be impatient at times with his cursing of 'slow' (*morantis*, 138) nature, even keen to work late into the night (132–3).[55] The old man's diligence is thus rewarded by the full realization of natural potential, i.e. every spring blossom bears autumnal fruit. Ironically, then, it is his awareness of his lack of time that actually pushes him to be 'ahead of the game' with his seasonal tasks.

We have already discussed how Virgil's characterization of old age within the georgic world promotes the idea that, despite coming to the end of his life, the old man in the *excursus* is actually the only figure within the *Georgics* with the time to garden: unlike Virgil, for example, the old man has no 'essential' agricultural task to complete, and thus he has the 'spare' time required to garden because he is no longer useful within the agricultural world. However, Virgil's description of the actual gardening process shows that, although the old man is limited in his old age in terms of lifespan, and although he may be useless for 'proper' agricultural work, he is also unlimited or perhaps unbound from the usual constraints of that agricultural work. His productiveness and usefulness in the garden, and the success he achieves, stand in stark contrast to the limitations discussed previously. Once we enter the garden, old age is no longer the barrier it was in the outer agricultural world. Our conception of the effects of age and time inside the garden is markedly different to the conception we had when we were 'outside' with Virgil looking 'in'.

It is worth unpacking this juxtaposition further by considering the contrast and difference between the gardener and the farmer, and their engagement with cyclical patterns of time. As previously noted, agricultural work is in general a product of task time that is assimilated to the natural rhythms of the earth, and this is reflected in the *Georgics*, wherein the poem's time markers are all 'natural': time is organized not by dates but by the constellations, the seasons, the forces of the wind and rain, the sun and the moon. However, although located within the same rural sphere, and adhering to the same broad principles of cyclical time, the activities of the gardener and the farmer do not simply co-exist: the gardener's uselessness in terms of the rest of the *Georgics* suggests to us that the natural cycles of the garden sit 'outside' (perhaps even 'below'?) the cycles of the farm in terms of priority, i.e. one can only participate in the garden cycle once the 'first' farming cycle is complete. The successes of the old man within his supposedly leftover piece of land, though, also 'implicitly invites us to reconsider the nature of the truly useful':[56] the old man is clearly useful in his garden, and so we must be careful not to judge his actions from a position of supposed farming superiority.

Furthermore, the differences between the harsh world of the farmer and the apparent bliss of the gardener shows us that the supposed limitations associated with Virgil's initial temporal framework disappear once you have the opportunity to step inside the garden. The old man's garden is shown to be both miraculous and non-commercial, as demonstrated by the succinct but telling phrase *dapes inemptae* (unbought feasts, 133).[57] In fact, there is no explicit reference to *labor* in the entire description of the activities. The old man, who seems to 'work' only for himself on his *relictus* plot, does not participate in any sort of commercial activity – compare, for example, his 'unbought feasts' with the description of Simulus in the *Moretum*, who produces a surplus to sell on, and Varro's description of two brothers who were able to make a large profit by keeping bees on their land and selling honey.[58] That the garden is non-commercial is important because we are left with the sense that 'such a place is meant to symbolise an idea of beauty'; and, therefore, the *senex*'s 'esthetic, materially superfluous goal and non-destructive relationship with nature' stands in stark contrast to the aggressive and *labor*-focused activities of the farmer (characterized by terms such as *capere, fallere, insectari, terrere* and *arma*).[59]

In fact, the gardening passage reminds us more of the mood of Virgil's earlier work, the *Eclogues*: not only does the gardener seem to enjoy a magical harmony with nature, but the garden itself also recalls the *locus amoenus*, especially with the mention of the shady trees (146).[60] As Gale has noted, Virgil's garden reminds us of Tityrus' farm in *Eclogue* 1, which is simultaneously poor and uncompromising, but also a haven of peace and beauty:[61]

Fortunate senex, ergo tua rura manebunt
et tibi magna satis, quamvis lapis omnia nudus
limosoque palus obducat pascua iunco.
non insueta gravis temptabunt pabula fetas
nec mala vicini pecoris contagia laedent.

fortunate senex, hic inter flumina nota
et fontis sacros frigus captabis opacum;
hinc tibi, quae semper, vicino ab limite saepes
Hyblaeis apibus florem depasta salicti
saepe levi somnum suadebit inire susurro;
hinc alta sub rupe canet frondator ad auras,
nec tamen interea raucae, tua cura, palumbes
nec gemere aeria cessabit turtur ab ulmo.

Happy old man! So these lands will still be yours, and large enough for you, through bare stones cover all, and the marsh chokes your pastures with slimy rushes. Still, no strange herbage shall try your breeding ewes, no baneful infection from a neighbour's flock shall harm them. Happy old man! Here, amid familiar streams and sacred springs, you shall enjoy the cooling shade. On this side, as of old, on your neighbour's border, the hedge whose willow blossoms are sipped by Hybla's bees shall often with its gentle hum sooth you to slumber; on that, under the towering rock, the woodman's song shall fill the air; while still the cooing wood pigeons, your pets, and the turtle dove shall not cease their moaning from the elm tops.

The similarities to Tityrus' farm demonstrate how Virgil's gardening interlude has something of the 'teasing, dreamlike quality so characteristic of the *Eclogues*', which similarly combine real place names with elements of fantasy.[62] In fact, as Armstrong has discussed, Virgil's *Georgics* garden also includes an 'interesting mix' of plant species, which straddle 'the different associations of the idyllic and the workaday'.[63] By straddling the line between fictive and real, the old man's garden once again demonstrates a rejection of any sort of strict categorization.

Time and land ownership

Finally, the juxtaposition between 'inside' and 'outside' the garden, between continuous natural cycles and strict teleological frameworks, can also be seen in the last two lines (147–8) of the passage, where Virgil returns to the issue of his poetic task and reiterates the supposed limitations he has on writing about gardens. Here, the poet claims that he is shut out by the unfair constraints of space (*spatiis exclusus iniquis*), but he also states that he is leaving the subject matter for later poets to discuss (*aliis post me memoranda relinquo*). *Memoranda relinquo* provides a neat closural point to the opening *memini . . . vidisse* at the beginning of the garden passage proper, and thus seemingly signals a finite end point to the gardening discussion; but, crucially, the neat enclosing frame of the *praeteritio* is undermined by Virgil's engagement with a continual process. By framing the description in terms of his memory, Virgil's backwards glance at the beginning of the passage becomes a forward one at the end, as he positions himself within a process of bequeathal, inheritance and continued cultivation.

His request that later poets pick up where he left off and cultivate the garden (as text) thus alerts us to the question of both text and land ownership – who will inherit Virgil's text, and who will inherit the old man's garden? A potential answer to this question may be found by considering the so-called *heredium*, a space that von Stackelberg has called the 'original Roman garden space'.[64] The *heredium* signified two acres of land (*bina iugera*) that traditionally corresponded to the original land grants assigned to Roman citizens by Romulus himself;[65] and, since it could not be bequeathed outside of the family, it was viewed as a symbol of the continuity of archaic agricultural land from one generation of the family to the next. However, although von Stackelberg rather neatly suggests that we can view the *heredium* as a sort of precursor to the *hortus* proper, Pliny the Elder complicates our picture of the *heredium-hortus* relationship:[66]

> *in XII tabulis legum nostrarum nusquam nominatur villa, semper in significatione ea hortus, in horti vero heredium.*

> In our laws of the Twelve Tables, the word farm (*villa*) never occurs – the word garden (*hortus*) is always used in that sense, while a garden (*horti*) is denoted by family estate (*heredium*).

The only aspect of this passage that is really clear is that the *hortus* and the *heredium* pre-date the *villa* as concepts, but does *villa* simply replace *hortus*? Should we actually see the *hortus* as part of the *heredium*? Or are *hortus* and *heredium* simply interchangeable terms?

This flexibility in terminology and the ensuing lack of definitive labelling for the most 'traditional' of Roman gardens is an important factor to keep in mind when reflecting on the closing lines of Virgil's description of the old man's garden. Virgil may position his text within a seemingly straightforward inheritance pattern, but the ambiguity of Pliny's categorizations, coupled with the realities of land ownership during Virgil's lifetime, present a more fraught and complicated picture. As Campbell has noted, between 41 and 14 BCE, some 200000 Roman veterans were allocated land through various processes of colonization; and Virgil himself famously took on this issue in his first work, the *Eclogues* (published *c.* 39–38 BCE), cutting to the heart of Roman fears regarding the potential disruption to traditional and land-holding patterns caused by the post-Philippi Triumviral confiscations.[67] In the *Georgics* (published in 29 BCE), though, Virgil appears to demonstrate a return to the more conventional pattern in the way he bequeaths his own garden (the text) to his (literary) successors, perhaps reflecting a conscious post-Actium desire to stabilize such traditional land ownership cycles.[68] And yet, Virgil does not actually designate his garden to anyone specific, both in the sense that he does not name a particular literary successor and in the sense that the old man seemingly has no relatives to leave his plot to. Is Virgil's bequeathal therefore a reflection of a new Augustan agenda to stabilize the system of land ownership, designation and maintenance? Or, does the fact that he 'self-consciously treads the boundaries between the world of *labor* and the life of ease of the *locus amoenus*' in this *excursus* reveal that this cycle of inheritance and continued cultivation is merely a fiction, an illusion, part of a bucolic dream that only exists within his own fleeting memory?[69]

I would like to end this section on Virgil by reflecting on a forceful statement made by Mynors in his commentary on the *Georgics*:[70]

> Gardening, as far as we can see, is to the Ancients, as to us, no part of agriculture ... and it forms no necessary part of the Georgica.

Based on the evidence discussed, I believe it is time that we revisited such a straightforward exclusionary understanding of the garden in relation to agriculture. My aim thus far has been to explore how the temporal structures at play in Virgil's garden *excursus* have the potential to inform us on the relationship between garden space and the wider agricultural network it is positioned within. The juxtaposition of teleological and cyclical structures points to a split between the time of the text (Virgil's agricultural task), which is limited, and the time of the actual garden, which is unlimited. The lack of 'text time' suggests that the garden is viewed as sub-*Georgic*, but the potential for continued cultivation and the fact that, ultimately, it is not completely excluded, shows us that it is still part of the agricultural world. We are left with the sense that, yes, there is no time for the garden *now*, but that does not mean there is no time *ever*. In fact, the story of the old man has shown us that what might be deemed unproductive and useless in one temporal framework can actually be very productive and useful in another – he succeeds in the garden, even though his time there could be categorized as useless in relation to other agricultural tasks and spaces. What we have here is an issue of perspective, and we tend to be drawn more towards viewing the garden within the overriding teleology of the *Georgics*, rather than as an entity in its own right. The garden is both parallel and alternative to agriculture, but it also has a continuous and contiguous relationship with it; and

Virgil expresses the oscillation between these two different relationships through his inclusion of opposing and alternative dimensions of time within the passage.

What happens, though, when someone does find the *right* time to 'garden'? Does this change the above interpretation of the garden space, or are the patterns expressed by Virgil merely repeated but on a larger scale? Does the garden-as-text continue to sit uneasily within its agricultural framework? It is time to turn to a Spanish writer from the reign of Nero, a certain Lucius Junius Moderatus Columella, in order to find out.[71]

Columella's *agricolatio*

In the opening preface and book of his sole surviving work (a twelve-book agricultural treatise published between 56 and 65 CE) Columella contemplates the immensity, or 'vastness', of his subject matter (*vastitatem corporis*, 1.pr.21), and wonders whether he will be able to cover the entirety of the agricultural discipline (*universam disciplinarum ruris*, 1.pr.21) before his time runs out.[72] Indeed, when he considers the detailed list (1.pr.22-8) of all of the individual topics (*singulorum membrorum*, 1.pr.21) he must deliver on in order to follow in the footsteps of previous agronomic writers without doing disservice to that literary tradition, he demonstrates the sheer scale of the project about to be undertaken.[73] However, Columella need not have worried. The finished product – *De Re Rustica* – is a comprehensive corpus of agricultural information: it treats the general layout and organization of the farm (Book 1), ploughing (2), vines and trees (3-5), animals and livestock (6-7), poultry, fish, game and bees (8-9), gardens (10),[74] and the role and duties of the *vilicus* (11) and his wife (12).[75]

In this way, Columella explicitly positions himself as a new 'helping hand' (*adiuvare promittunt*, 1.1.17) within a tradition of Roman technical agronomic literature that began with Cato's *De agri cultura*.[76] *De Re Rustica* is designed to be 'definitive' in that it covers the *universarum disciplinarum ruris*, but Columella does not seek to simply replace or exclude the knowledge of his literary predecessors. Instead, he views his text as a new and important addition to an ongoing agronomic conversation (*non profitura per se sola, sed cum aliis*, 1.1.17) that will be of benefit to those who wish to learn about agriculture now and in the future (*ideoque haec velut adminicula studiosis promittimus*, 1.1.17).[77]

The 'new-ness' of Columella's treatise is rather neatly summarized in his coining of a new term – *agricolatio* – to describe the endeavour, but it is most explicit when we arrive at Book 10, which jumps out at the reader immediately.[78]

For here, in comparison to the eleven other books all written in didactic prose, we find a prose preface followed by a 436-hexameter poem dedicated exclusively to the traditional *hortus* – a formal and rather obvious departure from the style and subject matter of the rest of the manual. The poem features a short discussion of the preparation of the garden plot and an invocation to the Muses, before continuing to chart the course of an entire yearly cycle, focusing for the most part on the set tasks that should be completed during each season to ensure the best results. We know from our discussions so far that the inclusion of a discussion of a *hortus* within an agricultural text is not, in itself, a surprising thing, but the length and format of Columella's garden-text has certainly raised commentators' eyebrows. For unlike other technical prose agricultural writers like Cato and Varro, who really only discuss it in passing, Columella dedicates an entire book to the topic of gardens, and a verse book at that.

Why? Columella offers a seemingly straightforward reason: picking up on the supposed challenge of *Georgics* 4.147–8, he is going to fill in 'in poetic measures' the 'missing' part on gardens that Virgil had to leave out (*ut poeticis numeris explerem georgici carminis omissas partes*, 10.pr.3). In doing so, Columella makes clear that, in order to achieve his new and improved *agricolatio*, he will engage not only with the technical writers of *agri cultura* or *res rustica*, but also with the tradition of didactic poetry. The overall nod to Virgil is stated at the outset of the entire treatise, when Columella includes him in the list of Roman authorities on agriculture (*mox Vergilium, qui carminum quoque potentum fecit*, 1.1.12); but it is here in Book 10 that Columella blurs the lines between the 'technical' and the 'didactic' the most.[79] The inclusion, style and length of Book 10 thus raise several questions about the relationship between Columella, his technical and didactic sources, and his attempt to create a new and definitive agricultural treatise.[80] Why does Columella have the time and space to dedicate an entire book to the garden when his literary predecessors did not? Is it simply a case of wanting to 'expand' the gardening *excursus* of the *Georgics*, or are there other additional motivations at play? And, by including the *hortus* as a striking shift to verse in an otherwise prose treatise, what can Columella tell us about the relationship between garden-as-text and the *agricolatio*?

A paratextual approach

In order to explore these questions, I am, perhaps rather surprisingly, not going to discuss the hexameter poem at all in this discussion, but, instead, focus solely on the prose preface to Book 10. There are two main reasons for this approach. First, this is where we can gain the most information regarding Columella's reasoning behind writing about gardens in this way. It is here that he sets out two distinct, but interrelated motivations for the presence and format of Book 10, which, in turn reflect two different relationships: Silvinus' request for the final 'payment' of work, which establishes a connection between Book 10 and the rest of *De Re Rustica*;[81] and Columella's self-appointed status as Virgil's 'heir', which creates a link between Book 10 and the *Georgics*. Second, the preface thus acts as an important threshold, or 'paratext' to the poem, the value of which has been underestimated in the past.[82]

So, what exactly is a paratext? For Genette, who coined the term, a text is rarely presented to us in an unadorned state, but, rather, has features – or paratexts – that surround it or extend it (such as a title, illustrations, table of contents or preface), and that enable it to become a book and be presented to its readers.[83] Key to our understanding of the paratext is the meaning of the word 'para'. Although this preposition is typically understood as 'beside' or 'next to', deconstructive thinking has pointed to the limitations of viewing 'para' objects as simply separate and detachable entities.[84] 'Para', therefore, according to Hillis-Miller, signifies 'proximity and distance, similarity and difference, interiority and exteriority'; and a thing 'in para' is not only 'simultaneously on both sides of the boundary between inside and outside', but it is also the boundary itself.[85] By mediating between what is strictly inside and outside of a text, the paratext thus operates as a liminal threshold.[86] Although it is not *the* text, it is still *some* text; and, as a verbal frame, it can 'enhance the text, it can define it, it can contrast with it, it may distance it, or it may even be disguised as to form part of it'.[87] The construction, placement and functionality of the paratext raises questions about the relationship between text and frame, between the creator of the text and the public, and between senders and receivers of the message of the text; and, perhaps most importantly, it has the potential to control one's reading of *the* text.[88]

It is in this context that we should consider Book 10 of *De Re Rustica*. Although we cannot completely ignore how Columella describes the *hortus* in the actual verse book, my primary concern is to consider how the garden-as-text is situated in relation to his agricultural treatise as a whole and to his literary predecessors, and whether or not the placement and construction of the text has implications for our understanding of the place of the *hortus* within agronomic literature. In its functional role as a paratext, and thus a 'conveyor of commentary that is authorial or more or less legitimated by the author', the preface is of the utmost importance to addressing these concerns; and, by focusing on a reading of Book 10 in terms of its margins or edges, my analysis supports the paratextual approach set out by Jansen in that it 'explores the nature of the relationship between a text's frame, its centre, and its context, as well as the way in which audiences approach and plot this set of relations'.[89]

Introducing the *cultus hortorum*

Columella wastes no time in the opening sections of Book 10's preface in explaining the urgent socio-political need for his lengthy garden discussion:[90]

[1] Faenoris tui, Silvine, quod stipulanti spoponderam tibi, reliquam pensiunculam percipe. Nam superioribus novem libris hac minus parte debitum, quod nunc persolvo, reddideram. Superest ergo cultus hortorum segnis ac neglectus quondam veteribus agricolis, nunc vel celeberrimus. Siquidem cum parcior apud priscos esset frugalitas, largior tamen pauperibus fuit usus epularum, lactis copia ferinaque ac domesticarum pecudum carne velut aqua frumentoque summis atque humillimis victum tolerantibus.	[1] Accept, Silvinus, the small remaining payment of your interest, which I pledged to you at your insistence, for I had repaid the debt in the preceding nine books, except for this part, which I now pay. Therefore, there remains the cultivation of gardens, which was formerly idle and neglected among farmers of old, but is now extremely popular. Indeed, although thrift was stingier in earlier generations, nevertheless, among the poor, their enjoyment of feasts was more extensive, with the highest and the lowest-ranking people maintaining a diet that included an abundance of milk and meat of both wild and domestic animals, as though on water and grain.
[2] Mox cum sequens et praecipue nostra aetas dapibus libidinosa pretia constituerit cenaeque non naturalibus desideriis sed censibus aestimentur, plebeia paupertas submota a pretiosioribus cibis ad vulgares compellitur.	[2] Soon when the following age, and especially our own, established arbitrarily high costs for banquets, and meals are judged not by natural desires but expenses, the common people, in their poverty, having been shut out from costlier meals, are driven to common fare.
[3] Quare cultus hortorum, quoniam fructus magis in usu est, diligentius nobis, quam tradiderunt maiores, praecipiendus est: isque, sicut institueram, prosa oratione prioribus subnecteretur exordiis, nisi propositum meum expugnasset frequens postulatio tua, quae praecepit, ut poeticis numeris explerem georgici carminis omissas partes, quas tamen et ipse	[3] For this reason, since the produce of gardens is more in use, I must prescribe their cultivation more accurately than our ancestors passed down to us; and, as I had decided it, it would have been tacked on to the preceding instructions in prose, if my purpose had not been defeated by your constant demand, which succeeded in getting me to complete, in poetic

Vergilius significaverat, posteris se memorandas relinquere. Neque enim aliter istud nobis fuerat audendum quam ex voluntate vatis maxime venerandi:

measures, the missing sections of the *Georgics*, which even Virgil himself had expressly stated were to be left to posterity. For I would not have dared such a thing except by the will of the most honorable poet;

[4] cuius quasi numine instigante pigre sine dubio propter difficultatem operis, verumtamen non sine spe prosperi successus aggressi sumus tenuem admodum et paene viduatam corpore materiam, quae tam exilis est, ut in consummatione quidem totius operis annumerari veluti particula possit laboris nostri, per se vero et quasi suis finibus terminata nullo modo speciose conspici. Nam etsi multa sunt eius quasi membra, de quibus aliquid possumus effari, tamen eadem tam exigua sunt, ut, quod aiunt Graeci, ex incomprehensibili parvitate arenae funis effici non possit.

[4] With his divine spirit, as it were, goading me on, I have approached – though doubtless sluggishly due to the difficulty of the task, yet not without hope of favorable success – a subject that was narrow and almost bereft of substance, and one that is so meagre that, on the one hand, in the completion of the entire work it can be reckoned as a small part of the task, but on the other hand, in itself bound by its own limits it cannot be the object of attention. For even if it has many limbs, so to speak, about which I can say something, nevertheless they are so slender that, as the Greeks say, one cannot make a rope out of an imperceptible bit of sand.

[5] Quare quidquid est istud, quod elucubravimus, adeo propriam sibi laudem non vindicat, ut boni consulat, si non sit dedecori prius editis a me scriptorum monumentis. Sed iam praefari desinamus.

[5] For this reason, whatever this is which I have composed by burning the midnight oil, it is so far from claiming the praise appropriate to it that I would take it as a good sign if it does not reflect badly on my earlier works. But let me now put an end to the preface.

To summarize, Columella says that the reason why he must prescribe the cultivation of gardens more accurately than before (10.pr.3) is because of the increase of banquets as a form of conspicuous consumption for the elites: previously, the rich and poor had both eaten well (10.pr.1); but, now, because the rich have driven up the price of food so high, 'common people' have been forced back to 'common fare' i.e. they have been forced back to gardening in order to be more self-sufficient (10.pr.2). So, although farmers 'of old' had neglected the practice of gardening (*neglectus quondam veteribus agricolis*, 10.pr.1), it is now extremely popular again through necessity and, thus, deserves our attention once more.[91] The justifications presented here align Columella's attitudes to gardening with his overall view and approach to agriculture, and his return to the *hortus* provides a perfect vehicle to promote his broader valorization of a self-sufficient agricultural way of life.[92] As Doody notes, Columella sees agriculture as 'emblematic of a traditional way of life', and so both 'agrarian morality' and garden culture can be 'set in opposition to the corruption' of the present-day Neronian period.[93] Columella's justifications for the timing of and the need for a more thorough treatment of gardening in this context thus appear entirely reasonable.

Virgil's heir

Such reasoning does not, however, explain the decision to write in verse and not prose; and so, Columella also sets out the context for this particular composition choice. It seems that, originally, he had set out to continue with Book 10 in the same manner as the previous nine books, but it was 'at the constant demand' of his patron, Silvinus, that he changed from writing in prose to verse (10.pr.3).[94] The patron's insistence on verse composition is then explicitly tied to a literary predecessor, when Columella states that he has been instructed by Silvinus to pay homage to Virgil by finishing 'in poetic measures the missing part of the *Georgics* (*ut poeticis numeris explerem georgici carminis omissas partes*). He then makes it clear that this 'missing' garden poem is a part of the *Georgics* that 'even Virgil himself expressly stated' was to be 'left to posterity' (*qua stamen et ipse Vergilius significaverat posteris se memorandas relinquere*). This particular statement is, of course, a reference to *Georgics* 4.147–8, with Columella's *memorandas relinquit* directly echoing Virgil's *memoranda relinquo* – and it appears from the preface to Book 10 that Columella is more than willing to fill in the apparent gap in the literary market left by Virgil's 'non-treatment' of the garden. In fact, he believes he has the express blessing of Virgil to do so (*Neque enim aliter istud nobis fuerat audendm, quam ex voluntate vatis maxime venerandi . . .*).[95]

Book 10, then, is meant to be viewed, according to Columella at least, as the fifth *Georgic* that never was – a bold claim, perhaps, to be filling in what Virgil 'left out', but not an entirely surprising move when we consider how Columella prepares his readers for it during the build-up to Book 10. Books 1–9 of *De Re Rustica* deal with the same general topics as treated by Virgil in the *Georgics*, and also in the same order: crops (Books 1–2), vines (Books 3–5), cattle (Books 6–8) and bees (Book 9). The proem of the garden verse (lines 1–5) also re-emphasizes this ordering of topics and the connection to Virgil, and repeats the phrasing of G. 4.147:

> *Hortorum quoque te cultus, Silvine, docebo,*
> *atque ea, quae quondam spatiis exclusus iniquis,*

cum caneret laetas segetes et munera Bacchi,
et te, magna Pales, necnon caelestia mella,
Vergilius nobis post se memoranda reliquit.

The cultivation of gardens I will now teach, Silvinus,
And those themes which Virgil once left behind to be recounted by us,
when, enclosed by narrow bounds,
he sang of flourishing crops and Bacchus' gifts,
and you great Pales, and heavenly honey.

The placement of Book 10 after a discussion of apiculture is another obvious nod to Virgil. Both Boldrer and Saint-Denis have pointed out that Columella could have logically dealt with gardens in or immediately after Books 1–5 because they deal with crops and soil, therefore offering a thematic connection to gardening;[96] but, instead, he chooses to exploit the connection between bees and gardens as set out by Virgil, in that gardens offer a way to provide flowers to support the bees with nectar and thus keep them safe and discourage them from wandering off. Columella additionally prepares the readers for his poetic gardening book by briefly discussing in Book 9 the sorts of flowers favoured by bees (9.4.4); by relating a myth concerning the origin of bees (9.2.2–3), which recalls Virgil's *bougonia* myth in *Georgics* Book 4 (4.281–314, 548–58); and by illustrating his discussion of apiculture with quotation from Virgil.[97] Thus, although Book 10 may not be positioned at the most obvious place within *De Re Rustica*, by mimicking the placement of the *Georgics* gardening episode, Columella has 'left his readers agog for Virgilian flights of fancy' by ending Book 9 with bees.[98]

Thus, as White notes, through the overall arrangement of *De Re Rustica* as a kind of reflection of the *Georgics*, by evoking the connection between bees and gardening as suggested by Virgil in *Georgics* 4, and by a brief restatement of his poetic purpose and of the themes of the *Georgics* in his proem, Columella has prepared his readers for his 'completion' of the *Georgics* by his poetic gardening book.[99] Book 10, therefore, will not just be a recapitulation of the *Georgics*, but a reimagining of it. That the first nine books of his treatise appear to build up to this climactic 'fifth Georgic' also suggests that Silvinus' supposed demand for verse-writing is more of a front for Columella's personal motivation to emulate Virgil. The decision to write a garden poem, when viewed in the context of an entire reimagining of the *Georgics*, was surely not the result of some last-minute pressure but, rather, a carefully managed and deliberate decision by Columella.[100]

To recap, the motivations for writing Book 10 appear, on the surface, to be relatively straightforward. Columella, as an agricultural writer, will include in his treatise a discussion of gardening, a topic that has been recognized as part of agriculture in various degrees by previous writers. His discussion, however, will stand out in two ways: first, in comparison to the 'neglect' of previous writers, Columella's discussion will be of a considerable and notable length; and, second, in comparison to the rest of his treatise, the garden discussion will stand alone as a verse book, surrounded by prose. Why these two changes? Columella would have us believe that gardening is of greater concern to his contemporary audience, and that his patron requested verse writing specifically so that he would create the 'missing' fifth Georgic of Virgil. On reflection, though, these two factors appear to be more of a front for Columella's own belief that he has a debt to literature, so to speak, to provide what Virgil could not and, therefore, emulate Virgil's poetic status.

These co-existing socio-political and literary motivations thus combine to suggest that the *hortus* now has value as a subject within agronomic literature. However, if we take a look at the specific language Columella uses to describe Book 10 as a part of his *De Re Rustica*, as opposed to an heir to Virgil, the issue of the garden's perceived 'place' within the new *agricolatio* becomes far less clear-cut.

The 'place' of the Hortus: *poeticis numeris* vs. *agri cultura*

The first lines of the prose preface present Book 10 as a payment from Columella to his patron Silvinus:[101]

> *Faenoris tui, Silvine, quod stipulanti spoponderam tibi, reliquam pensiunculam percipe. Nam superioribus novem libris hac minus parte debitum, quod nunc persolvo, reddideram.*

> Accept, Silvinus, the small remaining payment of your interest, which I pledged to you at your insistence, for I had repaid the debt in the preceding nine books, except for this part, which I now pay.

In this opening sentence, some key words stand out. First, he describes the payment as *pensiuncula* ('a tiny payment'): not attested to before Columella, this is a diminutive of *pensio*, and, taken together with *particula* (10.pr.4), it suggests that the subject of gardening (i.e. the payment) should be viewed as 'small' or even 'meagre'.[102] The emphasis on the size of the payment is then reiterated when Columella describes the individual topics, or 'limbs' (*membra*, 10.pr.4), within gardening as 'slender' (*exigua*, 10.pr.4);[103] and throughout Book 10 there is a continued emphasis on narrow and ordered elements: 'let him mark out a fine path' (*parvo*, 10.93), 'soil combed with clear marking' (*pectita*, 10.94), 'closely marked furrows' (*parvo*, 10.230).

Columella continues to downplay the garden by apologizing for its lack of substance: he says it 'cannot be the object of attention' (*nullo modo conspici*, 10.pr.4), and it 'cannot be viewed as a topic within its own limits' (*quasi suis finibus terminata*) because those 'slender (*tenuem*) limbs' are, in fact, so 'imperceptible' (*incomprehensibili parvitate*) that, even put together, they will amount to nothing. The use of *tenuis* here has an obvious programmatic function, in that it indicates Columella's desire for the concise, well-wrought verse favoured by Hellenistic poets and their imitators;[104] and this alignment with 'finely spun Callimachean poetry' is re-emphasized in the garden poem when Columella asks the Muses to 'spin him a slender song' (*tenui deducite carmine*, 10.40).[105] However, any notion that this sort of concise verse should be viewed positively is immediately undermined by the use of the metaphor 'you can't make a rope out of grains of sand'.

This use of terminology of meagreness for the garden-text 'payment' thus stands in contrast to Columella's bold claims elsewhere in the preface that gardening deserves to, or indeed *must*, be discussed more thoroughly than before. On the one hand, we are meant to view the stand out verse experiment as so substantial that it will 'complete' the *Georgics*; but, on the other hand, within the context of Columella's own treatise, it is still presented as a small and almost inconsequential part. In fact, at the end of the preface (10.pr.5), Columella worries that his verse book will reflect badly on the rest of his treatise:

> *Quare quidquid est istud, quod elucubravimus, adeo propriam sibi laudem non vindicat, ut boni consulat, si non sit dedecori prius editis a me scriptorum monumentis. Sed iam praefari desinamus.*

> For this reason, whatever this is which I have composed by burning the midnight oil, it is so far from claiming the praise appropriate to it that I would take it as a good sign if it does not reflect badly on my earlier works. But let me now put an end to the preface.

Columella seems to be suggesting that, no matter how much he writes about gardens, the topic just cannot amount to anything substantial on its own; or, to borrow a phrase from Pliny, it is 'helpful' but, ultimately, rather 'trivial'.[106]

Why, though, is this the case? The key here is the garden text's position in relation to the entire agricultural manual, and, more specifically, how we are forced to focalize our view of Book 10 from the vantage point of the *universam disciplinarum ruris*. Although Columella writes in more detail about the *hortus* than any Latin writer before, it is clear that he also remains bound by principles of marginality when attempting to define the garden text's position within the broader agronomic and technical literary tradition. This act of definition is then complicated further because Columella is also attempting to articulate his relationship to Virgil at the same time, which pushes Book 10 out of the margins in its 'completion' of the *Georgics*.

The complexities of these interconnected relationships are hinted at by a couple of key phrases. Firstly, it is important to return to the phrase *quasi suis finibus terminata* (10.pr.4). Here, Columella is not just emphasizing that his payment is small but, more crucially, that it is so small that *it cannot constitute a subject in itself*. The garden text, apparently, *has* to be viewed in relation to something else (in this instance, Columella's *agricolatio* and Virgil's *Georgics*); and so, although it is clearly set aside as something 'different' by the shift from prose to verse, this setting-aside does not constitute a complete separation from the broader framework. It seems the *hortus*-as-text cannot escape its smallness in relation to a broader literary framework no matter how much you write about it.

Secondly, if we return to the opening sentence of the preface, *faenoris* (10. pr.1) is particularly significant. *Faenus* generally denotes 'interest received on capital lent out', and it is clear that Columella, in line with the Roman approach to money-lending in general, viewed interest as a separate entity to the loan.[107] At 3.3.7–11, for example, he discusses agricultural loans and calculates his sum total by adding together two parts, principal and interest (*Fit in assem summa sortis et usurarum*);[108] and he also, rather tellingly, uses *faenus* at 10.140–3 to discuss abundant fertility – or 'crops with interest' (*ut redeant nobis cumulatio faenere messes*). Through the use of *faenoris* in the preface, Columella is thus clearly suggesting that the garden payment is an additional extra or 'bonus' element to *De Re Rustica*. Indeed, it is noteworthy that, when Columella lists all the *singulorum membrorum* he will need to include in his *universam disciplinarum ruris* (1.pr.21–8), the *hortus* is not explicitly named.

The notion of Book 10 as a bonus is further articulated in the preface (10.pr.3) through the use of a weaving metaphor:[109]

> *prosa oratione prioribus subnecteretur exordiis, nisi propositum meum expugnasset frequens postulatio tua* . . .

> would have been tacked on in prose to my opening books, if my purpose had not been defeated by your constant demand . . .

This type of metaphor is then repeated at the beginning of Book 11 (11.1.1) when Columella reflects back on his gardening verse:

cum praedictam materiam carminis legibus implicarem.

when I tried to enfold the said subject within the rules of verse.

Finally, even when the topic of gardening is brought up again as a subject in Book 11, it is still 'woven in' to the duties of the vilicus (*ut holitoris curam subtexerem villici officiis*, 11.1.2). It still remains unable to stand alone.

These repeated assertions of Book 10 (and its associated subject matter) as a bonus, however, stand in contrast to another financial metaphor used at the end of Book 9 (9.16.2) to describe the garden poem:

> *Sed iam consummata disputatione de villatici pecudibus atque pastionibus, quae reliqua nobis rusticarum rerum pars subest, de cultu hortorum, Publi Silvine, deinceps ita, ut et tibi et Gallioni nostro complacuerat, in carmen conferemus.*

> Having now finished the discussion of the animals kept at the farmhouse and their feeding, the remaining part of husbandry still to be treated, namely the cultivation of gardens, will now be presented in verse in accordance with the desire which both you, Publius Silvinus, and our friend Gallio were pleased to express.

Here, rather than a piece of additional interest, Book 10 is presented as the last part-payment to Silvinus.[110] It might appear insignificant, but the fact that Columella refers to Book 10 as the *reliqua ... pars* of *De Re Rustica* is telling, for what is 'remaining' is surely an integral part of the treatise, in that it would not be complete without it. There seems to be no question that Book 10 was going to be included in the treatise, that the subject would be gardening, and even that it would be dealt with in verse. Indeed, it is only at the beginning of Book 11 (11.1.2) that Columella states he has 'overrun' his original tally of books (*voluminum excessi*).[111]

There is clearly some conflict, then, in the terms that Columella uses to describe the small payment of Book 10. He initially presents Book 10 as an expected element of the treatise, but then it is described as just a small bonus element that is, as Gowers argues, merely 'tacked on in subordinate fashion to the rest of the work'.[112] Is it possible for Book 10 to be simultaneously essential (as part-payment of a whole) and also a bonus (as interest)? The inclusion of words such as *faenoris* and *subnecteretur* in the preface of Book 10 force us to address this question.

The *hortus* as supplement

What, then, can we deduce from this analysis of Book 10's prose preface? In its functional role as a paratext, how does the preface guide or control our perception of the garden text? It is clear from the discussion that Columella frames his verse experiment in two different ways – as a response to Virgil, and as a small payment towards the completion of his own manual – and it is the co-existence of these two relationships that creates such an intriguing dynamic between Book 10, Columella's literary sources, and the rest of *De Re Rustica*.

Following my analysis, it appears that the small payment of Book 10 is both inside and outside of Columella's remit as an agricultural writer. It is as if *De Re Rustica* would be complete without it, but also incomplete in some way. Book 10 is portrayed as a substantial necessity from the perspective of its relationship to Virgil, but also a small extra in relation to the rest of *De Re Rustica* – it relates to it, but it is on the edge (literally, if we believe it to be the original ending) – a peripheral 'bonus' concern. Nowhere is it suggested that a discussion of gardening simply does not belong as part of an agricultural treatise, but the value of this part does not appear to be significant. On the surface, Columella appears to be breaking with tradition by including a 436-hexameter verse gardening book in his otherwise prose treatise; but, despite the stand out nature of this verse book, and his desire to fill in the missing part of the *Georgics*, he continues to be bound by a framework of terminology that emphasizes the garden text's meagreness compared to the other *membra* within his *agricolatio*.

Returning to my initial characterization of the prose preface as a paratext, then, it appears that this textual tool not only controls our reading of *the* text (i.e. of Book 10); but, by articulating the intriguing dynamic between Book 10 and the rest of *De Re Rustica*, both of which must be read in relation to Virgil, the preface also informs us by implication of the position of the garden-as-text within agronomic literature. The positioning of Book 10 as both 'inside' the treatise, in that it is an expected payment to Silvinus, and yet also 'outside' the traditional remit of an agricultural writer, in that it goes above and beyond the norm as a 'bonus', reveals an ambiguous and often paradoxical relationship. In fact, the concept of the paratext, as both part of and not part of a text, turns out to be a useful metaphor for that ambiguity – in this agricultural text, the garden belongs without really belonging.[113]

In light of these observations, I would like to end by introducing Derrida's concept of the supplement – the 'critical idiom with which he describes the paradoxical nature of an extra element added to something that is supposed to be complete' – as a means of articulating this paradoxical relationship.[114] A supplement is defined as something that, allegedly secondary, comes to serve as an aid to something 'original' or 'natural', but this definition is ambiguous because it can be interpreted in two ways: first, that the 'natural' is lacking something and requires completion; or, second, that the supplement merely enriches the 'natural' as an 'add-on'.[115] A supplement to a dictionary, for example, is an extra section that is added on, but the possibility of adding that very supplement indicates that the dictionary itself is incomplete.[116]

Derrida uses the concept of the supplement as a deconstructive tool to show that what is claimed to be full can also be shown to be lacking, in that supplements can be viewed as either substitution or completion. As Reynolds has argued, we must recognize that Derrida's discussion reveals that there is a 'constitutive undecidability involved in the notion of the supplement'; and what is noticeable in his chosen examples is an 'ambiguity that ensures that what is supplementary can be interpreted in two ways'.[117] In fact, Derrida himself states that it is 'undecidable' whether the supplement adds itself and is a 'plenitude enriching a plenitude, the fullest measure of presence', or whether the supplement 'supplements ... adds only to replace ... represents and makes an image ... its place ... assigned in the structure by the mark of emphasis'.[118] Such a conflicting double-bind has thus led Culler to define the supplement as an 'inessential extra, added to something complete in itself' but 'added in order to complete, to compensate for a lack in what was supposed to be complete in itself'.[119]

The paradox of the supplement is thus also the paradox of Book 10. Columella's verse experiment exposes past agricultural texts as lacking, in that they neglected a thorough treatment of gardening, and therefore are requiring completion through the inclusion of a garden text; yet his description also maintains that the very thing designed to complete it is, in itself, still a 'small bonus', situated outside or, at the very least, on the edge of his treatise. Book 10 is both a supplement in that it fills in something lacking elsewhere, and also a supplement in that it merely enriches something already whole, of which it is a part. The two sides of supplementation are expressed through the two literary relationships of which Book 10 is a part of: one with Virgil (didactic poetry) and one with the rest of *De Re Rustica* (technical agronomic literature). Consequently, these two co-existing relationships exemplify the two determinate possibilities involved in the 'undecidability' of the supplement – Book 10 has the potential to be simultaneously 'added in order to complete' and also an 'inessential extra'. Perhaps it was always Columella's aim to keep us guessing about its place in his new *agricolatio*.

Both Virgil and Columella, then, inform us on the ambiguous relationship between the garden (as *hortus*) and the broader agricultural network within which it is situated. Through the deliberate and specific constructions of their gardens-as-text, they articulate a set of cultural perceptions regarding the supplementary status of the space in Roman thought, and demonstrate how temporal frameworks can provide insights into societal constructions of importance and value. What happens, though, when the garden takes on another form outside of this 'original' agricultural context? If it is no longer positioned as part of an agricultural network, does its supplementary status change? And do other, different, manifestations and representations of garden space continue to be guided by and understood within the specific cultural frameworks of their creators, as this chapter has suggested? With these questions in mind, it is time to turn to two case studies that demonstrate how gardens can move beyond a supposedly marginalized status and, more specifically, how garden imagery can become absolutely central to image-making within the Augustan period.

3

Augustus' Garden Room? Re-Framing the *Ara Pacis Augustae*

When Strabo describes his visit to Rome during the Augustan period, he appears immediately struck by the novel combination of monumental architecture and nature within the city as a whole and, more specifically, within the Campus Martius:[1]

> τούτων δὲ τὰ πλεῖστα ὁ Μάρτιος ἔχει κάμπος, πρὸς τῇ φύσει προσλαβὼν καὶ τὸν ἐκ τῆς προνοίας κόσμον. καὶ γὰρ τὸ μέγεθος τοῦ πεδίου θαυμαστόν, ἅμα καὶ τὰς ἁρματοδρομίας καὶ τὴν ἄλλην ἱππασίαν ἀκώλυτον παρέχον τῷ τοσούτῳ πλήθει τῶν σφαίρᾳ καὶ κρίκῳ καὶ παλαίστρᾳ γυμναζομένων· καὶ τὰ περικείμενα ἔργα καὶ τὸ ἔδαφος πόαζον δι' ἔτους καὶ τῶν λόφων στεφάναι τῶν ὑπὲρ τοῦ ποταμοῦ μέχρι τοῦ ῥείθρου σκηνογραφικὴν ὄψιν ἐπιδεικνύμεναι δυσαπάλλακτον παρέχουσι τὴν θέαν.

> The Campus Martius contains most of these [buildings], and thus, in addition to its natural beauty, it has received still further adornment as the result of foresight. Indeed, the size of the Campus is remarkable, since it affords space at the same time and without interference, not only for the chariot-races and every other equestrian exercise, but also for all that multitude of people who exercise themselves by ball-playing, hoop-trundling, and wrestling; and the works of art situated around the Campus Martius, and the ground, which is covered with grass throughout the year, and the crowns of those hills that are above the river and extend as far as its bed, which present to the eye the appearance of a stage-painting – all this, I say, affords a spectacle that one can hardly draw away from.

As Duret and Néraudau have noted, Strabo is clearly seduced by the successful dialogue between nature and art within the Campus Martius (*c'est le dialogue réussi entre la nature et l'art*) and the ways in which the monuments are inscribed into the landscape without spoiling its beauty. What Strabo describes is, in essence, a large-scale garden (*un jardin qui nous est décrit*), where art, men and gods meet in total harmony (*une totale harmonie, par l'intercession de l'art, les hommes, et les dieux*).²

It is unsurprising that these features struck such a chord with the geographical commentator, since the Campus Martius was a focal point for the deliberate green-scaping of Rome during the Principate (see Figure 1).³ In contrast to the monumentality of Pompey's theatre/portico complex and Caesar's planned *Saepta Iulia*, Augustus chose to aggrandize the Campus Martius not just by building but, rather, by opening areas up to create a new kind of 'semi-urban zone of recreational, sacred, and dynastic buildings together with open fields, gardens, and woodlands'.⁴ The opening up of the Campus Martius in this way not only tapped into the space's deep-rooted tradition of commonality, but also led Strabo to describe the newly landscaped space as 'the holiest of all':⁵

> διόπερ ἱεροπρεπέστατον νομίσαντες τοῦτον τὸν τόπον καὶ τὰ τῶν ἐπιφανεστάτων μνήματα ἐνταῦθα κατεσκεύασαν ἀνδρῶν καὶ γυναικῶν. ἀξιολογώτατον δὲ τὸ Μαυσώλειον καλούμενον, ἐπὶ κρηπῖδος ὑψηλῆς λευκολίθου πρὸς τῷ ποταμῷ χῶμα μέγα, ἄχρι κορυφῆς τοῖς ἀειθαλέσι τῶν δένδρων συνηρεφές. ἐπ᾽ ἄκρῳ μὲν οὖν εἰκών ἐστι χαλκῆ τοῦ Σεβαστοῦ Καίσαρος, ὑπὸ δὲ τῷ χώματι θῆκαί εἰσιν αὐτοῦ καὶ τῶν συγγενῶν καὶ οἰκείων, ὄπισθεν δὲ μέγα ἄλσος περιπάτους θαυμαστοὺς ἔχον. ἐν μέσῳ δὲ τῷ πεδίῳ ὁ τῆς καύστρας αὐτοῦ περίβολος, καὶ οὗτος λίθου λευκοῦ, κύκλῳ μὲν περικείμενον ἔχων σιδηροῦν περίφραγμα, ἐντὸς δ᾽ αἰγείροις κατάφυτος.

> For this reason, in the belief that this place was the holiest of all, the Romans created in it the tombs of the most illustrious men and women. The most noteworthy is what is called the Mausoleum, a great mound near the river on a lofty foundation of white marble, thickly covered with evergreen trees to the very summit. Now on top is a bronze image of Augustus Caesar, beneath the mound is a large sacred grove with wonderful promenades, and in the centre of the Campus is the wall (this too of white marble) round his crematorium; the wall is surrounded by a circular fence and the space within the wall is planted with black poplars.

The most noteworthy of the tombs mentioned here is, of course, the Mausoleum of Augustus, surrounded by a large 'sacred grove' (μέγα ἄλσος) and planted thickly up to the summit with trees in a way that mirrors the broader integration of gardens into tomb spaces outlined in chapter one.⁶ Even the exterior decoration of the monument itself alluded to the surrounding greenery, with fragments of marble blocks carved in relief with laurel branches and leaves creating the impression that the walls flanking the doorway were sculpted with a pair of laurel trees.⁷

Augustus' Garden Room? Re-Framing the Ara Pacis Augustae 63

To complement and enhance this zone, Augustus also made large amounts of green space throughout the city either completely public or, at the very least, made available to the public: his own garden and residence on the Palatine, the *Horti Pompeiani*, the *Horti Maecenatis*, the *Porticus Liviae* on the Oppian Hill and the new grove (the *nemus Caesarum*) dedicated to his grandsons, Gaius and Lucius (on land previously designated for the Transtiber *Horti Caesarum*), are all examples of this trend.[8] Augustus, then, perhaps inspired by Julius Caesar's public benefaction of green space, clearly realized the importance of providing public space to the Romans within the city.[9] As von Stackelberg points out, for the majority of Romans in the city, 'any experience of a garden was limited to small urban or suburban plots or to a collection of potted plants', and so, their admittance to this public green space 'promoted an atmosphere of social inclusion that generated political goodwill'.[10] These new and 'open' garden spaces

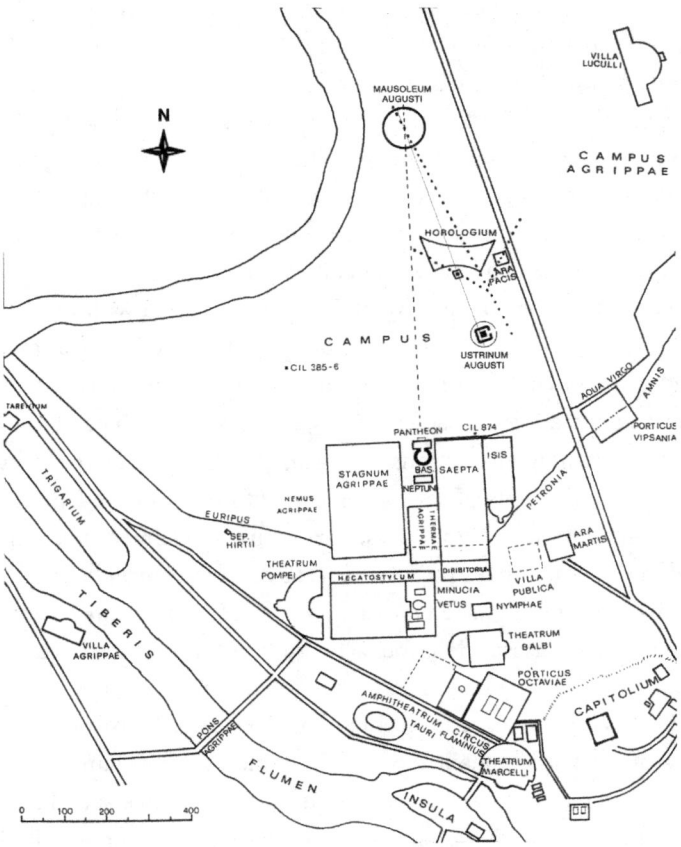

Figure 1 Map of the Campus Martius (from Pollini 2012).

provided Rome's residents with an escape from their crowded living conditions and positively transformed the cityscape.[11]

A botanic mythology

This injection of green space into the city can be understood as part of what Orlin has termed a 'reordering of Roman topographical and chronological space', that had 'profound implications for the reshaping of Roman identity' during the Augustan period;[12] and it was an especially powerful tool in the promotion of the new political and social ideals of the regime for two reasons. First, this approach seemed to find a happy medium between the two diametrically opposed views of garden space that took hold during the Late Republic: these garden spaces were not the productive but supplementary *hortus* found in agricultural settings, but neither were they the luxurious *horti* of elites that had elicited such negative moral invective from the ancient authors. In particular, by changing the emphasis from private *luxuria* to public benefaction, Augustus' green spaces became an apt symbol of his claims to be the sole provider and saviour of the Roman people. Augustus positioned himself as an ideal citizen, a shepherd herding the Romans into the new Golden Age; and these ideas complemented the traditional agrarian and pastoral associations of the garden to create a message of political renewal based on the language and imagery of cultivation.[13]

Second, Augustus' green-scaping of Rome also aligned with his overarching revitalization of traditional Roman religious practices and his focus on restoring *pietas* and 'old' Roman morality.[14] Key to this was to counteract the supposed disappearance of traditional sacred groves, the loss of which can be seen in the appearance of warning inscriptions imploring passers-by to leave the sites along, and also in the comments of several ancient authors from the Late Republican and Augustan periods:[15] Propertius, for example, claimed that shrines lay neglected in 'deserted groves' (*at nunc desertis cessant sacraria lucis*, 3.13.47) and that piety was being vanquished (*aurum omnes victa iam pietate colunt*, 3.13.48); Dionysius of Halicarnassus describes a 'far off holy place, arched over by a dense wood', said to be consecrated to Pan, that 'to be sure, no longer remains (*Ant. Rom.* 1.79.8); and Varro, who seemed to view sacred groves as a genuine expression of what little remained of the old Roman religion, laments at how sites of previous sanctuaries have been replaced by narrow streets, and how all that remains of the original groves are the street-name reminders symbolizing the trees which once stood there (*L.* 5.152).[16] Thus, just as Augustus' public benefaction directly counteracted the negative moralizing discourse of Republican *luxuria*, the apparently conscious effort to transform the Campus Martius into the 'holiest of all' spaces, with its very own 'sacred grove', also dealt directly with the Late Republican dismay at the disappearance of sacred landscapes.[17]

Underpinning this injection of green space was also a broader use of nature's symbols by the new *princeps*, a deliberate monopolization of specific plant types in order to establish a new botanic mythology that featured both himself and his family.[18] This new mythology, as an expression of imperial power through religious symbolism, is best encapsulated in the familiar story of the omen of the *Gallina Alba*: soon after the marriage of Livia to Augustus, an eagle flew down and dropped a white hen with a sprig of laurel right into her lap. She was advised by the *haruspices* to preserve the hen and its offspring, and to plant the laurel as religious obligation. Accordingly, to mark the spot of this *miraculum*, Livia planted the sprig of laurel at her villa near the ninth milestone of the *via Flaminia* (*iuxta nonum lapidum Flaminiae viae*, Plin. *Nat.* 1.137), where it subsequently flourished into a dense grove (*tale vero lauretum*, Suet. *Gal.* 1; *mireque silva provenit*, Plin. *Nat.* 1.137).[19] From this particular grove, Augustus took branches for his triumphal crowns, a practice which continued for all emperors until just before the death of Nero, when the grove and the Julio-Claudian dynasty simultaneously withered away.[20]

This neat little anecdote, whether true or not, was important for Augustus for several reasons. At its most basic level, the story behind the setting of the laurel groves of the Caesars was extremely useful in providing an auspicious sign for what was surely a controversial marriage at the time. Literary evidence makes clear that Livia was pregnant at the time of this betrothal with her former husband's child;[21] and yet, since Livia's marriage to Augustus would remain childless, it was the very child she was carrying when the omen took place who would go on to become Rome's second emperor, Tiberius.

The laurel featured in this story was also the perfect plant choice for re-affirming Augustus' position as Julius Caesar's rightful heir. Caesar himself had used the laurel as his personal symbol as *triumphator*;[22] and so it was a natural choice for Augustus and his heirs to continue this tradition using the laurel from the auspicious grove. Even more significantly, the Julio-Claudian emperors would replant the branch they had cut off for their crown after use, allowing it to take root again and grow into bushes that were marked with the individual's name.[23] Thus, as Flory suggests, the grove formed a living family genealogy of the *triumphatores* of the *gens Iulia*; and the ability of the cut branch to take root and grow again became a symbol of the perpetual rebirth of Julius Caesar through his family.[24]

Furthermore, the laurel's significance was in no way limited to this one story. The importance of the omen, laurel and the grove did not just lie in shaping the public opinion on the imperial marriage, but the imperial image as a whole. Indeed, so closely associated were Augustus and the plant that the depiction of the two laurel trees flanking his house served alone as symbol for him on coins.[25] In turn, these two particular laurel trees were themselves designed to recall the traditional use of the plant as a means of flanking religious buildings (like the Mausoleum);[26] and, as the Apolline symbol *par excellence*, the purifying and healing laurel was an extremely powerful visual device for establishing a link between the emperor and the divine. The crucial point here, then, is that the omen points to the potential of trees and plants as evocative visual stimuli which, in turn, create a public perception of a divine affinity between Augustus and tree. In this way, Augustus positions himself as part of a primitive Roman religious association between natural spaces and divine presence, outlined here by Pliny the Elder:[27]

> *Haec fuere numinum templa, priscoque ritu simplicia rura etiam nunc deo praecellentem arborem dicant.*
>
> The trees formed the first temples of the gods, and even at the present day, the country people, preserving in all their simplicity their ancient rites, consecrate the finest among their trees to some divinity.

This connection is then developed into the more specific category of the *lucus*, a wood, grove or thicket sacred to a deity:[28]

> *nec magis auro fulgentia atque ebore simulacra quam lucos et in iis silentia ipsa adoramus.*
>
> Indeed, we find ourselves inspired by adoration, not less by the sacred groves and their very stillness than by the statues of the gods.

Such groves tend to be singled out as 'inherently or *de facto* sacred';[29] although they may not be formally dedicated or consecrated to a god by a magistrate, they were set-aside in the minds of the Romans and perceived (and perhaps, more crucially, maintained) as sacred due to their numinous quality.[30] Indeed, Bodel argues that what makes an object or space sacred is someone *conceptually* setting it aside.[31]

This notion of an idealized connection between nature and the gods, as represented by the sacred *lucus*, thus brings us back to Augustus' redevelopment of the 'most holiest' green landscape, the Campus Martius, and his accompanying botanical mythology – both of which were designed as a way to position the new *princeps* within a tradition that recognized the numinous quality of trees and plants.³² It is against this backdrop that this chapter will analyse two garden-inspired displays from the principate in order to examine the centrality of botanic imagery to Augustan image-making at large, and to consider how the intersection of sacred space and garden space helps us explore the limits of what actually constitutes a 'garden' for the Romans of this period. My first example, the lower friezes of the *Ara Pacis Augustae*, is perhaps not an obvious choice in terms of a discussion on gardens (although they are certainly 'botanical'); but the monument's location in the Campus Martius, coupled with its obvious sacred function, does suggest it has the potential to play a role in a renewed Augustan cityscape that, as Strabo's description suggests, was consciously designed to evoke the primitive Roman connection between the natural world and the divine. In contrast, my second example, Livia's Garden Room, is not located in the Campus Martius, but it is far more obviously understood within the context of gardens and Augustus' botanic mythology. In fact, this room is located at the very same site as the omen of the *Gallina Alba*, in the underground apartments of the Villa of Livia.

It has long been recognized that the lower friezes showcase a particularly 'Augustan' garden-inspired theme, enhanced and informed by its compositional similarities to Livia's famous painted Garden Room at Prima Porta. Both compositions, through careful referencing to Augustus' botanic mythology, demonstrate the potential of plants and trees as evocative visual stimuli. I will argue, though, that it is possible to push this connection to garden space further if we view the lower friezes as part of carefully constructed spatial relationships, rather than just static artistic friezes, outside of time and space. More specifically, my analysis of the shared characteristics of hyperfertile abundance and contained profusion within the two compositions will reveal a complex balancing act, or perhaps even a deliberate collision, of supposed antitheses, with two types of temporal frameworks bound together in spaces that negotiate the boundaries between discipline and excess.

My discussion therefore moves beyond the purely visual by not only considering the lower friezes as a contained part of the sculptural programme, but also as a container for the altar complex itself; and I argue that the *Ara Pacis* does not just represent a distinct garden artistry, but also, in its position as both container and contained, replicates the spatial ambiguities of garden space at large. In doing so, I will demonstrate how the ambiguities of garden space, created by its destabilizing heterotopic nature, provide the perfect messaging vehicle for a new political regime that actively embraced ambivalence; and I will showcase how these two artistic displays contribute to the broader creation of a new sacral-idyllic cityscape within Rome. This will, in turn, allow me to reframe the *Ara Pacis* as a monumental *lucus* within this newly created landscape – a concrete reminder of the regime that transcended the transient nature of green space elsewhere in the city.

The *Ara Pacis Augustae*

The *Ara Pacis* is a monumental, free-standing altar complex, originally commissioned by the Senate in 13 BCE as a way of honouring Augustus for his military successes, and finally consecrated in its location on the Campus Martius in 9 BCE (see Figure 1).[33] Two separate festivals commemorated these two temporal milestones: the *constitutio* on 4 July commemorated the initial return of Augustus from his military campaigns, and the *dedicatio* on 30 January commemorated the consecration of the completed monument.[34] The structure has a 3 metres tall central altar, standing on a 6x7 metres podium, and is enclosed by walls composed of large rectangular slabs, measuring *c.* 11.6 metres from east to west, and *c.* 10.5 metres from north to south (see Figure 2).

Figure 2 3-D model of the *Ara Pacis* (from Pollini 2012).

There are two entrances to the inner altar space, one on the east and one on the west, with a short flight of steps leading up to the (front) east side.[35] The complex can be categorized as a free-standing altar, but it is also not untypical in its layout or structure as a Roman temple. It may not possess an *aedes*, or house a statue of a particular deity, but it does fulfil the strictest definition of a *templum* in that it is a space set aside for religious purposes and determined by ritual as a place for taking in the *auspices*.[36]

The interior of the precinct reaffirms the complex's sacred status (see Figure 3). Here, we find the representation of traditional wooden panels carved into the marble, above which 'hang' twelve garlands (two on each of the frontal sides, and four suspended on each of the longer sides) depicting a broad array of vegetation – laurel, ivy, grapevine, pine, pomegranate, poppies, olives, figs, myrtle, pears, wheat and nut-bearing trees. These garlands are fixed to the horns of dead cows (*bucrania*) with ribbons, and above each one is a sacrificial plate (*patera*) by means of which the *bucrania* are suspended. Research has indicated that such richly fruited garlands originated in much the same way as they appear here on the *Ara Pacis*, as internal decoration on religious buildings, and that they were

Figure 3 Interior wall decoration of *Ara Pacis* complex; representation of hanging garlands and wooden panelling.

offered to the gods and goddesses as a generic expression of fertility.[37] The interior sculptural programme, then, clearly represents a translation into stone of the natural embellishments of altars;[38] and is an appropriate form of decoration to help mark the sanctity of the interior precinct.[39]

Despite the fundamental sacrificial purpose of the altar, though, the *Ara Pacis* is most frequently understood in political, or perhaps more accurately, 'Augustan' terms; and scholars predominantly focus on its so-called 'message'. Indeed, the complex relationship between the establishment of the principate, the transformation of society and the creation of a new method of verbal and visual discourse during the age of Augustus is an important topic that has been well-examined over the years. Most notably, Zanker's influential study on *The Power of Images in the Age of Augustus* has been central to the assumption of many scholars that a key aspect of the new regime was a 'totalising visual imagery' that enabled a 'new mythology for Rome, and for the emperor, a new ritual of power'.[40] Zanker's focus throughout his work is not so much on individual monuments, but, rather, the totality of the visual imagery and the effect of this tapestry of images on the viewer.[41] The *Ara Pacis*, though, is repeatedly singled out as representative of this new 'communication', and it is easy to see why.[42]

The importance of the altar as part of Augustan verbal and visual rhetoric can be seen in the placement of his description of the complex within his very own *Res Gestae*, and in the physical location of the monument itself within the Campus Martius. In the first instance, Augustus' account is as follows:[43]

> *Cum ex Hispania Galliaque, rebus in his provincis prospere gestis, Romam redi Ti. Nerone P. Quintilio consulibus, aram Pacis Augustae senatus pro reditu meo consacrari censuit ad campum Martium, in qua magistratus et sacerdotes et virgines Vestales anniversarium sacrificium facere iussit.*

> When I returned to Rome from Spain and Gaul, having successfully accomplished matters in those provinces, when Tiberius Nero and Publius Quintilius were consuls, the Senate voted to consecrate the altar of Augustan Peace in the Campus Martius for my return, on which it ordered the magistrates and priests and Vestal Virgins to offer annual sacrifices.

This description is immediately preceded (*RG* 11) by that of another altar-based honour given to Augustus by the Senate (the *Ara Fortunae Reducis*), therefore linking Augustus' triumphs over the East and those in the West; and it is also significantly placed directly before Augustus' description of the closing of the gates of the Temple of Janus:[44]

> *Ianum Quirinum, quem clausum esse maiores nostri voluerunt, cum per totum imperium populi Romani terra marique esset parta victoriis pax, cum prius, quam nascerer, a condita urbe bis omnino clausum fuisse prodatur memoriae, ter me principe senatus claudendum esse censuit.*

> Janus Quirinus, which our ancestors ordered to be closed whenever there was peace, secured by victory, throughout the whole domain of the Roman people on land and sea, and which, before my birth is recorded to have been closed but twice in all since the foundation of the city, the senate ordered to be closed three times while I was *princeps*.

Thus, as Cornwell has noted, within the context of the *Res Gestae*, the *Ara Pacis* is 'testimony to the extent and completion of [Augustus'] *imperium*, as a display of *pax*, achieved through victory';[45] and so, the monument itself must be understood as an expression of *parta victoriis pax* ('peace through victory'), which secured the *imperium Romanum* on land and sea.[46] Augustus clearly took great pride in both the closings of the doors of the Temple of Janus and the establishment of peace, and these co-existing achievements are bound closer together both by the structure of the *Res Gestae* and also the stylistic similarities between the two sites: the *Ara Pacis*' form closely resembles that of the Temple of Janus, the double opening on the east-west axis of the altar complex mirroring the two openings of the Temple;[47] and reproductions of these two sites have also been found on coins minted during the age of Nero, in 66 CE, with each monument on opposing sides.[48]

The physical location of the *Ara Pacis* within the Campus Martius, and its close proximity to the Via Flaminia (which ensures high levels of visibility), also signify the altar's importance via placement. Although neither can be definitively proven, there are two theories in particular that demonstrate the potential significance and impact of this location as part of Augustus' new political mythology. First, it has been theorized that the altar was built exactly one mile from the pomerial line of the city, the boundary where a magistrate's power shifted from *imperium militare* to *imperium domi*.[49] The suggestion of this evocative and symbolic placement has subsequently been interpreted in two ways. Traditionally, the location was seen as marking Augustus' arrival into power, the deposition of the magistrate's warlike signs and powers, and the assumption of the peaceful *imperium domi*.[50] More recently, however, Rehak has argued that the location of the altar marks a shift in *imperium* for everyone else but, crucially, *not* for Augustus.[51] He notes that, in 30 BCE, the Senate decreed that the then-Octavian had tribunician power for life, and that this was renewed in 23 BCE with the addition of proconsular *imperium* 'so he did not have to lay it down upon entering the city'.[52] Thus, in this revised argument, the closeness to the *pomerium* is understood not as a symbol of the transfer to *imperium domi* but, rather, the continuity of Augustus' *imperium militare*.

Second, the altar's position in relation to the *Horologium Augusti*, a giant Egyptian obelisk dedicated to the sun-god Sol that formed a sundial, is widely understood as an expression of Augustus' appropriation of time.[53] Buchner, in particular, proposed that the locations of the *Horologium* and the *Ara Pacis* were specifically chosen due to the astronomical relation between the two monuments and their shadows; and he argues that, on 23 September (Augustus' birthday and the autumn equinox), the gnomon of the *Horologium* would project its shadow directly towards the interior of the *Ara Pacis*.[54] Thus, if we follow this interpretation, the *Horologium–Ara Pacis* complex can be read as a sort of giant 'cosmic clock', built to emphasize the climactic points of the solar year and their intrinsic connection to Augustus' own life.[55]

Such explicit positioning, both in the literary account of the *Res Gestae* and the physical layout of the Campus Martius, suggests that, if ever a monument was intended to be a 'locus … for the construction of popular discourse [on the Augustan political myth], verbal and visual', the *Ara Pacis* was it.[56] The imagery on display on the exterior walls also does little to detract from the apparent 'Augustan-ness' of the altar complex, with the upper sculptural registers of the exterior walls divided between allegoric and pseudo-historical relief panels (see Figure 4).[57]

The north and south upper walls depict a sacrificial procession, widely interpreted as showing the emperor and his imperial family on the south side, and officials (such as magistrates, priests, senators) on the north side.[58] The east and west walls, in contrast, consist of four panels, each depicting a more static allegorical or mythological scene: a version of the she-wolf nursing Romulus and Remus; the figure of Roma seated on a pile of armour, flanked by Honos and Virtus; a female figure, variously identified as Pax, Venus, or Tellus, with two children; and a male figure performing a sacrifice, traditionally interpreted as Aeneas sacrificing to the Penates, although also identified as Numa.[59]

The combination of these figural reliefs has been interpreted as a clear dynastic statement – the mythical and heroic past (east-west upper panels) is linked to the Augustan present (north/south walls), which will continue to be commemorated in the future (through on going religious ritual at the site) – and so, as 'the most complete version of the Augustan political myth to be found in visual rhetoric', it is unsurprising that scholars have focused their discussions of the *Ara Pacis* complex predominantly on these upper figural reliefs.[60]

Rather than examine these upper figural relief panels, though, this chapter will focus almost exclusively on the lower register of the *Ara Pacis*' exterior walls – a

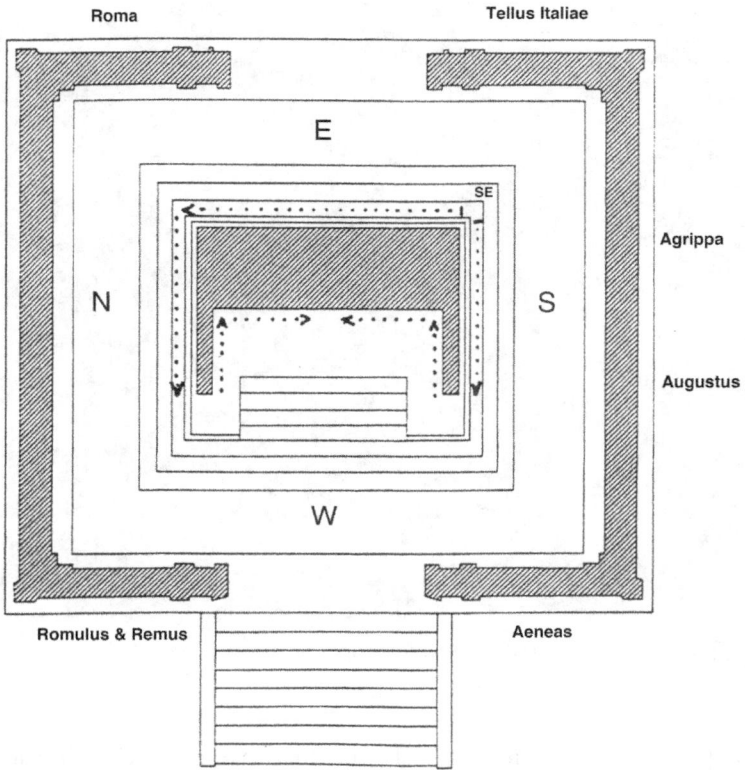

Figure 4 Plan of *Ara Pacis*, with identification of upper register panels (from Pollini 2012).

huge acanthus frieze that surrounds the entire enclosure (see Figure 2 and Figure 5). Each of the panels follows the same general pattern, with individual differences only coming in to focus upon closer inspection. The generating element of each lower frieze panel is an acanthus plant, with the large leaves at the base acting as a central focal point for the viewer. The acanthus plant then transforms into spiralling vines, which shoot off in all directions, before transforming again into a wider variety of tendrils and blossoms, all simultaneously in full bloom.[61]

This vibrant display of plant life is also populated by several animals, such as small reptiles (frogs, snakes, lizards), insects (snails, scorpions, crickets, butterflies) and birds (swans, sparrows). Each of the four walls of the frieze is bordered to the side by further vegetal ornament, and above by a geometric-type design, firmly separating them from the figural reliefs above.

Although this type of acanthus-centred ornament was extremely popular in ancient Greek and Roman art in general, and more specifically on Augustan

Figure 5 Lower-register frieze panel, *Ara Pacis*.

buildings in Rome, no other imperial structure carries so much of it:[62] at nearly two metres tall, the lower panels account for more than half of the outside façade (nearly fifty-five square metres of the decoration), with four rectangular panels (east and west walls), two lateral friezes (north and south walls) and the pilasters on all four corners of the enclosure. Furthermore, in its original location in the Campus Martius, the acanthus frieze would be at the eye-level of those approaching the west entry steps, those following the long sides of the enclosure along the ground sloping upward toward the Via Flaminia, or those standing street-side at the east-opening – and would therefore have a particularly strong visual impact.[63] The original colourful vibrancy of the frieze, with its deep blue background and bold greens, golds and reds, is now lost;[64] but it is still an eye-catching sight to behold.

Figure vs. ornament

These lower friezes were initially dismissed and believed to have no functional relationship to the rest of the monument. Early examples of scholarship on the lower panels tend to focus on the stylistic origins of the botanical ornament rather than any possible significance that it may have within the context of the monument as a whole.[65] Even in the 1970s, Bianchi-Bandinelli still maintained that the interest of the *Ara Pacis* resides chiefly in the decoration of the inside precinct and that the upper outside panels have a 'programmatic conformity which stamps all official art'; although he believed the lower friezes were a vivid feature, he argued that this was only from an artistic viewpoint and their functional relationship remains nil.[66] More recently, however, it is now widely accepted that the lower friezes cannot and must not be viewed as purely decorative. Caneva, for example, argues quite rightly that we cannot limit ourselves to viewing nature as simply decorative, for this hides the vision of the ancient man who uses plants as methods of communication by means of images that we have forgotten or made trivial;[67] and, in terms of the *Ara Pacis* specifically, we are not just dealing with a simply decorative message but, rather, an allegorical representation that transmits a symbolic message.[68]

One of the most in-depth examinations of this potential symbolism is Castriota's monograph on *The Ara Pacis Augustae and the Imagery of Abundance in Later Greek and Early Roman Imperial Art*, which deals almost exclusively with the study of what he calls the 'floral' ornament on the monument.[69] Throughout this work, Castriota places a strong focus on reconstituting the inherited tradition or 'interpretive strategy' that the wider Augustan audience would have bought to bear in responding to the imagery as a whole. Through long discussions of the divine associations of plants and an examination of the altar's stylistic predecessors, he ultimately argues that the imagery of the lower register is a 'harmonious assemblage of visual metonyms' that directs the viewer to their significative function.[70] It is for this reason that he distinguishes between the interior garlands, as general symbols of abundance to all deities, and the abstract and stylized form of the friezes, as specific symbols of an Augustan mythology based on botanical elements.[71]

The renewed focus on the lower friezes can perhaps be understood as part of a broader revisionist agenda to re-think the categorization of ancient materials as either simply 'figure' or 'ornament'.[72] Squire, in particular, notes two main problems in previous discussions of the relationship between 'figure' and 'ornament', both of which can be seen in the more traditional discussions of the friezes: first, scholars have uncritically imposed post-Enlightenment interpretative frameworks on what constitutes 'figure' and 'ornament' onto ancient materials; and second, scholars have approached 'ornament' as a means of categorizing materials, usually studying the decorative 'surrounds' in isolation from the figurative forms they frame.⁷³ These problems, in turn, led to continued 'anachronistic assumptions about form and value' that create 'hierarchical segregations' between the proper 'content' of the work and the 'superfluous frivolity' of its surrounding adornment.⁷⁴ However, over the last thirty years, there have been numerous calls, informed by Derrida's dismantling of Kantian aesthetics, to 're-evaluate the semantics of decoration' as part of a 'larger reorientation of aesthetics and art history, a movement from the centre to the margins'; and ornament has emerged as a means of 'deconstructing the ideological frameworks of post-Enlightenment aesthetics'.⁷⁵

It is in this context, then, that I too examine the *Ara Pacis'* lower friezes, focusing on how a revised understanding of this so-called 'ornament' and the movement of the traditionally 'marginal' to the 'central' both contribute to and open up new avenues of interpretation that are un-bound from the frameworks of Zanker's traditional narrative. It is always tempting to analyse the friezes, along with all of Augustan imagery, through a self-contained system of programmatic 'communication';⁷⁶ and there continues to be a sustained 'tacit assumption of communicated propaganda' and subsequent emphasis on the need to 'decode' a single prefabricated message.⁷⁷ My approach, however, aligns with those scholars who have recognized the need to question Zanker's totalizing view of Augustan imagery and embrace the potential for polysemy and ambivalence within the visual 'message'.⁷⁸ This is not about denying the existence of an Augustan 'message', but, instead, refining it by recognizing its exploitation of 'more subtle modes of visual ambivalence' and the resultant potential for more divergent viewer and scholarly responses;⁷⁹ or, to put it another way, the message itself is not ambiguous, but that very same message is also built on a series of premises where straightforward dichotomies just do not apply. To borrow Elsner's words, 'no society has ever been so efficiently dictatorial that the image propagated by the government of itself was at once the only image held of the government by every citizen', and so, to follow Zanker's interpretation, would be to 'deprive art of any subversive or conflictive viewings in a way that is culturally and sociologically too simplistic'.⁸⁰ Indeed, one could argue that Augustus' paradoxical position as *primus inter pares* ('first amongst equals') required a system of communication that embraced ambivalence.⁸¹

As we shall see, the lower register is an especially useful example for demonstrating how ambivalence was embraced and harnessed to create a new political discourse because of their inherent connection to garden space, which, in turn, lends itself naturally to a discussion on paradox and ambiguity. First, though, let us return to the site of the *Gallina Alba*.

Livia's Garden Room

The Villa of Livia, built in the early days of empire by Augustus for his wife, was located just outside of Rome on a large plateau dominating the Tiber valley.[82] Here, in the underground apartments, at the left of the vestibule, an open archway leads us into a large room (measuring 11.7 metres by 5.9 metres) where the walls are completely covered in one continuous painting of a garden scene.[83] This is the famous Garden Room at Prima Porta (see Figure 6).[84] Starting from the foreground and working out, the painting features a low wickerwork fence, beyond which is a clipped grass *ambulatio* featuring a selection of individually laid out small plantings. The wicker fence features three gates, one on each of the shorter walls, and one on the longer wall opposite the entrance archway. The grass *ambulatio* is again bordered on the far side by another wall, this one of stone, which has six recessed niches, each containing a tree (four spruces, one oak and one pine).[85]

Beyond the stone parapet is a dense thicket of closely packed plantings of many varieties. Our eyes are immediately drawn to the variety and density of this garden scene – tall trees interspersed with low shrubs, flowers of every colour, bountiful fruits, the delightful *ambulatio*, and also birds perching and

Figure 6 Livia's Garden Room, Museo Nazionale Romano (© ArchaiOptix 2015).

flying all through the vibrant shrubbery. The whole scene is topped by an expanse of blue sky; and a narrow band runs all around the top edge (the remains of an elaborate stuccoed vault), variously identified as either thatching or, more commonly, the rocky edge of a grotto or cave.[86]

It was certainly not unusual during this first-century BCE period to find depictions of garden prospects decorating the walls of domestic spaces.[87] Since around 80 BCE, so-called 'Second Style' landscapes had become a key feature of interior decoration, with Romans covering the walls of their houses with 'most pleasing landscapes, representing villas, porticoes, ornamental gardening, woods, groves, hills, fishponds, canals, rivers, sea-shored, and anything else one could desire' (Plin. *Nat.* 35.116).[88] Early examples of garden prospects within this style initially appear to depict garden elements as little more than a 'monochrome green fuzz' – they are 'occasionally specific' about the leafage, but generally only sketch the plants' botanical qualities, with 'individuated branch patterns and brushy green strokes or masses for foliage'.[89] A radical change, however, occurred in the 30s and 20s BCE, when painters developed their style to include clearer, specific representations of individual plants all distinctly shaped and coloured, with the aim of realistic portrayals of individual species.[90] The 'Auditorium of Maecenas' is a good example of this shift in representational content and pictorial means (see Figure 7).[91] This sunken pavilion features seventeen quadrangular recessed niches across three walls, each decorated with garden and landscape scenes, and therefore creating a *trompe l'oeil* window effect. In each niche, we can see a wall of densely packed shrubbery behind a lattice fence, featuring its own niche filled with a stone fountain – a composition that undoubtedly reminds us of the key compositional features within Livia's Garden Room.

In the context of this development of form and style, the garden prospect of Livia's Garden Room, with its realistic depiction of various cultivated botanical elements, is not unique. However, what *is* unique and most striking about this particular garden room is the way in which it carries the accepted illusionistic spatial prospect of the Second Style to its very limits. Scholars generally characterize this style by its creation of three-dimensional spaces from a two-dimensional plane, resulting in the sensation of being drawn out into a landscape framed by architectural devices.[92] The aim of these elaborate architectural frames depicted *on* the wall seems to 'lend the impression that the wall itself dissolves, allowing audiences isolated glimpses onto a world outside'.[93] In the House of the Fruit Orchard, for example, garden paintings include vertical architectural borders as framing devices for the landscape 'beyond'.[94] Here, the painting within the 'Blue' bedroom (I.ix.5, room off atrium) features a lattice fence in the

Augustus' Garden Room? Re-Framing the Ara Pacis Augustae

Figure 7 Niche painting featuring garden scene, 'Auditorium of Maecenas' (© Troels Myrup 2008).

foreground of the composition, beyond which is a lush garden of trees and flowers; and, in the 'Black' bedroom (I.ix.5, room off east portico of peristyle), the garden composition features a fence with recessed niches, close clipped grass in the foreground, and a denser thicket beyond the perimeter. In Livia's Garden Room, though, rather than being presented with a landscape vista as seen through colonnades, we find ourselves in a room with no visible vertical architectural supports at all. Instead, we are faced with a garden prospect that runs completely unbroken around the whole room – there are no columns, and the walls have all but disappeared – and so, rather than looking *out* at the garden, the viewer is now firmly placed *within* it. The only architectural elements to be found are the low wickerwork fence and stone parapet, both of which run around the room horizontally.[95]

In many ways, then, the garden room fits awkwardly into the Second Style classification, since it lacks 'the customary wall divisions in this traditional so-called "architectural" style';[96] but it can also be read in the context of another popular decorative choice from the time of the Late Republic onwards – the so-called 'sacral-idyllic', Third Style landscape.[97] Some of the best-known examples of these landscapes can be found in the Villa of Agrippa Postumus at Boscotrecase, and on the north wall of the so-called 'Red Room', we find a classic configuration of the components of the style (see Figure 8).[98] The painting depicts a statue of a goddess situated on a rocky island dominated by a large tree. In the background of the composition, we see a grove surrounding two temples, and the foreground is populated by figures – two female worshippers and a child crossing a bridge onto an island, and a goatherd lounging by one of the monuments. In this way, the 'Red-Room' aligns with the four basic components of such sacral-idyllic painted landscapes: 1) architecture; 2) sacred implements or sculpture; 3) figures; and 4) the handling of landscape nature.[99] In a departure from the Second Style, these paintings are often characterized by their inclusion of 'shadowy figures of farmers, shepherds, goatherds, wayfarers, and a variety of rustics' who represent 'morality, courage, and religiosity'.[100]

Although Livia's Garden Room does not include such religious monuments or rustic figures, it is perhaps the 'essence' of these sacral-idyllic landscapes that has drawn parallels with the garden scene.[101] As we shall see, the garden room is imbued with a divine aura through its representation of Augustus' botanic

Figure 8 'Red Room', Villa of Agrippa Postumus, Museo Archeologico Nazionale Napoli (© ArchaiOptix 2018).

mythology; and such a paradisiacal display reminds us of the idealistic sacral-idyllic form, itself an example of human acts and gestures of piety towards the *numen* of nature.[102] The painting, as an idealized garden fiction with links to divine authority but with some of the ordering principles of the architectural style, can thus be interpreted as the point where traditional Second Style framing meets the mythical and religious aura of the sacral-idyllic landscape.

Garden imagery as Augustan 'propaganda'

The sacred connotations of the room are further enhanced by the inclusion of specific 'Augustan' plant types within the composition, many of which form part of the same botanic mythology we have already seen expressed through the injection of green space in to the Campus Martius. In the first instance, and taking into account the location of the garden room as part of the villa site of the *Gallina Alba* omen, it is unsurprising that laurel features prominently throughout the composition. In fact, the laurel is shown in all its forms around the room – low shrubs, domestic and wild – and, thus, extends the link between Augustus and the sacred laurel grove at the villa to the garden room itself. Like Kellum, I do not wish to imply that the garden room is an attempt to recreate the laurel grove of the Caesars in artistic form; but the 'magical affinity' between Augustus and the laurel, so tied to this estate, certainly provides us with a pretext through which we should view the painting.[103]

The oak, too, holds a prominent position as a recessed tree in panel II (see Figure 9) and, when viewed in combination with the laurel, we are reminded of the central role of these two trees on the day Octavian was given the name Augustus:[104]

> For the right to place the laurel trees in front of the royal residence and to hang the crown of oak above them was voted to him to symbolize that he was always victor over his enemies and saviour of his citizens.

The laurel, as we know, had a strong religious significance to the Romans as a symbol of Apollo, and it was inherently linked to the Julio-Claudian line due to their use of the plant from their own grove to make triumphal crowns. The oak featured in this story, a traditional symbol of Jupiter, was similarly used in a symbolic crown, since a crown of oak (the *corona civica*) was traditionally awarded to a person who had saved a fellow citizen.[105] Thus, the combination of these two trees as part of Augustus' naming day advertised to the Romans 'in one

Figure 9 Panel II, featuring central oak tree, Livia's Garden Room.

leafy display' that he was 'both a hero of the Republic and the sacrosanct person of the populace';[106] and so the inclusion of these botanical species as part of the Garden Room could be interpreted as referencing this same message. In fact, every conceivable material from which a triumphal crown can be made is represented in the room – not just oak or laurel, but also ivy (depicted as part of the ambulatory), myrtle (in the dense thicket) and pine (in the recess of panel V – see Figure 10).[107]

Palms also feature at least four times within the composition, mostly as part of the dense thicket in the background, but also on panel III, where it sits behind the stone wall, seemingly flanking the central recess on both sides. In a similar fashion to the combination of laurel and oak, the pairing of palms and oaks

Augustus' Garden Room? Re-Framing the Ara Pacis Augustae

Figure 10 Panel V, featuring central pine tree, Livia's Garden Room.

within the painting is most likely an allusion to another anecdote involving Augustus and trees that, in itself, was regarded as a symbol of the rebirth of the state:[108]

> When a palm tree sprang up between the crevices of the pavement before his house, he transplanted it to the inner courtyard beside his household gods and took great pains to make it grow. He was so pleased that the branches of the old oak, which had already dropped to the ground and were withering, became vigorous again on his arrival in the island of Capri, that he arranged with the city of Naples to give him the island in exchange for Aenaria.

More generally, the palm also took its name from a symbol of rebirth – the Greek word for palm, φοῖνιξ, denoted the mythical regenerative Phoenix who was fabled to have built its nest atop the tree.[109]

The all-surrounding, botanically diverse prospect of Livia's Garden Room, with its inclusion of 'Augustan' elements, finds a parallel in the lower botanical friezes of the *Ara Pacis*. Here, the use of the acanthus plant as the central 'generating' element of the lower register is particularly important in establishing a specifically 'Augustan' feel to the whole composition (see Figure 11).[110]

Figure 11 Acanthus detail, *Ara Pacis*.

This plant is characterized by a loss of leaves and apparent death in the summer, followed by resurgence once the summer drought is over, and it is also notoriously difficult to eradicate (even if only the smallest part remains after an attempted extirpation, an acanthus has the ability to spring back to life);[111] thus, in a similar way to the palm tree, this regenerative plant form is a perfect choice for characterizing the supposed rebirth of Rome that played such a significant role within broader Augustan messaging.[112] Augustus may have claimed to simply be restoring the Republic, but we know that the political institutions of Rome underwent radical changes throughout his Principate. The transformative effect of this regime change is reflected in the way that the acanthus transforms, through a process of *anamorphosis*, into vines, which then shoot out in all directions, before transforming again into a wide variety of tendrils and blossoms at their end points (see Figure 12). Interestingly, a large proportion of these end shoots are identified as bulbous plants (characterized by full blooms and often

Figure 12 Spiralling vine tendril, transforming into oak leaves, *Ara Pacis*.

short or absent stems), which, taken together, allude to a general 'reflowering' of the earth.[113] These bulbous plants reinforce the message of rebirth started at the beginning of the tendril with the acanthus base; and so, as Pollini has argued, the symbols of *anamorphosis* also become a form of *anakyklosis*, i.e. the plants are quite literally 'wheeling about' and so representing an 'eternal return'.[114] The positioning of symbols of rebirth at the beginning and end points thus reminds us that the political transformation at hand during the Augustan regime was achieved through the pretext of restoration.

Furthermore, the end shoots of the acanthus tendrils so not just emit a random collection of blooming flowers designed to express a generic feeling of reborn prosperity. Instead, they emit a collection of distinct and distinguishable botanical species, which, once again, would be especially pertinent to a keen-eyed contemporary observer as symbols of Augustus' appropriation of botanical features into his public messaging.

For example, just as we saw in Livia's Garden Room, the laurel, oak and palm all feature on the *Ara Pacis*.[115] Although laurel is not as prominent on the lower frieze as one might expect considering the importance of the Augustus–Apollo connection it represents, its presence on the lower register is 'underscored by the laurel that is worn [as crowns] and carried in the figural procession frieze above'.[116] Apolline messaging may be read, however, in the presence of acanthus;[117] and the acanthus scroll motif made its earliest appearance in Rome as part of a tripod on the doorframe of the Temple of Apollo on the Palatine in 28 BCE.[118]

Alongside these typically 'Augustan' plants, the friezes also present us with a number of symbols – most notably, six large grapevines and at least ten recognizable sprigs of ivy – more typically associated with Dionysus, and therefore, not so obviously connected with the emperor. Augustus did not actively align himself with Dionysus as he did with Apollo;[119] and, indeed, Dionysus was often regarded as a symbol of Augustus' rival in the civil war, Marc Antony. Why, then, include such features as part of a composition if the artist was trying to portray an Augustan message?[120] Scholars who buy in to an Augustus/Apollo vs. Antony/Dionysus reading of the frieze have tended to see the inclusion of these Dionysian symbols as an examination of the relationship between Augustus and his former enemies, and also the establishment of divine support for Augustus' regime.[121] As such, by subverting negative associations with a whole composition of Augustan abundance, the 'power' of Dionysus is viewed as ultimately subverted under the new regime: Sauron, for example, sees in the contrast of Apolline-laurel and Dionysian-ivy a direct allusion to the struggle between Augustus and Antony;[122] and Caneva notes that the swans of Apollo 'overlook' the Dionysian elements of the frieze through their apical position, and that this could refer to the projection of Augustan values over the Roman people.[123]

Others, however, have posited alternative, and less antagonistic, interpretations of the Dionysian elements of the frieze. Both Castriota and Pollini, for example, argue for a post-Actian reconciliation of Apollo and Dionysus as a *numen mixtum* in Augustan iconography;[124] and Pollini, in particular, reflects on the positive rehabilitation of Dionysus as Liber/Pater during this period, celebrated as a god of wine, fertility and abundance in Augustan poetry and even compared to Augustus.[125] Kellum, meanwhile, points to quite a different reading of both the grapevine and the ivy, picking up on a potential connection to Augustus' wife, Livia. For Kellum, the vines of the *Ara Pacis* may have reminded viewers of the *Porticus Liviae*, where a miraculous giant grapevine growing from a single stem was said to provide shade for the whole structure and produce twelve amphorae of new wine every year.[126] She argues that this grapevine 'must have visually connected all four sides' of the

Porticus 'while functioning as a living symbol of the unity and fruitful concord of the state and all its citizens; and, thus, like the lower friezes, which also connect the *Ara Pacis* on all four sides, the presence of the grapevine could be interpreted as yet another reminder of the rebirth of Rome under Augustus.[127]

It certainly seems, then, that the *Ara Pacis* features a very specific array of plants and vegetation, many of which can be seen as alluding to Augustus' appropriation of natural features. It is no coincidence that Zanker used the lower register as another potent example of the political and totalitarian approach that he saw in Augustan art. Of course, taking all of the individual components of the frieze and constructing a singular coherent message has led to differences in interpretation, particularly in the exact emphasis of the combined symbolic elements; but there is now a broad acceptance that the friezes are images of a specifically Augustan abundance, with direct allusion to the gods and goddesses which were said to be linked to the emperor and the returning Golden Age. It is for this reason that the friezes have so often been read in conjunction with the imagery of Livia's Garden Room. Like the *Ara Pacis*, the garden room and its various painted plantings do not appear to be mere decoration or 'ornament' but, rather, a visual counterpart to the botanical mythology of the new emperor. In both instances, there appears to be an underlying ideological structure, a shared sense of 'garden artistry', and contemporary viewers of either example would surely be hard pressed not to see the significance of the Augustan message within either composition.

Hyperfertile abundance and contained profusion

It seems to me, though, that the connection between the two artistic displays does not stop at the inclusion of specific and symbolic plant types but, rather, extends to the ways in which each composition is actually constructed spatially; and it is through the comparison of these compositional characteristics that we can begin to see some of the ways in which ambiguity and paradoxes may actually deconstruct or, at the very least, reframe our initial Augustan reading.

Perhaps the most obvious characteristic of both compositions is how every vegetal and floral element is presented to us in full bloom, all simultaneously, regardless of the real-time life cycle of each individual plant. Although the design strives towards 'naturalism', both compositions involve an impossible synchronicity of nature that pushes them into a world of fantasy or, as Platt would term it, the 'marvellous'.[128] Each individual element may look *realistic*, but this does not result in a depiction of *reality*: we see plants that flower in the spring (periwinkles, laurel, iris, roses, poppies and daisies), alongside the oleanders of July, the chrysanthemums of September and the pomegranates of autumn.[129]

Just as in Virgil's *Eclogues*, all of nature is represented at once in perfect harmony, with the Nymphs able to collect both spring and summer blooms simultaneously:[130]

> *Huc ades, o formose puer: tibi lilia plenis*
> *ecce ferunt Nymphae calathis; tibi candida Nais,*
> *pallentis violas et summa papavera carpens,*
> *narcissum et florem iungit bene olentis anethi;*
> *tum, casia atque aliis intexens suavibus herbis,*
> *mollia luteola pingit vaccinia caltha.*
> *ipse ego cana legam tenera lanugine mala*
> *castaneasque nuces, mea quas Amaryllis amabat;*
> *addam cerea pruna (honos erit huic quoque pomo);*
> *et vos, o lauri, carpam et te, proxima myrte,*
> *sic positae quoniam suavis miscetis odores.*

> Come here O lovely boy: see the Nymphs bring lilies
> in heaped baskets for you: the bright Naiad picks
> pale violets and the heads of poppy flowers for you,
> blends narcissi with fragrant fennel flowers:
> then, mixes them with spurge laurel and more sweet herbs,
> embroiders hyacinths with yellow marigolds.
> I'll gather quinces, pale with soft down,
> and chestnuts, that my Amaryllis loved:
> I'll add waxy plums: they too shall be honoured:
> and I'll pluck you, O laurels, and you, neighbouring myrtle,
> since, placed together, you mingle your sweet perfumes.

Virgil's descriptions of burgeoning fertility are thus reflected in our two compositions, further enhanced by various symbols of love and fecundity (such as the quince, poppies, rose and myrtle), and bolstered by signs of miraculous transformation.[131] In fact, over one third of the identifiable plants in Livia's Garden Room, many of which are duplicated on the *Ara Pacis*, have stories of transformation attached to them:[132] the laurel, for example, is the metamorphosed form of Daphne, the nymph who was transformed into a tree by her father while fleeing Apollo; the pine tree was a transformation of Attis and the cypress was also said to have once been a boy, loved by Apollo.[133] It perhaps takes quite a discerning eye to recognize this transformative tone in the Garden Room, since it generally requires the knowledge to identify each plant type and know the associated stories. When physical transformation does occur in the Garden Room composition, it is only a small scale: violet flowers and ivy appear to be trained to graft together through the help of reed stakes in the bush, and other ivies also grow out of the acanthus bushes at the base of the central trees on the north and south walls. On the *Ara Pacis*, however, the transformation is obvious, since the generating central acanthus literally transforms before our very eyes into different flora and fauna as its tendrils expand. In this way, the transformative and hyperfertile abundance on the display has rightly been described as the 'ultimate metamorphoses of the natural into the marvellous'.[134]

What interests me most about this specific portrayal of nature, though, is how it appears to break down the usual constructs of time. It was noted in chapter two that the temporal structures at play within Virgil's gardening passage had a profound effect on how we interpreted the garden-agriculture relationship; and here, once again, understanding how time 'works' is crucial to understanding the significance of these garden-inspired compositions. But what conception of time are we actually dealing with on the *Ara Pacis* and in Livia's Garden Room? It is not enough to say that time is simply suspended here, because what we see in our two compositions are botanical displays that actually transgress the laws of nature.[135] If this were meant to be a 'snapshot' of time, then the plants would all be following their usual life cycle and would not be miraculously in full bloom together – and so the compositions are, in effect, actually *outside* of time.

The notion of a magical synchronicity of nature and its apparent location 'outside' of time poses a particular challenge to our understanding of the *Ara Pacis* because, from other perspectives, clear temporal structures appear to play an important role in defining the sacrificial complex. We have already noted how the altar's position in relation to the *Horologium Augusti* is widely understood in terms of Augustus' broader appropriation of time and the *fasti*. The altar was also built to commemorate specific Augustan victories in Spain and Gaul in 13 BCE, and both the foundation of the monument and its final dedication were annually re-commemorated through the ritual of sacrifice.[136] However, despite the monument's ties to specific temporal events, Ovid's description of the annual sacrifice on 30 January hints at some of the ways in which the 'message' of the altar complex undermines its own initially clear temporal framework:[137]

> tura, sacerdotes, pacalibus addite flammis,
>   albaque perfusa victima fronte cadat,
> utque domus, quae praestat eam, cum pace perennet
>   ad pia propensos vota rogate deos.

> Add incense, priests, to the flames that burn on the altar of Peace,
>   let a white victim fall after the sprinkling of its brow;
> and ask of the gods, who favour pious prayers,
>   that the House (of Augustus) that brings peace may last forever.

Here, although the monument's annual re-commemoration is based on a specific event in time, the peace resulting from these victories is clearly defined by Ovid as eternal – the ritual itself is at a specific moment in time, in honour of another specific moment, but the significance of that ritual attempts to transcend all of time.[138]

The mix of references to calendric events and eternity, as expressed by Ovid, is an issue that had been explored at some length by Holliday, whose article seeks to analyse the *Ara Pacis* as an 'intricate metaphor for the nature of the transitory moment in relation to larger cycles of time'.[139] Here, the author discusses how the contrast between the upper processional reliefs (representative of an exact moment in history, the founding of the altar) and the upper allegorical panel (representative of mythical and eternal characters) creates an intersection between two co-existent types of time, centred on the form of religious ritual. The ritual act of Augustus, as depicted on the processional reliefs, is seen as reproducing the primordial act of Aeneas' ritual, as depicted on the west wall; and thus, through ritual, 'profane sacred time and space are transcended into mythical ... time and space, [with] the duration of time temporarily suspended'.[140]

I find it surprising, though, that Holliday only includes a limited discussion of the lower friezes in his article, only briefly noting how the floral and botanical ornamentation indicates that Augustus' accomplishments were to be rendered eternal through their association with the sacred precinct. It seems to me that saying these friezes represent 'eternity' does not go quite far enough. The alignment of the *Ara Pacis*' botanic composition with the hyperfertile abundance we also see in Livia's Garden Room creates an ambiguous message that cannot simply be described as representing 'eternal abundance', because, as I have argued, the collective significance of the compositions actually shows a complete disregard for the seasonal understanding of time intrinsic to the plants' natural life cycle.

Such an 'absolute break' with 'traditional' temporal structures, in turn, reminds us of the fourth principle of Foucault's heterotopic discourse, a discourse that has been readily applied to studies of garden space.[141] As noted in chapter one, for Foucault, heterotopias are intrinsically linked to time, encapsulating either temporal discontinuity or accumulation, and such temporal discontinuity can certainly be seen in the construction of our two garden compositions – both the friezes and the garden room bring together different plants from different times into a single space that attempts to enclose the totality of time, a totality of time that itself is protected from time's erosion.¹⁴² In this way, the hyperfertility of the garden compositions reminds us of another of Foucault's heterotopias, the museum, which, according to Beth Lord, engages in a similar double paradox:¹⁴³

> [the museum] contains infinite time in a finite space, and it is both a space of time and a 'timeless' space. What makes it a heterotopia, then, appears to be threefold: its juxtaposition of temporally discontinuous objects, its attempts to present the totality of time, and its isolation, as an entire space, from normal temporal continuity.

The *Ara Pacis*, then, in its commemorative function towards the Augustan regime, parallels the function of the museum in general terms, but it is in the paradoxes of the botanical friezes that we see the temporal discontinuities of the heterotopic discourse at full force.¹⁴⁴ We should, therefore, view the magical synchronicity of the friezes as contributing to the overall message of the altar complex – as put forward by Holliday – which consistently challenges a straightforward understanding of time and its limits or boundaries.¹⁴⁵

The concept of boundaries also becomes important in the way the hyperfertile abundance within the two compositions is spatially represented. Evans' analysis of the *Ara Pacis* strikes me as a useful way of thinking about this issue.¹⁴⁶ She comments that, although the lower friezes represent a form of boundless fertility, it is telling that they are safely enclosed within the panels' borders, surmounted by orderly processions and sealed in with scenes which freeze moments of Rome's mythic life – it is 'a vision of nature energetic and productive, yet ultimately strictly controlled by the forces of the Roman state'.¹⁴⁷ In fact, however wildly the floral elements appear to burst forth, the chaotic swirls of the lower friezes do appear to conform to a pattern when viewed from a distance (see Figure 5); and so, somewhat paradoxically, we are presented with a display of unrestrained natural elements within a composition that demonstrates clear overall order.¹⁴⁸

Similarly, Evans points to how this 'contained profusion' is also repeated in domestic settings, notably in the Roman garden and the wall paintings which represent them. Gardens and their artistic counterparts are seen as a nexus of contradictions, which deliver the 'illusion of spontaneous growth within a fabricated frame'.¹⁴⁹ Livia's Garden Room, with its juxtaposition of 'wild' and 'tame' elements, is no different in this respect.¹⁵⁰ At first glance, the dense copse in the background may appear to be nothing more than a lush, tangled thicket, but elements in the foreground bring a sense of order and balance to the composition – not only do the four recessed trees provide a central focus to each 'panel', but the plants on the *ambulatio* (iris, ferns, ivy and violets) are set out in parallel sequences on either side of the recesses.[151] More specifically, recent analysis by Gleason has demonstrated how the fictional plants of Livia's Garden Room show clear signs of the pruning methods used by the Romans in material gardens (see Figure 13):[152] for example, the citrus and pomegranate trees are pruned to remove the leader branches and open up the centre of the tree, leaving the fruit clustered at the very ends of the branches; and, despite its small size, the pine tree's foliage is mature, raising the potential that these are examples of miniaturized or dwarfed coniferous trees. This type of pruning or shaping thus falls under the new art of *nemora tonsilia* or *silva tonsilis*, initiated by Gaius Matius during the Augustan period, which focused on pruning groups of trees and shrubs for ornamental presentation: this type of artistic rendering did not have to involve cutting plants into special shapes (like our modern understanding of topiary), but, rather, clipping and pruning to produce miniaturized trees and

Figure 13 Pruned fruit trees, Panel I, Livia's Garden Room.

shrubs that could be densely arranged, an effect that can clearly be seen in the lush thicket of Livia's Garden Room.[153]

The notion of contained profusion seems particularly important for the 'Augustan' tone of both the lower friezes and the garden room. We may associate the initial display of hyperfertile abundance with the perfect harmony of the utopian Golden Age, but the overall order of the compositions actually distances them from the characteristics often ascribed to that paradisical Golden Age. Tibullus, for example, describes the Golden Age as boundary-free, stating that 'no house had doors' and 'no stone was fixed in the earth to determine the fixed boundary of the field'.[154] For Tibullus, the Golden Age is situated *before* human intervention with nature and the resultant fertile abundance is seen as spontaneous, whereas the compositions, and especially the *Ara Pacis*, clearly demonstrate an element of restraint in their containment and order.

This sort of control can be seen as a mirror of the Augustan regime's control of sexuality, enshrined into law with the *Lex Iulia* in 18 BCE, just five years before the dedication of the *Ara Pacis*.[155] This law represented a 'major increase in state regulation of citizens' family lives', with clear privileges for 'acceptable' marriages and penalties for those 'who either did not marry, or married socially unacceptable partners', and also incentives to have children.[156] These laws, then, parallel the same close guard on fertility as is visually represented on the *Ara Pacis*, and it is perhaps no coincidence that Horace, writing during the Augustan age, used the term *fecundus* (fertile) to denote an 'era full of sin' when describing a wife who prostitutes herself out with her husband's full knowledge.[157] In order for the *Ara Pacis* to display the 'right kind' of Augustan paradise, then, it had to engage explicitly with the potential for dangerous overgrowth, and it does this through its connection to Livia's Garden Room and their shared contained profusion. As Evans has argued, like the Roman garden, the *Ara Pacis* determines strict limits for growth, providing the illusion of a spontaneous abundance that, in reality, could only be achieved by organization.[158] The friezes, therefore, are not designed as an abstract utopian paradise from a mythical Golden Age but, rather, as a specifically 'Augustan' rendering of miraculous fecundity.[159]

Ambiguous structures

The shared characteristics of hyperfertile abundance and contained profusion within the two compositions reveal a complex balancing act or perhaps even a deliberate collision of supposed antitheses – two types of co-existing temporal frameworks (calendrical and eternal) bound together in spaces that also represent a constant negotiation between discipline and excess. This balancing act highlights how the new Augustan age marked a turning point towards a 'boundless' prosperity, but also how this renewal and stability could not be possible without a distinct and essential order underpinning it. This notion of a specifically Augustan Golden Age relied on the careful renegotiation of normative categories, and the potent crux of this new ideology is summed up perfectly by Horace, who states that the sun rising over the 'new Rome' is 'ever new but changeless' (*aliusque et idem*).[160]

The fact that these ideas are visually encoded on the *Ara Pacis* through the use of a botanical frieze should not, therefore, be surprising, since the connection to Livia's Garden Room reminds us that the garden is surely the perfect model for representing such a nexus of contradictions. Gardens, after all, can appear static at any particular moment and yet are also constantly evolving due to nature's cyclical system of growth and decay; and, by their very nature, gardens are an attempt by humans to place a level of control over a natural process that arguably remains unrestrained and spontaneous. It is clear that the two compositions reveal the importance of the balance between abundance and control in achieving both a garden-inspired and an Augustan theme. Furthermore, the power of the botanical images cannot be limited to the symbolic value of individual elements, since the compositional configurations of space and time, their construction and deconstruction, are crucial for creating the Augustan part of that symbolism. How, though, do these ideas extend to the structural principles embedded in each composition? Does the physical framing of the spaces continue to subvert normative categories? And, if these more formal framing strategies are ambiguous, how are such 'games of destabilisation, provocation, and metamorphoses' to be interpreted in the context of the Augustan regime?[161]

Returning to Livia's Garden Room first, the depiction of boundaries here perfectly exemplifies the ambiguous sense of separation between garden and not-garden. The multiple perimeters on display not only define the garden as 'different', but also highlight the complex relationship between the garden and 'wild' nature beyond. The garden room itself was a sunken one that could only be entered through a small archway after a series of narrow passageways. Thus, the interior presents the occupant with a clear choice as to whether or not to enter it, and the crossing of the boundary into that space is emphasized by the special journey required to get there. This special enclosure of the garden room in turn reflects the commonly accepted definition of the garden as a space marked off for a particular purpose. However, the composition also demonstrates how the garden's enclosure is anything but straightforward. For, although this particular garden is positioned as part of a real interior space defined by its own concrete boundary wall, the unbroken and all-surrounding garden prospect we see in the room, bound neither by space nor time, 'effectively dissolves the wall (i.e., the boundary), transforming the space into an open-sided pavilion set in a paradise forest'.¹⁶²

Upon closer inspection, the notion of boundaries is then complicated further still by the inclusion of multiple perimeters within the 'open-sided' painting itself. Not only do the physical walls of the room act as a boundary to the rest of the house, but there is also the low wickerwork fence that dominates the foreground of the paintings, and the stone parapet further in the distance (see Figure 14). Between the fence and the stone wall, the plants are arranged in an ordered display, with close-clipped grass and individually laid out plants; and yet, in complete contrast, just behind the parapet flourishes a tangled thicket of a variety of plants, trees and bushes. Now, the inclusion of fences within interior garden paintings was certainly not unusual, but earlier examples not only lack depth but also include vertical architectural borders to create the illusion of

Figure 14 Multiple perimeters at work, Panel V, Livia's Garden Room.

looking out into the garden, rather than being surrounded by it; and so the inclusion of multiple perimeters in Livia's Garden Room, coupled with the lack of architectural framing devices, appears to be a unique innovation.[163] By juxtaposing 'wild' and 'tame' elements of the composition in such a vivid way, the duality of the garden's enclosure is emphasized – the garden is enclosing the room, while also being enclosed by the rest of nature[164] – and this, in turn, re-emphasizes the complex relationship between balanced order and abundance that was so important in visually encoding the Augustan Golden Age.

The use of these perimeters also forces us to question exactly what constitutes the garden proper within the paintings, and where we are in relation to it. Initially, when we enter the room, the all-surrounding prospect and the physical structure of the interior walls leads a visitor to feel 'inside' the garden. However, upon closer inspection of the painting's composition, we are, strictly speaking, actually *outside* the garden, looking *in*: if we follow the definition of the garden as a space marked off by a physical boundary, then the only part of the painting that is truly 'garden' is the close-clipped grass between the wicker and stone boundaries. Further complicating this inside/outside paradox is also the fact that, as a viewer of the painting, you undoubtedly include the 'wild' elements beyond the stone wall in your perception of the garden, therefore effectively dissolving the distinction between wild and tame as well.

The spatial complexities of the garden, as revealed by the multiple perimeters of Livia's Garden Room, are also evident in the structure of the *Ara Pacis*. For the *Ara Pacis* is separate from the rest of the urban space, yet still defined in relation to other monuments and its position within the Campus Martius, just as the garden is defined as separate but also perceived in relation to its surroundings. Like a garden, our understanding of the *Ara Pacis* as a sacred *templum*-like space hinges on its being set aside as a separate space and the enclosing boundary wall is the means for this particular separation. However, the lower friezes destabilize this straightforward sense of enclosure because of their dual status as two-dimensional framed ornament and three-dimensional frame for the altar itself. Even though the friezes are contained as part of the composition, it is this same 'garden' element that is also enclosing the rest of the sacred complex. In fact, the abundance and sheer size of the lower register actually creates the illusion that the garden has now become the supporting element of the entire enclosure. Is it possible for the frieze to be enclosed, enclosing and a support all at the same time? The friezes' paradoxical status as both contained and container, and the consequent subversion of structural norms, thus mirrors the ambiguous spatial status of Livia's Garden Room and, indeed, garden space in general.

Platt's exploration of how we might define the 'marvellous' is especially relevant for my discussion here, in which she seeks to locate the semiotic slipperiness of the marvellous within Augustan visual culture, and asks to what extent these forms either destabilize the normative classicism of Augustan art, or offer an alternative through fanciful escapism. For Platt, although it may be defined formally as simply a disruption of the laws of nature, we should also define the marvellous in terms of its affective qualities and the impossibility of an explanation of these qualities; and it is this impossibility, this resistance to language, which, in turn, lends visual manifestations of the marvellous a certain ambiguity, in that they are 'resistant to conventional practices'.[165]

It is, of course, this type of resistance that has featured so heavily in the discussion of the two case studies thus far. As Platt demonstrates, the prescriptive treatises of Horace and Vitruvius promote the idea that the marvellous (as *monstra*) embodies an 'aesthetic impulse that undermines the laws governing natural bodies and their organising systems', therefore 'generating a threat to the corporeal and structural integrity of the Augustan culture'.[166] In fact, Vitruvius particularly singles out vegetal and floral motifs as examples of this monstrous threat, focusing on their 'irrational' (*sine ratione*) use as structural elements within wall paintings – he argues that such images, although delightful to look at (*delectantur*), should not be tolerated because they transgress the rules of propriety and perspicuity as respects the subject.[167] What troubles Vitruvius the most, then, is not the use of such motifs *per se*, but, rather, the fact that such 'decorative' or 'ornamental' aspects have been reassigned to a structural role: the use of *monstra* as structural elements violates the Vitruvian principles of representational verisimilitude (*veritas*), rationality of design (*ratio*) and structural appropriateness (*decor*).[168] Within the context of his architectural treatise, Vitruvius thus aims to relegate the marvellous to one of two roles only – that of representational content or decorative motif.[169]

In this context, one would assume that Vitruvius would not have approved of the ambiguous status of the *Ara Pacis*' lower frieze. As part of the monumental structure, and a prominent part at that, the use of garden-inspired elements creates a 'play between the vegetal as structural or ornamental, and the vegetal as realistic or fantastical, in which the conventional categories of plausible structure and fantastical decoration' are subverted.[170] However, as we have seen through the comparison of the shared characteristics of our two compositions, the resultant ambiguity that Vitruvius attacks as a potentially destabilizing force is also the same factor that provides such an effective motif for the Augustan age:[171]

When traditional mechanisms of power had literally been supplanted, it is not surprising that conventional representational categories were being radically rethought, especially when the new order sought both to emphasize the extraordinary status and to render such status normative.

As part of the *Ara Pacis*, then, it is the very reimagining of the ornament as structure, its status as 'marvellous', that creates the perfect balance between hyperfertile abundance and contained profusion so essential to its interpretation. The entire composition's resistance to conventional categories simultaneously promotes an Augustan 'message', but also consistently fights a totalizing discourse. To put it another way, the 'message' itself is not ambiguous – in that we know it is Augustan – but that same 'Augustanism' is actually built on, and relies on, normative dichotomies and categorizations not applying. Garden-inspired imagery, then, with its heterotopic destabilizing of time and space, provides the perfect vehicle for this type of messaging.

Gardens and sacred groves – the *Ara Pacis* as *lucus*

My discussion thus far has demonstrated what we might call the 'formal framing strategies' of my two case studies. By examining the ways in which boundaries are constructed, represented and contested within each composition, and how these boundaries reflect some of the ideological principles of the Augustan regime, I have highlighted how the physical frames on display have the power to 'make visible the conceptual frameworks structuring [these] visual representation[s]'.[172] My comparison of Livia's Garden Room and the lower friezes of the *Ara Pacis* has also demonstrated how Augustus' botanic mythology was transformed into a series of evocative visual stimuli that harnessed the ambiguities of garden space as a messaging vehicle for the paradoxes of the new political system.

Finally, then, I would like to return the *Ara Pacis* to its physical location within the Campus Martius, that 'most holiest' landscape discussed at the opening of this chapter, and reconsider its position as part of the landscape in light of my analysis. In this way, I seek to move beyond the purely visual and re-frame the botanical friezes as part of carefully constructed spatial relationships within the landscape of Augustan Rome. My comparison to Livia's Garden Room focused on the *Ara Pacis*' similarities to garden space, but how do these similarities sit with the complex's function as an altar space within the Campus Martius? How should we interpret the suggested intersection between garden space and sacred space? And what impact does this intersection have on our understanding of the complex within the wider landscape of the Campus Martius? As an alternative, but complementary, interpretation to previous approaches, I would like to end by reframing the *Ara Pacis* as a sacred grove (*lucus*) or planted temple enclosure dedicated to Augustus, and one that forms a central part of the construction of the new sacral-idyllic cityscape of Rome.

As the introduction to this chapter laid out, Augustus consciously set out to 'open up' Rome to the people during his Principate, and a key part of this approach was the public benefaction of garden (or more broadly, green) space within the city. This strategy, in turn, found a happy medium between the two diametrically opposed views of garden space that had taken hold during the Late Republic. Augustus' green spaces were neither the morally dubious and luxurious *horti* of the elite, nor were they that 'poor man's farm', the *hortus*. Instead, Augustus appeared to tap in to the religious associations of green space by counteracting the disappearance of sacred landscapes through the redevelopment of the Campus Martius as a botanically infused sacred space; and, underpinning all of this, was the creation of botanic mythology that established and promoted a divine affinity between Augustus and specific botanical species.

It was certainly not unconventional for Augustus to align his green-scaping with these sacred or religious associations. As previously noted in the survey of different types of Roman gardens in chapter one, Roman religion was deeply connected to agricultural and vegetal deities; and, thus, it comes as no surprise that *religio*, the sense of divine reverence, also extended to many garden spaces. At its most primitive level, the association between natural spaces and divine presences seems to stem from Pliny the Elder's assertion that trees occupied an honourable place within the system of nature;[173] and this connection is then developed into the more specific category of the *lucus*, as described earlier in this chapter.

This notion of an idealized connection between nature and the gods, as represented by the *lucus*, was also replicated in a more concrete form through the creation of planted temple enclosures. Depictions on Roman coins and illustrated maps show that temples were regularly flanked by trees and situated within a colonnaded grove:[174] three sites at Pompeii demonstrate the existence of a sacred grove – the Sanctuary of Venus, the Temple of Dionysus at Sant' Abbondio and the Temple of Apollo;[175] and, in Rome, we find a temple dedicated to Venus Erycina within the *horti* of Sallust, as well as evidence for the worship of Phoebus Apollo/Pallas Athena and Venus in the *horti* of Maecenas and Caesar, respectively.[176] Such planted temple enclosures can generally be characterized by a formal *porticus* structure, usually in a tripartite form, with tree plantings that correspond to the columns. Augustus' victory monument at Nikopolis, for example, built to celebrate his victory at Actium, was laid out as a *porticus triplex* with an altar at the centre of the courtyard space – this precinct was open at one end, and ceramic planting pots have been found inserted in to the ground parallel to all three porticoes.

In all of these cases, then, it appears that 'only in mythical retrospective' did religious experiences of nature ever take place in completely untouched wilderness – in reality, they always happened in 'more-or-less ordered environments, in nature treated or tamed by human hands'.[177] At the most basic level, natural spaces believed to be 'auto-consecrated' were conceptually set aside in order to maintain their inherent relationship with the divine *numen*. This intrinsic relationship between nature and the divine was then replicated through the construction of formal temple enclosures featuring clearly designed plantings. Furthermore, regulations found in sacral law highlight that the establishment of precise property borders was of fundamental importance to such sanctuaries: the designated plot of land was set aside by the means of ritual *effatio*, and then fenced off in order to enact the transfer into its new sacred use; and the frequent references to fences, walls and gates on inscriptions finds an obvious parallel in the importance of boundary elements to delineate and define garden space.[178] Thus, as a form of constructed nature, based on the fundamental action of 'cutting out' a specific area of land and designating it as 'other', such sacred groves clearly fall under our definition of garden space.

Interestingly, Livia's Garden Room has been read in the context of such sacred groves before.[179] As was previously noted, the painting has been interpreted in the context of the sacral-idyllic landscape painting style due to its inherent idealized or paradisiacal nature. Kellum, meanwhile, in the opening paragraph of her article, contextualizes her entire approach to the Garden Room in relation to the fabric of the Augustan city, where 'sacred groves and individual trees provided not only much-needed shade and urban punctuation, but also a living link with the purity of the city's primeval past'.[180] It seems odd, then, that, despite its connection to Livia's Garden Room and its fundamental function as a sacred altar, the *Ara Pacis* has not been interpreted more explicitly in the context of sacred groves. If we reflect back on the basic components of sacral-idyllic Third Style paintings – architecture, sacred implements, figures, landscaped nature – it is clear that the Campus Martius, particularly as described by Strabo, can also be read as a sacral-idyllic landscape: it, too, is a garden-like, green space, not quite wild but not fully tame either, punctuated by monumental sacred sites all with links to the 'divine' authority (here, Augustus).

Within this broader landscape, one particular monumental structure is set aside – defined by and annually re-commemorated through ritual, the design of the *Ara Pacis* is a powerful representation of the ways in which the Romans thought about the intersection of the natural world, the world of the divine, and the power of a political message based on the language and imagery of cultivation.

The relationship between garden space and sacred space represented by the structure, its location within the new Campus Martius sacral-idyllic park and the underlying botanic mythology represented within its imagery thus all point to the notion of the *Ara Pacis* precinct as akin to that more formal type of grove, the planted temple enclosure. This interpretation also accounts for the paradox of a dominating garden-inspired frieze that surrounds or, potentially, supports the entire altar structure – rather than being enclosed within a boundary, planted temple enclosures demonstrate that garden space can also be an *enclosing* structure that surrounds a space.[181]

This reframing of the *Ara Pacis* as a sacred grove thus enhances both the political and the sacred dimensions of the altar complex – it should not be viewed exclusively as an altar to peace or just a piece of propagandistic art, for it is a concrete monument that transcended the transient nature of green space elsewhere in the city. In fact, although we, as modern viewers, are able to use the similarities between the *Ara Pacis* and the Livia's Garden to inform our interpretation of the lower friezes, would Roman viewers have been able to use the same interpretative process? Would the average Roman citizen have ever seen the Garden Room? Would every person walking through the Campus Martius recognize, let alone be able to 'read', the individual parts and collective message of the Augustan political myth on display?[182] Based on the presumed lack of access to the room, and the primary intended audience of the altar complex (elite, educated and probably senatorial), I would argue that the answer to both of these questions is 'no';[183] and so, if we are going to think about the multiple interpretations open to individual viewers, then we must surely consider how the friezes would be read in light of the interpretive aids actually available to the majority of Romans.

The garden-inspired frieze can, of course, still be understood as a symbol of Augustus' botanic mythology and, thus, a key aspect of the Augustan system of visual communication – long after the physical gardens and groves of this period changed owners, changed imagery, or even just disappeared altogether, the imagery of the lower friezes of the *Ara Pacis* could still be a concrete reminder of the utilization of garden space during the Principate. However, as a marble manifestation of the *lucus*, the altar complex can also be understood outside of an Augustan context – you do not need to be able to interpret the Augustan 'message' in order to identify or appreciate this sacred association, or its allusions to the sacral-idyllic landscapes represented in art. Therefore, if we understand the *Ara Pacis* as a monumental sacred grove, situated within the sacral-idyllic Campus Martius, the altar maintains its connection to garden space beyond an exclusively Augustan reading, and it is the co-existence of these broad and specific framings that ultimately lead to the success of the monument as such an evocative piece.

In my analysis of Virgil and Columella's gardening texts, it became clear that the supplementary classification of those texts demonstrated the interstitial nature of the *hortus* in that this literary space sat neither truly inside or outside the temporal and spatial frameworks of agronomic literature. In this chapter, then, even when garden-inspired spaces moved from a marginal position to take centre stage as part of a new political regime, the associated imagery still challenged straightforward delineations in its destabilization of normative categories of time and space. The Augustan botanical motifs thus also highlighted the heterotopic discourse of garden space, where binaries are held in productive suspension. What happens, then, when we take this destabilizing and paradoxical imagery and integrate it into the domestic context of elite ornamental villas? How does this affect our perception of the spaces that we find there? And, if garden boundaries are repeatedly contested, how are we able to establish a clear sense of division between what is inside or outside any individual space? Do we even need to be able to divide them? With these questions in mind, I now turn to my final pair of case studies, Villa A at Oplontis and the villa letters of Pliny the Younger (2.17 and 5.6), in order to explore the issues raised thus far in the specific context of elite Roman villa culture.

4

Distinguit et Miscet: Framing Roman Villa Gardens

As the all-surrounding, visually enticing frescoes of Livia's Garden Room suggested, elite Romans of the Late Republic and Early Empire took clear delight in decorating interior rooms with illusionistic garden rooms that played with, or intentional destabilized, a viewer's sense of time and space. Furthermore, the detailed rendering of the individual plants, trees and birds, coupled with the owner of the villa location, have all contributed to this fictive representation becoming one of *the* icons of Roman art history and of garden paintings in general; and in a similar way to the impact of Virgil's garden *excursus* on literary representations of the *hortus*, the room has become, intentionally or not, a starting point or frame of reference for a majority of scholarship on Roman garden paintings. However, as discussed, despite its iconic status, Livia's Garden Room is in many ways unusual in its composition and layout. In particular, the combination of the underground and completely interiorized location, the unbroken and all-surrounding prospect, and the lack of vertical architectural framing devices results in a distinctly unique viewing experience for any visitor.

A close parallel to Livia's Garden Room, though, can provide us with a more 'typical' example of Roman garden paintings within an elite domestic context. Painted just a few decades later than the Prima Porta site, in the early to mid-first century CE, the garden scenes of the *triclinium-nymphaeum* complex in the House of the Golden Bracelet (VI.17) at Pompeii showcase the same skilled rendering of naturalistic plant forms and many of the same compositional features discussed in the previous chapter; but, additionally, they also demonstrate how Romans of this period regularly integrated such fictive displays into real outdoor garden spaces as well.

Located at the rear of a three-storey structure, the *triclinium-nymphaeum* complex of the House of the Golden Bracelet features a painted chamber that opens out onto a planted garden with views of the bay below. Excavations of this garden suggest it featured a geometric planting design of slightly raised beds at each corner, perhaps defined by box hedges, and complemented by fruit-laden branches trained to climb up the exterior walls.[1] The centrepiece of the garden is undoubtedly the lavish fountain that flows into a rectangular pool below, also fitted with jets to continue the bubbling effect.[2] The arched apse behind the fountain is decorated with a mosaic featuring two large panels bordered by geometric designs, each depicting a lush green garden behind a lattice work fence, and set against a vibrant blue background. The mosaic panels also feature a central fictive fountain, thus mirroring the real fountain that once flowed in front.

Figure 15 Garden fresco, *oecus* 32, east wall, House of the Golden Bracelet (© S. Bolognini 2009).

To complement further the landscaped greenery in the exterior space, and the garden-themed mosaic within the *nymphaeum*, a chamber to the north of the garden features a set of incredibly well-preserved garden frescoes that far surpass the density of detail and high quality of workmanship of other Pompeian examples (see Figure 15).[3] This narrow *oecus* chamber had a white marble floor interspersed with coloured fragments and a vaulted mosaic ceiling depicting a rose trellis, and all of the walls are painted with garden scenes.[4] These scenes are filled with a dense and lush set of plantings featuring a huge number of diverse, naturalistically rendered and identifiable plants species (laurel, poppy, date, palm, oleander, viburnum, periwinkles, plan, ivy, roses, pine, violets and calendula, to name a few), all separated from the viewer by a horizontal fence.

In the centre of the north-wall scene, we also find the familiar marble basin, enjoyed by one of the many birds that populate the composition (nightingale, rook, pigeon, jay, water rail, oriole, thrush, blackbird and partridge). Flanking the water basin on this north wall are two features unique to this particular garden painting, designed to mirror the marble statuary so often found in Roman gardens – fictive pilasters, topped by herms (one of a young girl and one of a satyr), which, in turn, support *pinakes* displaying reclining and semi-nude maenads. All of the garden scenes in this *oecus* are then topped by an expanse of blue sky, featuring a series of hanging masks.

The coherence of the design across the entire *triclinium-nymphaeum* site – particularly the vibrant colour combinations of glistening white marble, lush greenery and deep blues – must have created a visual delight for any visitor to the house; and the fluidity between the interior and exterior garden spaces was surely an integral part of any individual's experience of the complex. Indeed, the integration of garden paintings and mosaics into this linked indoor-outdoor space represent a common trend across the remains of ancient domestic sites, in that fictive representations of gardens embellish the walls of spaces already partially open to exterior landscaped space. In this way, such murals differ from the interiorized example of Livia's Garden Room by providing an opportunity for painters and viewers to create 'interactions between the painted illusion and its immediate natural context';[5] and, although we may wonder how the paintings in Livia's villa might have complemented or competed with the real plantings above ground, it is within the multimedia environments of sites such as the House of the Golden Bracelet where the play between the real and the fictive, the interior and the exterior, is most obvious.[6] Furthermore, such integrated displays also raise a pertinent question about the purpose of garden paintings in elite domestic settings: clearly, at both the House of the Golden Bracelet and the Villa of Livia, the owners had the means *and* the space to create lavish landscaped and cultivated green spaces – so, if paintings aren't included *in lieu* of real garden space, what is their function? What do garden paintings contribute to the experience of the owner and/or the visitor when real garden space is also available?

It is in this context, and with these questions in mind, that I now turn to the analysis of my final two case studies – Villa A at Oplontis, and the villa letters of Pliny the Younger (*Ep.* 2.17 and 5.6) – in order to explore integrated and multimedia garden environments within some of the most lavish domestic settings of the Roman world, namely the ornamental villa gardens of elite Romans along the Bay of Naples. In line with the focus of the previous two chapters, my analysis here will primarily focus on the ways in which garden boundaries operate across the two case studies by questioning the extent to which elite Roman villa owners of the early imperial period regarded their gardens as objects of artificially constructed viewpoints, and exploring the impact of this framing (both metaphorical and physical) on our perception of these spaces. More specifically, I will demonstrate how the garden boundary operates as a porous membrane within the villa, a membrane that mediates between a series of oppositions – not only inside and outside, but also architecture and horticulture, and art and nature – and how this blurring of distinctions creates garden spaces that consistently multiply the perspectives on offer. I will thus display how the garden boundary, functioning as a frame, draws attention to itself, while also deconstructing itself, to the point where the garden can simultaneously be a framed space and the frame itself. In this way, this chapter will continue my exploration of the destabilization of normative frameworks within the garden; but here, in contrast to the earlier case studies, we will see less of a focus on temporal structures and more of an emphasis on how optics (and optical illusions) can frame our perspective of place and space.

By focusing on these elite villa gardens, this chapter also concludes my overall analysis of the three broad sub-categories of Roman garden space identified in chapter one – agricultural (chapter two), sacred (chapter three) and now domestic. As with the previous chapters, I have chosen to explore one type of garden through the comparative analysis of two examples. However, unlike the previous two pairs, the two case studies here are not like-for-like. In order to consider the *hortus*, I examined two literary representations of the space; and, for my analysis of Augustan sacral-idyllic greenspace, I compared two artistic depictions of gardens. Here, though, I have the opportunity to compare the same type of garden across literary and material evidence. Although, as Bergmann has noted, it is tempting to see these different types of media as 'existing in alignment, as mutual confirmation of a cultural phenomenon', it is important to remember that they can also be contradictory; thus, my own comparative analysis will follow Bergmann's approach, in that I argue for neither confirmation nor contradiction, but, instead, hope to expose 'parallels in order to raise larger questions about representation, aesthetic experience and environmental values'.[7] Such an approach is thus reminiscent of the framework provided by Soja's Thirdspace, discussed in chapter one, which encourages us to locate the 'true essence' of the garden space *between* the real and the representational; and, in this way, this final chapter provides a fitting conclusion to my multimedia analysis in that it allows me to truly 'test' how concepts of boundedness within the Roman garden translate or operate across different media.

Seeing and reading the villa

My choice of case studies here is primarily driven by scope. Villa A at Oplontis, or the 'Villa of Poppaea', is one of several large establishments along the Bay of Naples buried by the Vesuvian eruption of 79 CE, and is located in the modern town of Torre Annunziata (fourteen miles south of Naples and three miles north of Pompeii).[8] Both the name 'Oplontis' and the villa's ownership are somewhat mysterious: there is only one mention of the place in the ancient sources, on the Peutinger Table (itself a thirteenth century copy of a fourth century road map);[9] and, in terms of ownership, scholars have tended to attribute the villa to Poppaea Sabina, consort of the emperor Nero from 62 CE, although this is only on the basis of fragmentary evidence.[10] However, despite this ambiguity, it is clear that the villa typifies many of the characteristics of setting, architecture and decor that we have come to associate with Roman luxury villas and the life of *otium* along the coast.[11]

It is quite difficult to imagine the once-impressive original setting of Villa A. Now more than 500 m inland, and buried within the urban fabric of the modern town, this ancient maritime villa once perched on the edge of the ancient coastline, some 14 m above the beach.[12] The remains of the villa suggest a multi-storeyed structure at the intersection of countryside and sea. The location provided panoramic views of the sea to the south and Vesuvius to the north, and the site also aligned with the larger landscape through a pattern of centuriation (its east–west axis following major arteries into outer towns and connecting with other suburban villas).[13] This positioning within the wider Campanian landscape reflects many of the criteria of the 'ideal villa' set out by Latin writers from the second century BCE onwards: Cato, for example, states that an estate should lie at the foot of a mountain and face south, and be near a flourishing town, or the sea, or a navigable stream, or a good or much-travelled road;[14] and Varro not only supports Cato's suggestion, but also argues for an east–west orientation in order to optimize sunlight and observation.[15]

Just as impressive as its location is the scale of Villa A (see Figure 16). The excavated area covers approximately 8,500 square metres, and consists of ninety-nine excavated spaces; and, yet, this is only part of the original estate, since at least half is still either situated under modern streets or was destroyed by the construction of the Sarno Canal in the sixteenth century. Excavations of the site suggest it originated in the middle of the first century BCE – a foundation wall in the northeast corner of the east peristyle marks the original limit of the villa – and was then gradually refurbished and enlarged over time in three main building phases.[16] Finally, excavations suggest that a fourth phase of renovations and repairs were ongoing at the time of the Vesuvian eruption of 79 CE, possibly as a result of damage from the earlier earthquake of 62 CE; and it appears that nobody was living in the villa during the renovations, since no human remains nor furniture have survived.[17]

Complementing the villa's grandiose architecture were a vast number of interior and exterior garden spaces, all of which were initially excavated by the

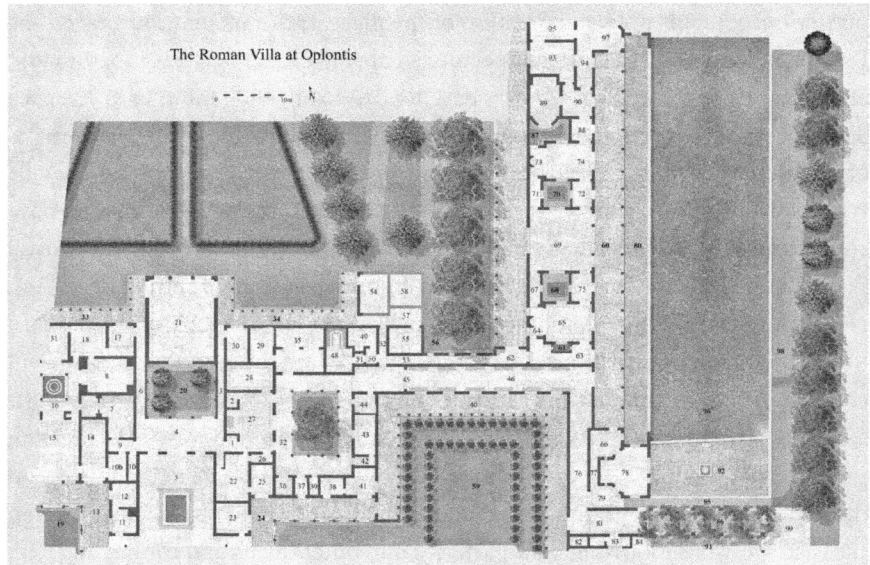

Figure 16 Plan of Villa A at Oplontis (produced by Victoria I and James Stanton-Abbott).

pioneer of garden archaeology, Wilhelmina Jashemski.[18] Jashemski documented thirteen garden spaces within the villa, an unprecedented amount for a single complex (and this, of course, excludes the potential of an unearthed west wing), and she was able to confidently reconstruct the gardens' design and plantings through the study of root cavities, planting pots, and soil, pollen and plant analysis.[19] In fact, as Gleason notes, Oplontis provides optimal conditions for garden archaeology, because the best conditions for recovering gardens buried by Vesuvius are found immediately after the removal of lapilli, and before the daily processes of weathering resume.[20] Whereas the majority of gardens at Pompeii had been previously excavated and often replanted before Jashemski began her analysis, the gardens at Oplontis were often analysed directly after the removal of lapilli or, even in the worst cases, within two years.

Finally, one of the most exciting aspects of Villa A is the extensive collection of frescoes still preserved. Out of the ninety-nine excavated spaces at the site, sixty have preserved painted surfaces (walls, columns, ceilings or floors);[21] and sixteen of these spaces have wall paintings featuring either 'garden' scenes or, at the very least, representations of plants.[22] The collection thus provides us with an opportunity to see the changing fashions and shifting tastes within a single complex: out of the four canonical styles of wall painting, only the First Style (200–80 BCE) does not appear as it predates the villa as we know it; Second Style paintings, dating from *c.* 50 BCE, and thus contemporary with the initial construction of the villa, are located in *atrium* 5, *cubiculum* 11, *triclinium* 14, *oecus* 15 and *triclinium* 23; Third Style paintings, dating to *c.* 1–15 CE, are found in rooms 8, 10, 12, 17, 25 and 30; and, finally, the predominant Fourth Style decoration, dating from between 45 and 79 CE, is featured in nearly forty separate rooms.[23] Many of the oldest rooms also feature a combination of older and newer styles, and, as Gee notes, the evidence of retention and restoration in these examples demonstrates the owner's desire to 'maintain the integrity of the visual fabric of the villa over time' – the fact that older paintings were either replaced, refreshed, or restored speaks to their status as 'markers of prestige', as well as the villa's long life.[24] Furthermore, the authorities' decision to leave the paintings *in situ* allows us, even as modern visitors, to gain a unique insight into how these paintings were 'built in' to the fabric of the villa and the visitor's experience of it.[25]

Thus, the combination of the sheer scale of Villa A, the preservation of its garden spaces, and the continued presence of wall paintings allows us to make observations at this site rarely possible about multimedia environments created by the Romans in their own land – the consistency and coherence of the architecture, painted designs and garden spaces create a unique opportunity to analyse and visualize the villa space as was originally intended, and, considered together, they 'manifest a unified vision of planning and design, and suggest an absorbing experience for inhabitants and visitors'.[26] However, despite the vast range and variety of scholarship on individual components of the complex – such as sculpture, mosaics, paintings, architecture, gardens, etc. – there have been relatively few examples where scholars have taken a fully multimedia approach to Villa A. Bergmann and Zarmakoupi are two such examples, with both authors choosing to focus on the correlation of different media, the importance of the framed view, and the integration of interior and exterior space within the villa complex, and how these factors can be then be connected to a broader Roman ideology of landscape.[27]

Picking up, then, on the notions of integration and mediation, as highlighted by both Bergmann and Zarmakoupi, I seek to continue to explore the multimedia environment of Villa A through a critical analysis of specific garden spaces and, perhaps more importantly, garden *views*. My analysis will move between two ways a visitor can encounter garden space as part of the complex – seeing an actual garden from the vistas embedded in the villa, and seeing the associated gardens painted on walls – and I will examine how the layering of boundary elements within the villa creates framing effects which, in turn, affect our perception of the space. Using garden 20, the connected east-wing room series centred around room 69 and the exterior dado paintings of room 78, I will consider how visitors are faced with multiple possible interpretations of the garden boundary within both a single complex and, sometimes, even within a single space; and I will demonstrate how the construction and orientation of garden spaces and paintings within the villa are purposefully designed to multiply our perspectives and defuse oppositional categories. In this way, this chapter will complement the previous multimedia approaches to the villa by analysing the real and fictive green space at the site in conjunction with one another. However, I will also expand these approaches by integrating a literary counterpoint – the villa letters of Pliny the Younger – into my analysis. Although Pliny's letters post-date the Vesuvian eruption by almost thirty years, they still crystallize imperial villa culture during the first century, and therefore offer a significant literary reception of many of the principles and features we see in Villa A. My approach will therefore not only demonstrate the multimedia effects on offer at Oplontis, but also consider the implications of analysing these effects *cross-media* with a complimentary literary source on elite villa gardens.

Although Pliny's most valuable house may well have been the one he owned on the Esquiline in Rome, it is two of his country residences that he chooses to describe in most detail:[28] *Ep.* 2.17, published in *c.* 104–5 CE, focuses on his *villa maritima* on the coast of Laurentum (on the beach to the south of Ostia), a winter retreat just seventeen miles from Rome, while *Ep.* 5.6; published a few years later and the longest letter in the entire collection, focuses on his summer villa in Tuscany, located at the foot of the Apennines near the town of Tifernum Tiberium (modern day Città di Castello).[29] Both letters share a similar grand structure:[30] an opening friendly response to an earlier query or remark (2.17.1–2/ 5.6.1–3); a description of the surrounding locality (2.17.2–3/ 5.6.4–13); a central section focusing on the villas' interior and grounds (2.17.4–24; 5.6.14–31); and, finally, a return to the surrounding locale and its amenities (2.17.25–9/ 5.6.32–40). In the central section of 2.17, Pliny focuses on the principal apartments and courts of a main block, followed by a description of the grounds and the *cryptoporticus*, and then a detached pavilion that lies at the far end of the grounds; and, in the central section of 5.6, the description of the main building is sandwiched between two accounts of different gardens and their related buildings. Most significantly for the purpose of my study, descriptions of the wider landscape setting of the villas and their individual garden spaces feature 'prominently, if not predominantly' in both letters: ten out of twenty-seven paragraphs in 2.17 describe the Laurentum villa's locality and grounds, and, in 5.6, twenty-one out of thirty-seven.[31] The letters thus provide us with the first full-scale descriptions of villa gardens and, as such, Pliny's villas have become the quintessential model against which Roman villas and their gardens have been measured.

Although scholars initially pushed to locate both of these villas in reality, debates have since shifted away from simply trying to answer whether or not Pliny's country estates actually existed and, instead, have focused on the literary aspects of the letters.[32] Both villa descriptions fall under the category of ekphrasis, a descriptive speech that aims for a 'verbal representation of a visual representation.'[33] the term is generally used now to refer almost exclusively to a literary description of a work of art, but the ancient concept encompassed descriptions of all types in several different formats.[34] Our essential 'definition' of ancient ekphrasis comes from the *Progymnasmata*, a series of rhetorical prescriptions aimed at training budding orators.[35] Here, Theon, 'Hermogenes', Aphthonius and Nikolaus each set out the features they view as being integral to the concept.[36] According to their definitions, ekphrasis is a 'special form of descriptive speech' (λόγος περιηγηματικὸς) that 'transforms the subject described from something figuratively "shown" (τὸ δηλούμενον) into a sort of literal apparition "before the eyes" (ὑπ' ὄψιν).[37] For the ancients, it appears that they were 'less interested in the subjects of ekphrasis than in its effects on the audience':[38] what was important was the ability of the speaker (or, in our case, writer) to create an image in the mind's eye of the listener (or reader), making them 'see' whatever it was being described.

This process of *enargeia* should, according to Nikolaus, 'bring the subjects of the speech before our eyes and almost make speakers into spectators';[39] and this, in turn, should allow the listener/reader to arrive at the same 'inner vision', or *phantasia*, that was originally experienced by the speaker/writer.[40] *Phantasia*, however, is not merely an imitation of what can be seen, but it also encompasses the vision of what *cannot* be seen with the eyes. The description of a work of art, for example, should not only express the totality of that object, but also convey the original vision, the original *phantasia*, that gave rise to it in the first instance.[41] Thus, as Newlands has argued, ekphrasis is not simply an objective conveyance of a visual reality but, rather, a verbal interpretative strategy for the ideas and feelings expressed through the object being described to us – ekphrasis tells us not so much about appearance, but the way in which objects were *perceived*, and, in this way, it has a sophisticated function as an 'interpreter of attitudes'.[42]

It is in this context, then, that we should understand Pliny's descriptions of his two villas. Although he does not use the term ekphrasis specifically, his confession at 5.6.41 that he wants to set 'the entire villa before [our] eyes' (*totam villam oculis tuis subicere*) clearly 'recalls the technical language of the *Progymnasmata*', as well as that used by Latin authors like Cicero and Quintilian.[43] Furthermore, in both instances, Pliny explicitly frames the villa letters with evocations to the ekphrastic form: at 2.17.1, he uses the term *miraris* ('wonder') in order to signal that an ekphrasis is about to begin;[44] and, when defending the length of his description at the 5.6.43, he draws upon the sizes of the shield accounts in Homer and Virgil to illustrate the power of his own verbal description.[45]

Pliny's desire, though, to bring the villas 'before our eyes' should not be understood simply as an attempt to create verbal 'floor plans'. Indeed, as we shall see, neither of his villa descriptions provides us with enough information to create accurate reconstructions of the sites;[46] and to focus on floor plans is to misinterpret the nuances of Pliny's ekphrases, since, as demonstrated above, this format is not simply about appearance, but, more importantly, the *perception of* that appearance.[47] Therefore, rather than concentrating on the 'realism' of their architectural details, we should instead understand the villas' properties as part of an ideological or symbolic code.[48] As Chinn has noted, if we cannot fully conceptualize the physical details of the villas, then the descriptions must have some other purpose.

What might this purpose be? What does the villa represent and what is the 'inner vision' that Pliny is trying to evoke? Scholarship on the villa descriptions is plentiful and varied, but the various approaches do tend to fall into one of four broad categories (although each of these categories does contain many overlaps). First, both letters have been read as a kind of self-fashioning political metaphor delineating a Roman aristocratic villa lifestyle, within which Pliny presents his daily life of *otium* and the spaces that facilitate it.[49] Such an approach focuses on the way in which Pliny's words 'register not only the values associated with villa life, but also the experiences and gratifications generated by the villas'.[50] Closely related to this approach is the second category of scholarship, which focuses on the ways in which Pliny's letters act as a response to his own 'anxiety' concerning his own wealth within the 'Roman rhetorical abhorrence for ostentation'.[51] As such, the villas (and letters) become powerful symbols of an 'acceptable' form of 'learned leisure' that is 'distanced from suggestions of political disapproval or resistance'.[52] For Pliny, the production of literature is of central importance to this intellectually driven *otium*, since literary creation 'balances and justifies the luxurious life of *otium* in the countryside and gives structure to the day';[53] and this sort of activity, in turn, is evoked specifically through the use of ekphrasis, which suggests that the letters can also be read as 'self-reflective models of the text itself as a work of art'.[54] Pliny's focus on literature as an intellectual pursuit also contributes to the third category of scholarship, which looks at the ways in which the letters reflect contemporary rhetorical practices and theories, and suggests that the letters may constitute rhetorical *laudes locorum* or *descriptiones regionum*.[55]

Finally, the letters have become a key example within broader discussions on the Roman understanding of luxury, ornamental villa gardens and the importance of the surrounding landscape to the overall villa experience. Indeed, an analysis of the gardens and landscapes described within the two villa letters reveals these spaces to be of central concern to many of the scholarly debates already noted, since Pliny clearly uses them as a means of articulating and promoting specific aspects of his own self-representation. In general terms, the very choice to feature these spaces so prominently allows Pliny to make such detailed descriptions without the fear of moral opprobrium often attached to descriptions of luxury buildings and architectural details.[56] Indeed, it is particularly noteworthy that, among all of the 'ornamental' gardens of the villas, Pliny still includes a *hortus* at 2.17.5, seemingly located near the front of his Laurentum estate; and scholars have read this inclusion as a further attempt to counteract any negative moral invective on *luxuria*.[57] The phrasing Pliny uses (*hortus alius pinguis et rusticus*) appears only once elsewhere, at Virg. G. 4.118

(*pinguis hortus*), therefore clearly aligning this particular garden space on the estate with traditional and productive values. Furthermore, in an attempt to align his gardens with morally appropriate pursuits, Pliny also goes out of his way to showcase his green spaces as a fitting setting for his intellectual pursuits by consistently emphasizing their 'superior' qualities through the use of elitist terminology, both obscure and unique (e.g. *cryptoporticus, gestatio, areola*), and also Greek (e.g. *xystus, zothecula*).[58]

My own analysis of Pliny will continue to follow this tradition of understanding gardens and landscapes as powerful vehicles of meaning. However, rather than focus on what the gardens and landscapes tell us about Pliny, I will examine what Pliny tells us about these spaces and how they are conceptualized. If 2.17 and 5.6, as ekphrastic accounts, are representative of how the author perceives garden space, what do they reveal more broadly about the perception of gardens within the villa lifestyle? How are these types of spaces integrated into the villa, both physically and figuratively? How are they used? And what do Pliny's descriptions tell us about the relationship between garden space and not-garden space in this specific context?

By exploring these types of questions, my analysis focuses on the ways in which Pliny 'frames' his discussion of villa gardens and the surrounding landscape of each site. I will demonstrate how this has the potential to inform us on the importance of the physical framing of views in the construction of garden space. Such an exploration will help to establish a cultural perspective on the thematics of viewing that, in turn, can be used as a platform to analyse and appreciate the garden spaces we encounter in the real site of Oplontis. In particular, I will focus on the ways in which Pliny uses specific language to programme our 'viewing' of green space by establishing key interpretative principles, namely the importance of the framed view and the potential of nature to become 'artificial'; and I will demonstrate how, despite a clear interest in 'framing' *natura* in relation to *ars*, Pliny also paradoxically makes it increasingly difficult for us to recognize these frames of reference because he consistently blurs the distinction between a series of categoric opposites.

Pliny, the framed view and 'artificial nature'

What do Pliny's letters tell us about how he perceives (and how he wants his readers to perceive) the 'natural' world around him? And how does that inform our approach to and interpretation of the garden spaces he describes to us within the villa proper? Two descriptions of triple vistas in the Laurentum villa provide us with a good introduction to these issues. First, at 2.17.5, Pliny describes the view of the sea out of a set of windows in a dining room, the partitions of which create the illusion that you are looking out on to three, distinct, seas:

> *Undique valvas aut fenestras non minores valvis habet atque ita a lateribus a fronte quasi tria maria prospectat.*

> It has folding doors all round, or windows as large as doors, so that at the front and sides it seems to look out onto three seas.

Similarly, at 2.17.21, he also describes a suite of rooms which features windows on three outer walls, this time featuring three different potential 'scenes':

> *Lectum et duas cathedras capit; a pedibus mare, a tergo villa, a capite silvae: tot facies locorum totidem fenestris et distinguit et miscet.*

> It is large enough to hold a couch and two chairs, and has the sea at its foot, the neighbouring villas behind, and the woods at your head, views that can be seen separately from its many windows or blended into one.

In both instances, Pliny demonstrates his desire to define the villa in terms of its views, which not only reflects the 'ekphrastic drive' powering the letters, but also demonstrates a conscious desire to partition the natural world into a series of framed vistas;[59] and he thus appears to celebrate a 'domestic context in which architecture imposes order on the land and nature is shaped into a series of perfect views'.[60] In fact, elsewhere, Pliny even goes as far as to suggest that another dining room within the Laurentum villa actually 'owns' (*possidet*, 2.17.5) the view of the sea and the shoreline outside.[61] Furthermore, both of these triple vistas emphasize not just the importance of the simple act of viewing, but also the importance of providing a *multiplicity* of views to the occupant of these rooms – at 2.17.21, in particular, it is the variety of the countryside/villa/sea view (emphasized by the tricolon *a pedibus mare, a tergo villa, a capite silvae*) that appears to delight Pliny the most.

Similar effects and 'visual programming' are at work in the opening sections of 5.6, where, once again, Pliny's descriptions of the surrounding locale of the villa encourage us to think about issues of spectatorship and the 'artfulness' of the landscape. At 5.6.7, for example, Pliny comments on the exceptional beauty of the surrounding landscape:

> *Regionis forma pulcherrima. Imaginare amphitheatrum aliquod immensum, et quale sola rerum natura possit effingere.*

> The region is exceptionally beautiful. Picture for yourself a vast amphitheatre such as could only be the work of nature.

In this example, although he claims only nature could achieve something so beautiful, Pliny invites us to recognize this beauty in comparison to a man-made structure specifically designed for spectatorship. Here, then, as Spencer argues, Pliny programmes us to recognize nature's beauty via comparison with an artificial structure – the form of the villa's location is beautiful, but this beauty has to be 'qualified by a defined visual frame of reference and described using an architectural overlap'.[62]

At 5.6.13, Pliny takes the artificiality of the landscape even further by directly comparing the landscape surrounding the villa to a picture:

> *Magnam capies voluptatem, si hunc regionis situm ex monte prospexeris. Neque enim terras tibi sed formam aliquam ad eximiam pulchritudinem pictam videberis cernere: ea varietate, ea descriptione, quocumque inciderint oculi, reficientur.*

> It is a great pleasure to look down on the region from the mountaintop. For you would think you were looking at a picture of unusual beauty rather than a real landscape, and the harmony to be found in this variety refreshes the eye wherever it turns.

Pliny's choice of language and metaphor in this passage is striking for a number of reasons. First, as in the description of the triple vista at 2.17.21, Pliny finds delight not just in the view of the landscape, but in its variety (*varietate*). Although it is only a single vista here, this variety would be achieved simply by the natural rhythms of the landscape – seasonality and weather changes prevent Pliny's 'picture' from ever being static.[63]

However, in conjunction with this actual view, it is also the description (*descriptione*) that refreshes the eyes – within the letter a viewer's eyes are depicted as both looking around the scenery, and also as being 'somehow affected by the textual description of this very scenery' – and by merging visual and descriptive acts here, Pliny creates a 'single perceptual experience'.[64] This mixing up of visual and textual forms, so central to the ekphrastic form, coupled with the use of *cernere* ('to distinguish through the sense of sight, perceive, discern) to describe the resultant perceptual experience, thus alerts us to the fact that Pliny's *phantasia* encompasses not only looking or seeing, but also 'understanding and making a judgement through the faculty of sight'.[65] Pliny does not want us simply to 'look' at the landscape in this passage, but, instead, he actively encourages us to view it in artificial terms, so artificial that it actually takes on the form of a picture (*formam ... pictam*). Looking back at the triple vistas of 2.17, we might now understand the framing of these views by windows as akin to a framed piece of art; or, at the very least, we are certainly reminded of man's ability to create aesthetic pleasure by turning nature into art through the creation and placement of clear and structured borders.[66]

Thus, in both 2.17 and 5.6, the descriptions of the surrounding landscape inform us of two overarching principles that guide Pliny's approach to landscape – the importance of the framed view, and the consequent potential of nature to become 'artificial'. It is with these two principles in mind that I would like to turn to our first 'real' example of a villa garden in this chapter, garden room 20 in Villa A, and consider how framing features impact the 'visibility' of this garden space. Is Pliny's perception of nature as a series of artificially constructed views reflected in reality, as Newlands' definition of ekphrasis as an 'interpreter of values' suggests? And, if his description of landscape gives us an insight into *how* to view garden spaces, can Oplontis similarly point to how these cultural perceptions work in action?[67]

Visual openness vs. spatial segregation

Entering the Oplontis complex through the *atrium*, we find a variation of the *fauces-atrium-tablinum* axis deemed 'typical' of many Roman houses and villas from the first century BCE:[68] a visitor's gaze would undoubtedly be drawn to the penetrating visual axis running north from the *atrium* (5), through room 4, through an enclosed garden (20) and a large room (21), eventually opening up onto a sprawling rear garden (see Figure 16). The visitor's eye is clearly directed here through the use of framing features. First, columns frame the view from the *atrium* into garden 20 (see Figure 17).

From here the view is focused even further, directed through a single window in the north wall of the garden; and this window directs you into room 21, where further columns on the north side both frame and also allow an opening-up of the view onto the rear garden (see Figure 18).[69] In addition to framing views of the outside rear garden, the painted walls of garden room 20 also mimic the effect of the window in the north wall: the murals on the east and west walls are separated into a tripartite formation by engaged columns, with each of the three panels representing a 'garden' scene with a fountain as its central feature;[70] and the contrast between the highly stylized deep red backgrounds of the outer panels and the more 'realistic' blue/green background of the central panel creates

Figure 17 Framing features, garden room 20, Villa A at Oplontis.

Figure 18 West wall, garden room 20, Villa A at Oplontis.

the impression that, once again, we are 'looking out' through a window onto a real garden scene in the distance.[71]

This room series, then, clearly parallels Pliny's predilection for framed views of the 'natural' world. What we see here, in particular, is a garden space (20) being used as a visual marker with cleverly focused surrounding frames that invite the visitor to the villa directly into the rear garden from the *atrium* in one continuous movement. However, once the visitor begins their physical journey towards that end goal, it becomes clear that the sequence of openings allowing them to see through the building were designed for viewing and viewing alone. Despite appearing very open from the entrance point of view, garden 20 is in fact almost completely enclosed: both the east and west walls have no openings at all, only the illusionistic 'windows' detailed above; the north wall features just a single, albeit quite large, window; and the south façade columns are joined together by a low wall. The room was open to the sky, and an opening in the south-east corner allows access to the garden (presumably for maintenance of the original plantings), but, crucially, there is no through route.

Thus, in order to actually reach the rear garden, the visitor to Villa A is forced to circumvent garden 20 entirely through a series of passageways on either the east (passage 3) or the west (passage 6) side of the enclosure (see Figure 16). These walkways do not, however, bring the visitor into room 21, but, rather, into porticoes that border the rear garden – from passageway 6, you enter portico 33, and from passageway 3, you enter portico 34 – and from these porticoes you can either enter the rear garden or enter room 21 through doorways in its east and west walls. On the physical journey, then, the visitor completely loses their original sight line and enters the rear garden from an altered perspective. It appears that the architect has designed the spaces specifically in order to achieve the sort of variety and visual delight that pleased Pliny so much. Here, the visitor is drawn in through the long axial perspective towards an end goal, the careful framing paradoxically suggesting openness and a lack of boundaries. This visual temptation controls movement from the *atrium* to the rear garden, but, ultimately, it also controls vision, since it forces the visitor to question what they think they saw when forced into an altered perspective. Such variation and visual trickery would have added to the delight of the visitor navigating their way through the complex for the first time, and these effects would surely have been enhanced even further through the use of 'temporary' partitions (such as curtains) that could have been strategically opened and closed to create multiple and varied viewing experiences each time you entered the villa.[72]

The disparity between the visual connectivity of the garden spaces in this *atrium*-core room series and the accessibility for movement to and through these spaces is repeated in the east-wing of the villa, where we find a fascinating series of interconnected rooms and gardens that rely on a 'clear and intentional connection to *each other* and a complex relationship of views through other spaces'.[73] Here, room 69 acts as a remarkable central axis point surrounded by a variety of different garden spaces and views – the room's 'special status' is marked by its central location, its elevated roof and its inlaid marble floor, all of which help demarcate it as 'the most important of the entertaining spaces' in this wing of the villa.[74] In this one room, the visitor can turn in every direction and enjoy a far-reaching 'green' vista. The west window, for example, exposes a wall of green trees on the eastern edge of the same rear garden that we encountered in the *atrium*-core series, and this green wall is punctuated by the columns of the portico (56) adjacent to the west. Looking east, our line of sight is also directed through more framing portico columns (60) into another huge garden (96) featuring what appears to be a swimming pool (see Figure 16).

Both of these east and west views remind us of the directed and framed views through the *atrium*-core series into the rear garden. Furthermore, the eastern view in particular seems purposefully designed to include the *varietas* Pliny highlighted as so important. Excavations of the root cavities of the trees planted on the far eastern side of garden 96 suggest that the plantings were carefully chosen to create a natural 'still life', a subtle 'moving picture', wherein the order of the trees was staggered to create an orchestrated gradual blossoming from the centre to the edges over time:[75] in the centre of these plantings stood two lemon trees, which flowered in the spring; then, moving outwards, we find clusters of oleanders, which bloom in June and July; and, finally, the outer positions were occupied by dark and shady plane trees.

In contrast to these views, which focus on a line of sight towards a real garden, the north and south viewing axes from room 69 feature a different and somewhat unique vista – here we find increasingly narrow framing devices focusing our gaze through a combination of real and fictive gardens to a specific end point of another garden painting.[76] The two axes mirror each other in a number of ways. Situated on either side of room 69, we find two courtyard gardens, one to the north (70) and one to the south (68), both fully decorated with garden paintings, and both with large windows in their north and south walls. Looking north from room 69 (see Figure 19), the gaze is directed through garden room 70 by means of the large windows, through room 74 and finally into a further garden room 87, where we catch a glimpse of another garden painting on the back (north) wall.

Figure 19 View from room 69, looking north into room 70, Villa A at Oplontis.

Similarly, looking south from room 69, we encounter another continuous visual axis, this time from 69, into garden room 68, through room 65 and finally into a small garden room (61), which features a garden painting on the back (south) wall (see Figures 20 and 21).

Using the same effect as the *atrium*-core series, these continuous visual axes are achieved through the use of window openings: in order to view from 69 to 70 to 87, there is an alignment of the windows of 70 with the opening of the southeast corner of 87; and to view from 69 all the way through to 61, the windows of 68 align with the windows of 61. Furthermore, in this east wing series, we are introduced to more novel viewing angles, since none of the windows is in absolutely direct alignment with each other, and the 'whimsical' concave and convex architectural forms of rooms 87 create new variety in the axial perspectives (see Figure 16).

However, just as we saw previously, these continuous visual axes north to south are not mirrored by continuous physical access. All four garden spaces (61,

Figure 20 View from room 74, looking south, Villa A at Oplontis.

68, 70, 87) are only fully open to the sky – the only 'entry' points are the windows – and so you cannot follow the north or south sight lines *through* the spaces as described, but, instead, you must move *around* them in adjacent passageways. In fact, the difference between visual and physical access is so extreme here that, if you move northwards – through passageway 72, into room 74 and then 88 and 90, finally turning left into room 89 – you can actually find yourself looking into room 87 southwards from a completely new angle. Furthermore, the garden rooms here are even more physically enclosed than garden 20 since, unlike the one access doorway for maintenance in that example, these east-wing rooms can seemingly '*only* be enjoyed through picture windows that punctuate the walls'.[77] Paradoxically, then, the axes create the illusion of ever-expanding space into the distance, while the physical frames of the rooms become narrower and more focused as we reach the final 'goal' of the back wall paintings in either room 87 or room 61 (see Figure 21).

Figure 21 Rear (south) wall painting, room 61, Villa A at Oplontis (© S. Jashemski).

So, what can we take away from these two room-series? The disparity between the visual connectivity and physical access here creates what Bergmann has termed 'architecture for ventilation, illumination, and viewing' – the visual continuity of the spaces, the alternation between completely roofed rooms and garden rooms open to the sky (and the subsequent creation of light and air wells), creates the impression that the structure can 'breathe', thus breaking down the normal function of architecture as a firmly bounded enclosure.[78] The Oplontis complex's ability to 'breathe' appears to be made possible specifically through the use of garden spaces, since their placement suggests that the garden boundary lends itself perfectly to transforming what could be a harsh and concrete boundary into a more permeable entity.

Reflecting back on the visual programming at work in Pliny's letters, it appears that his desire to mould the natural world into a series of framed views is reflected in the architectural forms of Villa A. Seeing how these frames work in action, however, demonstrates to us that such a desire does not necessarily lead to the creation of enclosed, static, or unchanging scenes. In this east-wing room series, the various boundaries to each room operate as 'porous membranes' rather than 'impassable frontiers', transforming the intermediary garden spaces into liminal zones designed not only to be looked *at*, but also to be seen *through*.[79] Furthermore, if we return to one of the triple vistas at 2.17.21, we see that Pliny's description actually alludes to the porous nature of these boundaries:

> *Lectum et duas cathedras capit; a pedibus mare, a tergo villa, a capite silvae: tot facies locurum totidem fenestris et distinguit et miscet.*

> It is large enough to hold a couch and two chairs, and has the sea at its foot, the neighbouring villas behind, and the woods at your head, views which can be seen separately from its many windows and blended into one.

The last three words of this passage are key because, despite his delight in them, Pliny immediately undermines the potential impact of such framed views: the three vistas of sea, villa and woods can certainly be distinguished (*distinguit*) from each other, but, crucially, they can also be blended (*miscet*) into one another. In this way, these words encapsulate the paradoxes of our two room-series – in both cases, physical barriers create division and diversion, but the visual openness (also created by a series of 'barriers', or frames) allows the blending of multiple prospects into a single axial perspective.

Blurred lines

It is with this 'blending' in mind that we now return to Pliny's descriptions – this time to a series of green spaces in his Tuscan villa – and consider the ways in which these descriptions reflect the garden's liminal nature in their mediation of categoric opposites. In fact, the blending of the three vistas in 2.17 actually foreshadows many of the themes we see in 5.6, where Pliny consistently blurs the distinction between architectural and horticultural features. Towards the beginning of his description of the villa's interior and layout, for example, he introduces us to a terrace garden, or *xystus*:[80]

> *Ante porticum xystus in plurimas species distinctus concisusque buxo; demissus inde pronusque pulvinus, cui bestiarum effigies invicem adversas buxus inscripsit; acanthus in plano, mollis et paene dixerim liquidus. Ambit hunc ambulatio pressis varieque tonsis viridibus inclusa; ab his gestatio in modum circi, quae buxum multiformem humilesque et retentas manu arbusculas circumit. Omnia maceria muniuntur: hanc gradata buxus operit et subtrahit. Pratum inde non minus natura quam superiora illa arte visendum.*

> In front of the portico is a terrace laid out with box hedges clipped into different shapes, from which a bank slopes down, also with figures of animals cut out of box facing each other on either side. On the level below there is a bed of acanthus so soft one could say it looks like water. All round is a path hedged by bushes which are trained and cut into different shapes, and then a drive, oval like a racecourse, inside which are various box figures and clipped dwarf shrubs. The whole area is enclosed by a dry-stone wall which is hidden from sight by a box hedge planted in tiers. Beyond is a meadow, as well worth seeing for its natural beauty as the features just described for their artificial beauty.

A similar effect can also be seen at 5.6.36, where, at the end of the *stibadium*, columns of Carystian (green) marble topped with ivy surround a dining couch (*in capite stibadium candido marmore vite protegitur, vitem quattuor columellae Carystiae subeunt*). These green columns, in turn, are perhaps designed to mimic the ivy-draped trees of the hippodrome garden (5.6.32), which act as 'columns' of enclosure around the space:

> *illae hedera vestiuntur utque summae suis ita imae alienis frondibus virent. Hedera truncum et ramos pererrat vicinasque platanos transitu suo copulat. Has buxus interiacet; exteriores buxos circumvenit laurus, umbraeque platanorum suam confert.*

> It is encircled by plane trees, green with their own leaves above, and below with ivy that climbs over trunk and branch, and links tree to tree as it spread across them. Box shrubs grow between the plane trees, and outside there is a ring of laurel bushes, which add their shade to that of the planes.

Pliny is not alone in referencing the nurturing of a vine to grow around a tree trunk or a column shaft: Cicero, for example, remarks that an expert gardener had trained ivy to cover architecture and statues; and Columella actually gives practical advice to his readers on the procedure for training vines around trees.[81]

Several expressions of this motif can also be found at Oplontis, where the image of the painted vine winding around columns and tree shafts is repeated across various spaces within the villa. On the engaged columns in the east and west walls of garden room 20, for example, the coloured lower sections are covered in painted vines (although this is difficult to see now due to exposure damage) (see Figures 22 and 25);[82] and the marble pillars framing the rear garden were also carved and painted with clinging vines and leaves.[83] Furthermore, this motif found a 'living parallel' in *portico* 40, where Jashemski found flowerpots and roots of climbing ornamentals (clematis, honeysuckle, ivy), presumably trained to scale the nearby columns.[84] Thus, across Oplontis and throughout Pliny's descriptions, we see sustained multimedia expressions and visual cross-referencing of the same motif.

More generally, and returning to the description of the hippodrome garden, it appears that, in a similar way to the *xystus*, the structures that help to delineate and define this garden space are created out of several 'green' elements. However, whereas in the *xystus*, when the *maceria* was simply *disguised* by a box hedge,

Figure 22 Painted column detail, south-east side of garden room 20, Villa A at Oplontis (© S. Jashemski).

here in the hippodrome garden, the architectural feature is actually *replaced* entirely by natural elements: instead of actual columns, the plane trees act as a border, and are joined together by ivy, 'forming a wall or continuous border and functioning as "dressing" (*vestiuntur*) for them', thus creating a sort of natural or green architecture.[85] The juxtaposition created by this green architecture is also especially stark in this garden space because of the terminology Pliny uses to denote it – *hippodromus*. By creating a space modelled or named after a riding ground, Pliny clearly wants to evoke the grandeur of public architecture, and yet the formality of this architectural style has been created out of plantings, as opposed to actual material structures.

In both the *xystus* and the *hippodromus*, then, Pliny has mentioned boundary or bounding elements in relation to the spaces, but, crucially, they are almost always constructed out of materials that can be found as part of the garden or, at the very least, blend into it. Subtle changes in the choice of materials creates a camouflaging effect, whereby the very natural elements that grow in the garden now become the elements that also contain it. By blending the 'architectural' and the 'natural', Pliny elides two opposite descriptors, and thus suggests that, although boundaries are still important in providing structure, there is also a desire to 'soften' the edges of each space – again, then, *distinguit et miscet*.

To complicate these issues, though, the green features of these spaces are anything but 'natural'. Almost every plant and tree detailed in the description is either trimmed into intensely stylized shapes (such as animals), or, at the very least, heavily pruned (for example, into box hedges). Thus, although nature is used to 'soften' traditionally architectural features, this in turn appears to encourage, or perhaps even lead directly to, the increased artificiality of those very natural elements. This is particularly evident in part of the description of the *hippodromus* (5.6.35):

> *Alibi pratulum, alibi ipsa buxus intervenit in formas mille descripta, litteras interdum, quae modo nomen domini dicunt modo artificis: alternis metulae surgunt, alternis inserta sunt poma, et in opere urbanissimo subita velut inlati ruris imitatio.*

> Between the grass lawns here and there are box hedges clipped into innumerable shapes, some being letters which spell the gardener's name or his master's; small obelisks of box alternate with fruit trees, and then suddenly in the midst of this ornamental scene is what looks like a piece of rural countryside planted there.

Here, the artifice of the garden is taken to such extremes that some box hedges have actually been trimmed to spell out Pliny's own name, as well as the name of his gardener – quite literally, then, 'signing' the garden and marking it out as an artificial creation. However, just as Pliny affirms these artificial qualities, he then swiftly juxtaposes them with a description of a little 'piece of the countryside' (*ruris imitatio*) in the middle of this 'ornamental scene' (*opere urbanissimo*).[86] This direct contrast of *rus* and *urbs* continues to play with the representation of the natural world and our concepts of what constitutes 'wild' or 'tamed' green space; for, here, rather than being enclosed, as formal definitions of garden space would suggest, the ornamental garden is now the space doing the enclosing, and the very thing 'inside' it is the type of space that you would expect to be shut 'outside' and surrounding it.

We also saw a similar juxtaposition of different categories of nature at the end of the *xystus* description (5.6.16–18, quoted above), when Pliny describes a meadow that stretches out beyond the terraced area. What is especially interesting here is that Pliny simultaneously suggests that the meadow is less appealing than the *xystus* garden, but that it is also comparable. He says that the meadow is no less of a must-see (*visendum*) on account of its nature (*natura*) than the artfulness (*arte*) of its artificial terraced space. This suggests to us that Pliny assumes we, as readers, would automatically see the artifice of the *xystus* as superior in some way to the more 'natural' meadow; and yet he also makes both *ars* and *natura* subject to the force of the gerundive *visendum*, therefore also equating the beauty of the meadow with that of highly stylized topiary.[87] This, in turn, reminds us of the visual programming at the beginning of the letter, where Pliny used the amphitheatre and the notion of a picture to quantify the beauty of the surrounding landscape. Once again, any strict delineation between the categories of art and nature continues to be blurred.

One of the main consequences of this continual blurring between architecture and horticulture, and art and nature, is that it becomes increasingly difficult to determine exactly where each garden space begins and ends. This is evident in the vagueness of the distinction between *xystus* and meadow: it is not only unclear where the meadow is – it simply stretches out 'from there' (*inde*), but it is also unclear whether we are meant to view it as part of the garden at all.[88] Pliny sets up a distinction between the two spaces but this distinction is undermined in two ways: firstly, through the shared gerundive in the description; and secondly, in the garden itself, where the box hedge concealing the stone wall tricks the eye into including the meadow within your experience as an extension of the terraced space. This, in turn, may remind us of one of the effects of Livia's Garden Room. Here, the 'wild' and 'tame' elements of nature were separated by the use of barriers (a stone wall and a lattice fence) within the composition; but these barriers were effectively dissolved by the all-surrounding experience of the continuous wrap-around frieze, thus tricking us, as viewers, to include the 'wild' elements in our conception of what constitutes the garden space. In all these instances, then, different categories or types of nature are contrasted but also elided, and this forces us to question what is really 'the garden' and what is not.

The difficulty in determining clear boundaries and edges for garden space continues in Pliny's descriptions of his own 'garden rooms' within his Tuscan villa. At 5.6.20–2, for example, Pliny discusses a suite of rooms that surround a courtyard (*areola*) shaded by four plane trees and centred on a small fountain. In one of these rooms (*cubiculum*), already green and shady due to the outside trees, is an 'eye-deceiving' wall painting (*aves imitata pictura*) of birds perching along a series of branches:

> *Contra mediam fere porticum diaeta paulum recedit, cingit areolam, quae quattuor platanis inumbratur. Inter has marmoreo labro aqua exundat circumiectasque platanos et subiecta platanis leni aspergine fovet ... Est et aliud cubiculum a proxima platano viride et umbrosum, marmore excultum podio tenus, nec cedit gratiae marmoris ramos insidentesque ramis aves imitata pictura.*

> Almost opposite the middle of colonnade is a suite of rooms set slightly back and surrounding a small court shaded by four plane trees. In the centre a fountain plays in a marble basin, watering the plane trees round it and the ground beneath them with its light spray ... There is also another bedroom, green and shady from the nearest plane tree, which has walls decorated with marble up to the ceiling and an eye-deceiving fresco (no less attractive) of birds perched on the branches of the trees.

As Spencer notes, this room is 'enthusiastically artificial in its transportation of a profusion of nature indoors and onto the walls'.[89] Not only does this transportation dissolve the wall surface by connecting viewers to an imaginary landscape that knows no bounds, but it also dissolves the distinction between the 'outside' *areola* and the 'inside' *cubiculum*, since the continuation of branches from the outside plane trees onto the interior painting creates a single seamless motif across the two spaces (similar to the repeated representation of the climbing vine at Oplontis). The effect you perceive here, then, depends entirely on orientation. From a position inside the courtyard, the wall paintings draw the viewer into the *cubiculum* and connect them to an imaginary prospect; whereas, from the *cubiculum* looking out, the plane trees appear to bring the painting to life. The result of this complex interplay of interior and exterior, real and represented, artificial and natural is an 'enhanced living *tableau*', designed to delight its occupants with *varietas* and playfulness.[90]

The effects that Pliny describes here also find a real-life counterpart in the room series at Oplontis already discussed.[91] The disparity between visual openness and spatial segregation in these room series transformed the intermediary garden spaces into liminal zones with porous membranes; but, in light of Pliny's description, we should also be aware of how this liminality challenges the very basic distinction between what is supposedly 'inside' and 'outside'. Garden rooms 20, 68 and 70, for example, all designed to be looked at and (more crucially) *through*, clearly play with our conceptions of these categories: we think of gardens as 'outside' – and, indeed, these courtyards are open to the sky – but, at Oplontis, they function as an integral part of the interior of the house, and are also interiorized by their own structural location within the villa. This play, then, between interior and exterior space is heightened even further in the east-wing room series because of the interaction between multiple versions of the same effect across the north–south axial perspective.

A final example of these effects can be found at 5.6.37–40, where Pliny describes another *cubiculum*, this time paired with a *zothecula*, that are designed to be a continuation or extension of the *hippodromus* garden:

> *E regione stibadii adversum cubiculum tantum stibadio reddit ornatus, quantum accipit ab illo. Marmore splendet, valvis in viridia prominet et exit, alia viridia superioribus inferioribusque fenestris suspicit despicitque. Mox zothecula refugit quasi in cubiculum idem atque aliud. Lectus hic et undique fenestrae, et tamen lumen obscurum umbra premente. Nam laetissima vitis per omne tectum in culmen nititur et ascendit. Non secus ibi quam in nemore iaceas, imbrem tantum tamquam in nemore non sentias.*

> Facing the seat is a bedroom, which contributes as much to the beauty of the scene as it gains from its position. It is built of shining white marble, extended by folding doors, which open straight out into greenery; its upper and lower windows all look out into more greenery above and below. Next, a small alcove, which is part of the room but also separated from it. Here there is a bed, and, although it has windows on all its walls, the light is dimmed by the dense shade of a flourishing vine, which climbs over the whole building up to the roof. There you can lie and imagine you are in a grove, but without the risk of rain.

Initially, in this *cubiculum*, we notice the same sort of intentionally framed view onto a 'natural' or green landscape that we have come to expect within the villa setting – here, the folding door and series of windows all provide a bounded structure through which to focus our gaze onto the greenery outside. However, once again, we also see the same play between oppositional categories, producing a counterpoint to the notion of intentional division evoked by the very same boundaries, and an elision of indoor and outdoor space. Within the alcove, for example, the vine covers the building so much that you can lie inside and imagine that you are not in a room at all but in a grove (*nemore*); and, from a position outside looking into this alcove, one can imagine that the vine hides the architectural structure of the building entirely, perhaps suggesting a naturally occurring canopy of vine, as opposed to an actual marble room. Furthermore, Pliny's choice of vocabulary for the outside 'greenery' suggests, rather paradoxically, an immersive quality. *Viridia*, linguistically, suggests *viridaria*, a term used to denote small, enclosed gardens that made ornamental greenery the star turn and were often covered in frescoes also decorated with garden images;[92] and, indeed, it is a term that could quite easily be used to describe the interior courtyard gardens (20, 68, 70) that we have seen at Oplontis. By using the evocative term *viridia* to describe an *outside* and, presumably, open space, Pliny quite literally turns our notions of interior and exterior space inside-out.

The two garden-room series at 5.6.20–2 and 5.6.37–40 thus demonstrate that, by blurring the distinction between architectural and horticultural elements, Pliny also blurs the distinction between concepts of *ars* and *natura*, and between inside and outside space. Although the inside rooms here are described as distinct and separate spaces, different in some way to the outside greenery, they also simultaneously become part of that outside greenery as an extension. In both instances, we are left questioning where each garden space truly begins and ends – and, despite a consistent emphasis on framing green spaces into constructed views, Pliny also, paradoxically, makes it increasingly difficult for us to recognize those frames.

Challenging perspectives

If our frames of reference become less clear, how do we conceptualize the spaces presented to us and how do we perceive each individual space in relation to one another? In this final section, I would like to return to Oplontis and unpack the seemingly straightforward lines of sight previously discussed by analysing the impact of the intermediary garden paintings in rooms 68 and 70 on these axial perspectives. The *cubiculum/areola* room series described by Pliny at 5.6.20–2 has already drawn our attention to the interplay between real and represented gardens – by merging the branches of the outside plane tree with the fictive branches of the interior fresco, Pliny challenges any strict delineation between the two spaces by creating a single, seamless intermedial motif. The phrasing Pliny uses here (*imitata pictura*), in turn, reminds us of the visual programming set out earlier in the letter, where he actively encourages us to view the natural landscape like a picture (*formam ... pictam*, 5.6.13). However, if Pliny wants us to view real gardens like pictures, how should we view actual pictures (or frescoes) of said gardens? And what impact do such garden paintings have on our perception of the space they decorate and the spaces around them?

In both room 68 and 70 of the east-wing room series, garden paintings cover every surface of the walls (see Figures 23 and 24). The north wall of room 70, specifically the panel to the left of its north window (the predominant view when looking through from room 69) is representative of the series of repeated motifs we find across all of the painted surfaces of these two rooms.

The garden scene depicted on this room 70 panel (see Figure 23) is centred on a marble crater with spiral handles, sitting atop a tall base. The crater itself features a carving of a male hybrid with swirling snake legs, and is filled with bubbling water, and myrtle shrubs completely surround the ornamentation. Two birds also punctuate and bring life to the scene – on the right side, a high bright blue peacock perches on the edge of the basin, and, to the left, a smaller bird hovers, as if waiting its turn to take a drink from the water. The entire scene is set against a bright yellow background and framed with contrasting red borders. Painted vines climb up the vertical sides of the panel, and the lower border is also decorated with a pattern of low-lying shrubs.

All of the panels in room 68 and 70 follow this general pattern – a marble fountain surrounded by plants and birds, set against a yellow background and framed by red borders. This pattern is also repeated in rooms 61 and 87, the 'end points' of the vistas, with the exception of the south wall of room 87, where the colour scheme is reversed and we find yellow borders surrounding a scene set against a red background. Within this repeated pattern, the artist creates *varietas* across the rectangular panels through small variations in form. The fountains, for example, vary in shape, size and design, and some emit jets of water while others feature a still pool. The plant types on display are also equally varied: across the range of panels, we can identify myrtle, oleander, berry bushes and pine surrounding the basins, and fern, hart's tongue and iris feature along the bottom red border, as well as vines on the vertical borders. There are also further, but unidentifiable, species depicted on the yellow backgrounds. As Young notes, upon closer inspection of the compositions, more plants emerge – 'hazy and barely visible, quick brush strokes in darker shades of yellow paint outline additional leaves and branches, creating greater depth'.[93]

Figure 23 Garden painting, north-west wall of room 70, Villa A at Oplontis.

Figure 24 Garden paintings, south-west corner and west wall of room 68, Villa A at Oplontis.

Several compositional features of these decorative schemes are worth noting. First, there is a clear emphasis on structure and order throughout: the repeated, rectangular panels surrounded by borders create a visual spectacle that reflects both Pliny's desire for partitioning views of 'natural' spaces into purposefully framed tableaux, and the broader definition of garden space as that which is marked off or set aside by means of a clear boundary. The choice of a bold red colour for these borders is particularly noteworthy, since this creates a much more vibrant and stand out effect than, say, a plain white or cream surround. Similarly, the choice of yellow as a background colour for these garden fountain scenes is another bold choice, and one that makes us question how we are meant to perceive the 'interior' space of these rectangular panels.

If the artist had used a more naturalistic blue background, like the one on the east and west walls of garden room 20 (see Figures 18 and 25), one could argue that the framed scenes on the north and south vistas of this east-wing series were designed to mirror the 'real' garden prospects to the east and west; but the choice of yellow, however, is anything but 'natural'. Are we, then, meant to view these red/yellow panels in the east wing as 'windows', offering us a glimpse 'outside'? Or are they 'marked as "inside" and integrated into the interior built-space'?[94] In the context of the styles of Roman mural frescoes, we can certainly view these garden

Figure 25 West wall panel with engaged columns featuring painted ivy detail, garden room 20, Villa A at Oplontis (© S. Jashemski).

panels as an example of the Second Style tendency to transform the wall into a 'series of make-believe vistas' in which the 'elaborate architectural frames depicted *on* the wall lend the tantalising impression that the wall itself dissolves, allowing isolated glimpses into a world "outside"'.[95]

The notion that these panels are windows, however, is brought into question by the inclusion of vines and plants on the red border, another example of the intermedial 'climbing vine' motif we have seen in Pliny's villa descriptions and across the Oplontis complex. Although the contrast between the red and yellow colours initially reinforces a sense of clear division between the external 'frame' and the view 'inside' the 'window', this division is undermined by the inclusion of plant elements in both areas. Are the vines meant to represent painted decoration in contrast to the 'real' fountain scenes? Are they simply additional decorative plant life? By including plants as part of the red borders, it seems to me that the artist sought to blur the distinction between frame and interior; and this, of course, provides a real-life counterpart to the blurring of boundaries between architecture and horticulture, between *ars* and *natura*, which played such a huge part in Pliny's two villa letters.[96]

It is one thing to perceive each panel individually, or even as a painted series, as part of a single flat wall surface, but what happens when we reintegrate these two-dimensional surfaces into their three-dimensional structural surrounds? We cannot, and should not, view these painted panels alone because of the interconnected of the east-wing rooms, which is so significant that you can actually see from niche 61 all the way through to room 89, traversing six other spaces in the process (65, 68, 69, 70, 75, 87) (see Figures 19, 20 and 26). It is through this reintegration of the panels back into the room series that notions of framing become far more complicated because, when we consider rooms 68 and 70 as part of the north–south visual axes from room 69, we see that the garden paintings within these rooms not only are bounded themselves, but also act as boundaries for other rooms.

The paintings within 68 and 70 of course feature the individually framed fountain scenes already discussed, and they are also framed by the window openings from room 69, creating a sort of double enclosure as we look into the rooms from the central point of 69. These paintings, however, also frame the windows looking through into rooms 87 and 61, which again feature the same yellow/red repeated garden composition. The positioning of garden paintings at the intermediary and end points of these visual axes creates a contradiction where the 'garden' element is both frame and the thing being framed, and at the same time, dependant on perspective (see Figure 26);[97] and this 'hall of mirrors'

Figure 26 Inside room 68, looking through in room 65, with room 61 in the distance, Villa A at Oplontis (© S. Jashemski).

effects thus creates a form of *mise en abyme* 'where the ontological status of two-dimensional painting and three-dimensional garden (not to mention interior and exterior space) continually shifts as each frames the other'.[98]

The same effect is created by the paintings on the exterior walls of room 78 (facing onto the swimming pool garden, specifically area 92) and room 66 (facing onto portico 60 and area 80), paintings often overlooked in comparison to the lavish examples in the east-wing series but equally important in terms of demonstrating the contradictory messages of framing, as well as the challenging sense of perspective, that I have been discussing thus far (see Figure 27).[99] Here, at the base of the east wall of room 78, and underneath a window that provides a view into the interior space, we find a painted garden motif that extends along the entire exterior wall, crossing over onto the eastern section of the exterior of room 66, and also wrapping round onto the north exterior wall of that room. In the foreground of the painting, there is a brown lattice fence, behind which is a series of low-lying green shrubbery surrounded by flying birds, and all set against a white/cream background; and, as such, these naturalistic scenes reflect the stereotypical features we have come to recognize in Roman garden paintings. Due to their exterior location, these paintings are not as well-preserved as those in the interior, and they generally lack the level of detail that would give them a

Figure 27 Painted detail under window, exterior wall of room 78 facing on to large swimming pool garden, Villa A at Oplontis.

proper three-dimensional appearance but the life-like size of the plants, the location of the mural close to the ground, and the accompanying birds in the scene all prevent these borders from slipping into the category of fully abstract pattern.

These particular exterior garden paintings highlight the constant play between inside and outside, framing and framed, enclosing and enclosed space that we have encountered elsewhere at Oplontis and in Pliny's descriptions. From inside room 78, we are presented with a relatively straightforward, framed view out on to the exterior garden;[100] but, from a position inside the exterior garden, framing once again becomes far more complex, and specifically because of the placement and compositional characteristics of the garden paintings. First, the walls in question – the physical architectural structure – surround the interior room, but these walls also contribute to bounding the outside garden, creating a double enclosure; and the garden scene on display on the exterior face of the wall (itself confined within the two-dimensional plane) both encloses the exterior space and acts as a surrounding frame into the interior one. This, in turn, reminds us of the paradox of the *Ara Pacis* structure, where we saw plants as enclosed within the confines of the lower frieze panels, but also as the enclosing element of the altar space proper, surrounding the interior as a container.

Second, the inclusion of a fence within the composition of the wall paintings at Oplontis also reminds us of the multiple perimeters at work in Livia's Garden Room, and, particularly, their ability to challenge or confuse a viewer's perspective. Is the painted fence on the dado of the exterior wall of room 78 meant to reiterate keeping us hemmed 'inside' the real, outside garden? Or is the fence a reminder that the viewer is being kept at a conceptual distance 'outside' of the represented garden beyond the fence? We, as viewers, are simultaneously inside the outside garden, but also outside the painted garden. Which is the 'correct' viewpoint to take with these differing perspectives on offer, if there is one at all? Or are we meant to view them in conjunction with one another? What these particular paintings demonstrate is how the combination of garden paintings and garden spaces at Oplontis appear purposefully designed to multiply our perspectives and challenge our sense of spatial delineation. We are left constantly questioning where we are in relation to each garden space, and, despite the emphasis on apparently clear and structured vistas, we are constantly required to realign our focus again and again.

At the beginning of this chapter, I set out to examine the extent to which elite Romans of the first century CE regarded their villa gardens along the Bay of Naples as objects of artificially constructed viewpoints, and to explore the impact of this framing (both metaphorical and physical) on our perception of the space. More specifically, through a comparison of Pliny the Younger's ekphrastic villa descriptions and the material remains of Villa A at Oplontis, I sought to establish a cultural perspective on the thematics of viewing garden space that could then be used a platform to analyse views of real and fictive gardens within an actual villa site. In turn, I set out to demonstrate how a multimedia examination of these types of gardens enables us not only to envisage the physical appearance of said gardens; but, perhaps more importantly, how this appearance was perceived phenomenologically by the occupants of the villa site.

Throughout the course of my analysis, it became clear that both Pliny and the designers of Villa A were guided by a central desire to partition the natural world into a series of framed vistas – and the remains of green spaces at Oplontis undoubtedly demonstrate how a play between visual openness and spatial segregation, created through the use of various boundaries, can be utilized to direct and guide the visitor's lines of sight, ultimately controlling their movement to and through different areas of the villa. Paradoxically, though, despite an insistence on the apparent proliferation of framing devices in the construction of villa gardens, the boundaries set up in Villa A do not operate as finite divisions but, rather, as porous membranes that mediate between a series of oppositions (or, as Pliny states, '*distinguit et miscet*'). In particular, it is the creation of a 'green architecture' that dissolves the distinction between architectural and horticultural elements, which, in turn, blurs the lines between interior and exterior space, and our perception of what truly constitutes either *ars* or *natura*.

This blurring of boundaries, then, along with the orientation of garden space and paintings, creates a series of spaces at Oplontis that consistently multiply the perspectives on offer and challenge our sense of orientation: we saw a disparity between physical and visual boundaries; enclosing boundaries to one space acting as windows on to another; and paintings that are enclosed within a two-dimensional plane both 'enclosing' a physical space, while also connecting us to an imaginary landscape that has no bounds. Thus, across the complex, the garden boundary seems to draw attention to itself, while also deconstructing itself, to the point where the 'garden' element can simultaneously be framed space and the frame itself. Indeed, the idea of a boundary has been completely flipped on its head in the villa context, since the paradoxical perspectives offered to us create a viewer experience that does not provide a clear delineation between what is 'inside' or 'outside' any particular garden space. Where does one garden begin? Where does it end? Once again, then, it remains unclear.

Conclusion: Seneca's *Thyestes* and the Anti-Garden

The aim of this book has been to interrogate the notion of 'the boundary' as an essential characteristic of the Roman garden and to explore the perception of Roman garden space in response to its limits – both temporal and spatial. Using six case studies from both literature and material and visual culture, my study was designed to examine the status of individual garden sites by providing answers to the following key questions: what purpose do boundaries serve in each individual garden? Why are they constructed in the way that they are? How do they affect the relationship between the garden and the not-garden, the garden and the visitor, or the garden and the viewer? And how does the notion of boundedness translate across real, represented and textual garden forms? In posing these questions, I sought to demonstrate the potential for furthering our understanding of individual Roman gardens by combining critical and nuanced analysis of each site's boundaries within an overall theoretical framework that allowed for intermedial analysis at the level of space.

The preceding chapters have explored the status of three of the sub-categories of garden space from the Late Republic and Early Empire – agricultural, sacred and ornamental villa – as they relate to, or are framed by, their contexts. Although, due to the limited available evidence, it was not always possible to achieve an intermedial analysis within each of these sub-categories, the potential for intermedial study was demonstrated by the integration of examples from literature, art and archaeology across the three chapters as a whole. Of course, as with any intermedial investigation, there was potential difficulty in moving across analysis of different media, produced in different contexts and for different audiences; and yet the formulation of my six chosen case studies into three sets of comparative pairs has demonstrated a productive method for focusing on the key issues at stake, while also providing a flexible enough model for use in complementary further research. By focusing on a common characteristic (the boundary) across a variety of examples arranged by theme, I was able to ground my wide-ranging analysis through the use of a clear anchoring principle. Furthermore, the three sub-categories chosen represented just three of the several categories of Roman garden space identified in chapter one, and the choice of case studies within these sub-categories could have also been different, thus demonstrating the potential of this structural framework for future enquiry. My investigation has shown that, although Roman gardens of the Late Republic and Early Empire all demonstrate a basic adherence to the transcultural understanding of the garden as a marked-off and 'separate' cultivated space, they also operate within broader spatial networks; and it is the relationship with these networks that creates such intriguing ambiguity within each individual garden site. In fact, it became clear that the ambiguities of garden space at-large stemmed from the permeability of its edges, albeit permeability expressed in different ways depending on individual context.

In chapter two, for example, we saw how Virgil and Columella, through the construction of their gardens-as-texts, articulated a set of cultural perceptions regarding the status of the 'original' *hortus*; and how these perceptions did not allow us to draw a definitive line between garden space proper and agricultural space at-large. The *hortus* was shown to be neither truly 'inside' nor 'outside' of agriculture, but, instead, a supplement to it. This supplementary classification, in turn, became a useful critical concept for unpacking and understanding the often paradoxical and ambiguous spatial and temporal structures within other, and later, manifestations of garden space.

Indeed, the ways in which garden space of this period challenged straightforward delineations of normative categories of time and space was made abundantly clear in my examination of the garden-themed compositions of the *Ara Pacis* and Livia's Garden Room in chapter three. Here, through the analysis of the ways in which boundaries were constructed, represented and contested within the two compositions, I demonstrated how Augustan image-makers harnessed the ambiguity of garden space in order to reflect the ideological structures at work within the new regime. This ambiguity, in turn, created an intersection between sacred space and garden space; an intersection that allows us to reframe the *Ara Pacis* as a monumental sacred grove to Augustus that compensated for the transient nature of green space elsewhere in the city by translating the imperial botanical mythology onto stone.

In this way, the case studies of chapters two and three showcased the heterotopic nature of garden space in their relational disruption of time and space; and the heterotopic dislocation of space, in particular, was also a key feature of the elite villa gardens discussed in chapter four. In both the material remains of Villa A at Oplontis and the ekphrastic villa letters of Pliny the Younger, it was clear that garden boundaries had been constructed in such a way as to consistently challenge our sense of perspective and realign our focus again and again. We were then left unable to make a clear distinction between a number of categoric opposites, which then made it increasingly difficult to determine the limits of any given individual garden space.

My analysis of these case studies has thus demonstrated how the Romans of the Late Republic and Early Empire constructed garden boundaries specifically in order to open up or undermine the division between a number of dichotomies, such as inside/outside, practical/aesthetic, sacred/profane, art/nature and real/imagined. Although the extent of this deconstruction, and the ways in which it was accomplished, varied between the individual garden sites and across the different media, it was clear that, across the board, the garden boundary did not just simply police access and control, but rather, acted as a porous membrane that mediated between a series of oppositions. The resultant liminal and interstitial nature of the garden led me to conceptualize its boundaries as more akin to frames, in that they not only delineated the space, but also loaded that space with meanings. In fact, when the garden space was at its most destabilized state, the garden boundary, functioning as a frame, was shown to draw attention to itself, while also deconstructing itself – to the point where the garden was simultaneously a framed space and the very frame itself.

In this way, despite the natural assumption that a boundary inherently involves some sort of tangible barrier, this book has demonstrated that the notion of a *garden* boundary moves far beyond an act of discrete spatial division. It is for this reason that I chose not to actively engage with Hillier and Hanson's space syntax model as part of my analysis, even though this had been utilized by scholars previously to analyse the social organization of garden space. As detailed in chapter one, proponents of this theory view garden boundaries as akin to architectural boundaries in that they enclose a 'definite region of space' and segregate it 'from what would otherwise be undifferentiated space';[1] and, following this, they have used the process of 'access analysis' to quantitatively define levels of access and control across garden boundaries within the Roman household. Although insights can be gained from this approach, particularly in relation to the domestic sphere, it was too restrictive as a model to consider both the physical *and* the conceptual boundaries at work in individual garden sites, and it was also not flexible enough to account for both real *and* representational garden spaces. Garden boundaries are fundamentally not the same as architectural boundaries, despite some overlap, and so it was clear that I should seek to establish a series of analytical tools that work for gardens on their own terms.

Through the selection and evaluation of my chosen case studies, I have suggested new ways of understanding Roman gardens at-large by refining the use of previous theoretical methodologies and proposing new ones; which, in turn, has provided fresh insight into individual garden sites, and also created a framework for future research. Following the so-called spatial turn, scholars have used increasingly sophisticated methods to analyse ancient gardens and landscape, both at an individual and intermedial level. In particular, as discussed in chapter one, Soja's Thirdspace has become the dominant model for approaching garden space and the interplay of its multiple associations; and scholars have demonstrated the usefulness of this approach in allowing us to step back from individual sites, texts or representations and 'relocate' garden space 'within the wider framework of conceptual space'.[2]

This Thirdspace model is indeed useful for considering the interaction between different types of gardens (in this instance, agricultural vs. sacred vs. ornamental villa) and also different types of media (literary vs. artistic vs. archaeological) because it allows us to locate the 'essence' of the garden space *between* these categories, without naively forcing them together. It is this very model that allowed me to consider the Roman delight in playing with Roman garden boundaries across all of the chosen examples in this book, while still appreciating that these games may be presented to us in wide-ranging formats. There are, however, limitations to the way in which Thirdspace can be utilized in the analysis of Roman gardens, and my investigation has demonstrated that other complementary theoretical frameworks provide more clarity on both the status of the garden within the Roman imagination, and also the ways in which temporal and spatial boundaries intersect with one another as part of individual Roman garden sites.

In the first instance, Derrida's formulation of the concept of supplementation appears to be the most valuable in articulating the relationship between individual garden sites and their surroundings or, more broadly, the individual garden sub-categories and their wider 'networks'. In all three case study chapters, the individual gardens were simultaneously inside and outside a broader network, both related to that network and yet also on the edge, part of and yet also 'extra' somehow. These markers of supplementation were most explicit in chapters two and four, made manifest by the paratextual construction of garden texts and the creation of 'green architecture', respectively; but the deconstructive focus of Derrida's approach also played a key role in the reconfiguring of frame and ornament in chapter three in order to demonstrate that the parergonal status of garden imagery need not render it simply marginal. In this way, I have demonstrated that the logic of supplementarity can be utilized as an effective interpretative strategy for understanding the continuous and contiguous relationships between gardens and their surroundings.

Following such a deconstructive approach naturally destabilizes traditional hierarchies and dichotomies, and yet it was clear through my analysis that the destabilization within garden space need not be understood as an accidental and unfortunate outcome. In fact, the creators of each individual garden seemed to actively embrace the ambiguity that resulted from the deconstruction of normative categories, and harness it in order to load the space with multiple and complex meanings. It is at this point that we need to return to the framework of Foucault's heterotopic space; for, although Derrida gives us the deconstructive tool to understand the relational aspects of garden space, we still require a means of conceptualizing the destabilization *within* that space.

It is in this instance that the concept of 'the heterotopia' is most useful. Foucault's categorization of the garden as a heterotopia had previously found its ways into the analysis of Roman gardens, with such analyses tending to focus solely on the garden as a site of resistance, picking up on the association between heterotopic discourse and notions of transgression – this is perhaps unsurprising, since garden spaces are defined by boundaries, and boundaries invite transgression. My analysis, however, has demonstrated how heterotopic discourse can also be put to use in understanding the 'relational disruption of space and time' within garden space.[3] Each of the garden sites explored engaged with a combination of different, and often conflicting, spatial and temporal boundaries, and understanding how these 'worked' in conjunction with one another was crucial for uncovering the layers of meaning within the space. The concept of heterotopia, in which boundaries and binary thinking are held in 'productive suspension' within an overarching ambivalence, thus provides a useful model for conceptualizing how games of destabilization have been put to use in any given garden site.[4]

Returning, then, to the initial definition of garden space laid out in the introduction to this book, we can now reflect on the garden's status as a bounded space, operating within the broader remit of landscape; and reconsider how useful such definitions are in helping us distinguish what is garden space and what 'not-garden' space. My analysis has highlighted that what was significant for the Romans of the Late Republic and Early Empire was not so much the garden boundary itself, but, rather, the delight in playing with concepts of boundedness and separation. This is not to say that defining the garden as a bounded space is incorrect or simply not useful. Indeed, it is actually *necessary* to continue to conceptualize the space in this way; for the traditional spatial divisions and conceptual boundaries still exist – they are still set up – but they are also constantly undermined, reworked or played with in new and provocative ways. The creators of each of the gardens analysed, whether real or representational, all established spaces wherein perspectives usually considered incompatible or oppositional could be encompassed to create 'both/and also' analyses, rather than simple 'either/or' conclusions. We should, therefore, continue to focus on the 'grey' areas between the apparent 'black-and-white' divisions within garden space, since my analysis made clear that evaluating and understanding the role of ambiguity is crucial in determining the role, status and perception of each individual garden.

Moving forward, though, there is still a need for further clarity regarding the most essential division of them all – garden vs. not garden. Although this book provides a series of theoretical tools for examining the role and function of boundaries within individual garden sites across different media, and for considering how these gardens relate to the networks they are situated within, it is still unclear in some contexts the point at which we can designate a bounded and cultivated space as garden proper. The garden may be a microcosm of the ideal landscape, but at what point does a space change from being a mere landscape to an actual garden? The challenges in answering such a question were most evident in chapter three, where the intersection between sacred space and garden space was shown to create a sense of uncertainty in the divisions between areas that had previously been deemed 'sacral-idyllic' and those that have been termed 'a garden'. I have proposed the concept of supplementation for understanding the garden's relationships with its surrounding networks, but is garden space a supplement of the sacral-idyllic, or vice versa? Since no comprehensive intermedial study of Roman sacred groves currently exists, this question is perhaps the most provocative to arise out of the conclusions drawn in my analysis.

As a means of drawing this book to a close, I would like to briefly draw our attention to another landscape-based ekphrasis – the description of the royal palace of Atreus from Seneca's *Thyestes* (641–82), which is delivered as part of a messenger speech in Act Four of the play.[5] Although traditionally dismissed as an example of Seneca's rhetorical flourishes, only loosely attached to the real subject-matter of the play, more recent scholarship has highlighted the significance of such *descriptiones loci* as 'structural pivots' within the overall drama.[6] Schiesaro, for example, argues that, in privileging such 'detached scenes' within his plays,

Seneca alerts his audience to the 'constructedness of the performance' via a series of internal framing devices;[7] and such devices, in turn, have an 'unusually emphatic role' in the emotional dynamics of the play.[8] Such frames, as we know, 'define boundaries and thus mark separation', but here they also highlight the 'inevitable collision of dramatic levels and the relentless conflicts that plague the successive generations' within the drama.[9] Indeed, in line with Newlands' definition of ekphrasis as an interpreter of attitudes, and as represented in Pliny's process of *enargeia*, it is now widely accepted that Seneca, too, utilizes the 'emotive quality of visual scenes' in order to create a 'correlative for the psychological events [of the play] and images of place and landscape'.[10] The detachment of these ekphrastic tableaux in space is thus reflective of the alienating effect of the horrors we witness on stage, and it is also underpinned by Seneca's unconventional approach to dramatic time – rather than a coherent succession of scenes in an undisturbed linear structure, we are forced to try and comprehend the 'sometimes loose ... often puzzling' temporal connections between the acts.[11]

In this context, then, the 'predatory palace' of Atreus becomes a symbol for the tyranny of its owner – it is not only the setting for the crimes of the Tantalid dynasty past and present, but it is also a mirror of those crimes:[12]

> *In arce summa Pelopiae pars est domus*
> *conversa ad Austros, cuius extremum latus*
> *aequale monti crescit atque urbem premit*
> *et contumacem regibus populum suis*
> *habet sub ictu; fulget hic turbae capax*
> *immane tectum, cuius auratas trabes*
> *variis columnae nobiles maculis ferunt.*
> *post ista uulgo nota, quae populi colunt,*
> *in multa dives spatia discedit domus.*

> In the highest citadel of Pelops' house, there is a place, turned to the south, whose outer wing rises up like a mountain and presses upon the city; and holds the people, contemptuous of their rulers, beneath its stroke. Here the monstrous roof gleams, containing multitudes, and multi-coloured columns bear its gilded beams. Beyond this public landmark, which nations tend, the house sprawls in every direction.

In contrast to the balanced, even blended, relationship between architecture and horticulture that we saw in Pliny's villa ekphrases, here Seneca opens his description with a clear hierarchical statement: this expansive complex (*multa dives spatia discedit domus*, 649) dominates the landscape from on high, pressing down (*premit*, 643) on both the city and the people who live there.[13] This palace does not work *with* nature, but, instead, actively tramples all over its boundaries.[14]

As the messenger continues his description of the palace, we learn that there is a grove (*nemus*) at the centre of the complex:[15]

> *arcana in imo regio secussu iacet,*
> *alta vetustum valle compescens nemus,*
> *penetrale regni, nulla qua laetos solet*
> *praebere ramos arbor aut ferro coli,*
> *sed taxus et cupressus et nigra ilice*
> *obscura nutat silva, quam supra eminens*
> *despectat alte quercus et vincit nemus.*
> *hinc auspicari regna Tantalidae solent,*
> *hinc petere lassis rebus ac dubiis opem.*
> *affixa inhaerent dona; vocales tubae*
> *fractique currus, spolia Myrtoi maris,*
> *victaeque falsis axibus pendent rotae*
> *et omne gentis facinus; hoc Phrygius loco*
> *fixus tiaras Pelopis, hic praeda hostium*
> *et de triumpho picta barbarico chlamys.*
> *fons stat sub umbra tristis et nigra piger*
> *haeret palude; talis est dirae Stygis*
> *deformis unda quae facit caelo fidem.*
> *hinc nocte caeca gemere feralis deos*
> *fama est, catenis lucus excussis sonat*
> *ululantque manes. Quidquid audire est metus*
> *illic videtur: errat antiquis vetus*
> *emissa bustis turba et insultant loco*
> *maiora notis monstra; quin tota solet*
> *micare silva flamma, et excelsae trabes*
> *ardent sine igne. Saepe latratu nemus*
> *trino remugit, saepe simulacris domus*
> *attonita magnis. Nec dies sedat metum;*
> *nox propria luco est, et superstitio inferum*
> *in luce media regnat. Hinc orantibus*
> *responsa dantur certa, cum ingenti sono*
> *laxantur adyto fata et immugit specus*
> *vocem deo soluente.*

In the deepest recess lies a secret place, a high wall enclosing a sacred grove: the innermost part of the realm, where no trees stretch out branches nor are tended to by the knife; but there are yews and cypresses and a dark thicket of black ilex, above which a towering oak looks down and dominates the grove. Here the Tantalids inaugurate their rule by custom; here they seek aid in dilemmas and disasters. Here votive gifts are fastened: war-trumpets and wrecked chariots hang, spoils from the Myrtoon Sea, wheels defeated because of rigged axles, and all the crimes of the family; here the Phyrgian cap of Pelops, here the spoils from his enemies, and an embroidered cape from his triumph over the barbarians. Beneath the shadows is a gloomy spring and it oozes slowly into a black pool: such is the formless water of the Styx, which makes oaths in heaven. Here in the blind night, it is said the gods of the dead groan, the grove rattles its chains, and the spirits howl. Anything fearful to hear is seen here. Released from ancient tombs, a crowd bursts out and things monstrous beyond conception caper about. In addition, flames flicker throughout the wood and lofty tree-trunks burn without fire. The grove booms with the howls of three throats and the house cowers at huge apparitions. Even daylight does not allay the fear, the grove has a night of its own. Here, those seeking oracles are granted infallible answers, their fate revealed by a thundering voice, and the cavern booms as a god unleashes his voice.

In its structurally significant location at both the centre of the physical palace complex being described (*penetrale regni*, 652) and the ekphrastic description itself, Atreus' *nemus* is clearly meant to evoke the typical inner courtyard garden of a large Roman *domus*, surrounded by its enclosing wall.[16] However, in contrast to the abundant, but carefully maintained, garden spaces I have examined in this book, we see no signs of expert cultivation here at all: the trees are so lifeless that they do not need to be pruned (*nulla ... qua coli*, 652–3); and yet, perhaps paradoxically, an oak that remains is so tall that it dominates the entire seat of power (*vincit*, 656), transporting the trees into the same atmosphere of violence as the palace itself (*premit*, 643).[17] Rather than highlight the 'natural' role of an abundant oak as a symbol of the earth's bounty, Seneca instead picks up on the association between trees and the underworld, which, in turn, violates the boundary between the upper and lower realms.[18] Furthermore, unlike the shady plane tree that gave respite to the *senex Corycius* in Virgil's gardening passage (*iamque ministrantem platanum potantibus umbras*, G. 4.146), here the *umbra* signals the shadows that cast darkness over the River Styx. This is not the pleasant shade of a life of a leisure, but a darkness that attempts, but fails, to hide the horrors all around (*quidquid audire est metus illic videtur*, 670–1) – the 'shade' is so severe here that there appears to be an inversion of the natural cycles of day and night (*nec dies sedat metum: nox propia luco est*, 677–8).[19]

The grove also completely undermines our positive perception of nature's cyclical pattern of renewal and growth. As the starting point of the reigns of the kings of Argos (*hinc auspicari regna Tantalidae solent*, 657), the *nemus* represents a source of sin for the House of Pelops and thus acts as the 'perfect symbol' for the 'hereditary evil of dynasty'.[20] The grove's symbolism regarding the dynasty is also strengthened by the description of the trophies hanging from the trees, which link the past crimes of the family to the ones enacted within the play.[21] These hereditary cycles are therefore an inversion of the type of transformative renewal we saw visualized as part of the garden-inspired scenes on the *Ara Pacis* and within Livia's Garden Room – the cycles of power here are not regenerative, but, rather, a sign of the family's continual degeneration.[22]

Such a dark and ominous grove, then, not only acts as a microcosm of the 'gothic and disjointed' world of the *Thyestes*, but it also demonstrates the powerful effects of a world in which the 'boundaries of the civilised and the barbarous' have completely broken down;[23] and, unlike the spaces encountered in this book, where binaries of space and time were held in productive suspension, this 'anti-garden' provides us with a stark warning of what happens when the discourse of garden space is taken to its most negative extreme.

Notes

Introduction

1 Repton 1816: 141–2.
2 Hunt 2000: 14. Cf. Ross 2007: 256 and Cooper 2006: 12–21.
3 Miller 1993: 15.
4 Pagán 2006: 8 (emphasis my own).
5 On the *pairidaeza*, see Moynihan 1979. On the *paradeisos*, see Farrar 1998: 9–10; cf. Tuplin 1996. Ziegler 1979, *sv.* '*paradeisos*', deals mainly with the biblical use of the term, although they do consider the attitudes of the Greeks towards these types of garden-parks (also identified with *kēpoi* and *alsoi*).
6 Lane Fox 2014: 296–7 notes the distinction between Christian 'paradise' and the loose use of the term in non-Christian images, which he argues should be called simple 'scenes of abundance'.
7 See Ernout and Meillet 1959, *sv.* '*hortus*'. The Latin noun *cohors*, closely related to *hortus*, can also mean 'enclosure'. Cf. von Stackelberg 2009: 9–21, who charts the concepts and terms related to the garden in the Roman imagination and, in particular, the similarities and differences between the Latin *hortus* and the Greek *chortos*: in the Greek, the term seems primarily utilized in relation to animals (in Hom. *Il.* 11.774 and 24.640, it is used to designate the area of the courtyard where the cattle were kept), with the produce from the space mostly used for livestock; whereas the *hortus* seems more intimately connected with domestic space and human food production. Both terms, however, maintain the notion of enclosure.
8 van Erp-Houtepen 1986.
9 It is noteworthy that one of the common Japanese terms for garden (*teien*) derives from a combination of two terms meaning 'wilderness' and 'control'.
10 Pagán 2006: 1.
11 Ross 1998: 176.
12 Spencer 2010: 5.
13 McIntyre 2008: 3 similarly defines landscapes as spaces 'shaped by the imposition of boundaries and frames'; and, according to Benjamin 1985: 78, this means that we tend to 'read' landscapes 'inwards' from the perspective of their edges.
14 I borrow this phrasing from Larmour and Spencer 2007: 11 and their discussion of landscape. Cf. Augé 1995: 42–4, who sees landscapes as a series of places, or 'ethnoscapes', given shared meaning as a territory by a community and providing a

shared frame of reference or point of origin for that community. Postcolonial criticism, following the work of de Certeau 1984, makes a fundamental distinction between 'space' and 'place', with the former defined as a more abstract concept that can refer to an area, a distance or even a temporal event, and the latter as a more tangible entity, often linked to a specific location.

15 For this reading of landscape, see also Tuan 1979: 90 and Bender 2006: 303.
16 Lefebvre 1974.
17 Valentine 2001: 5–6.
18 Cf. Spirn 1998 on the concept of 'cultural landscapes'.
19 Scott 2013: 1.
20 Hunt 1992: 6.
21 Cosgrove and Daniels 1988: 14.
22 Francis and Hester 1990: 8.
23 Berleant and Carlson 2007: 25.
24 This passage was bought to my attention by von Stackelberg 2013. For the original Sumerian text of the *Lugale*, see Black et al. 1998–2006.
25 For definitions from the Sumerian language, see Halloran 2006.
26 The quoted lines can be found in 'The Exploits of Ninurta', 1.6.2.
27 The Sumerian *kiri* is formed of the noun *ki* ('place') and the verb *ru* ('to send forth shoots, buds, blossoms), and this is probably the root of the Assyrian *kirû* ('garden, grove, or tree plantation') and *kirimāhu* ('pleasure garden'). Phonetic closeness and semantic associations also suggest a relationship between *kirû* and the Hebrew *kar* ('pasture, enclosed pasture'), *karmel* ('plantation') and *kirem* ('vineyard'), all of which are derived from the verb 'to dig'. For *kirû* and *kirimāhu*, see Wiseman 1983; and for *kar*, *karmel* and *kirem*, see Brown, Driver and Briggs 1996.
28 von Stackelberg 2013: 134.
29 Jones 2016: 30.
30 Bodel 2018: 209.
31 On the figure of Priapus, see Herter 1932; O'Connor 1989 and Uden 2010.
32 Col. 10.30-4. In a similarly crude fashion, the statue of Priapus features in Hor. *Sat.* 1.8, where the god (as a statue) is tasked with warning off thieves in the newly converted Gardens of Maecenas; see Pagán 2006: 37–64 and Uden 2010.
33 On Priapus in art, see Stewart 1997 and Clarke 1998: esp. 48–9, 174–7, 187–94.
34 See, for example, the studies of Richlin 1992 and Elomaa 2015.
35 The most comprehensive and up-to-date survey of Roman gardens is Jashemski et al. 2018. Other important contributions to scholarship include, but are not limited to, Grimal 1943; Jashemski 1979, 1993; Bowe 2004; Carroll 2003; Cima and La Rocca 1998; Coleman 2014; Farrar 1998 and Gleason 2013.
36 This is evident, for example, in the chapters in Jashemski et al. 2018, which include 'Produce Gardens', 'The Garden in the *Domus*', 'Representations of Gardens in Roman Literature' and 'Frescoes in Roman Gardens'.

37 The analysis and exploration of ancient city space has been a particularly popular avenue for such spatial analysis: see, for example, Laurence 1994; Edwards 1996; Edwards and Woolf 2003 and Larmour and Spencer 2007. More generally, the 'production of space in Latin literature' has been the subject of a recent edited volume by Fitzgerald and Spentzou 2018. Many of these works have been influenced by the growth of interest in the 'psychogeographies' of urban form, which refers to the effect of geographical setting on the mood and behaviour of individuals (as defined in *Internationale situationniste* 1, 1958).
38 Pagán 2006 examines four 'garden texts' (Col. 10; Hor. *Sat.* 1.8; Tac. *Ann.* 11; Aug. *Conf.* 8) in order to consider how the garden, 'with all its physical and metaphysical meanings', shapes the 'ideological import of a work of literature' (2).
39 Spencer 2010: esp. 113–34 (on Pliny's villa gardens) and 161–71 (on the *Horti Salustiani* and the *Porticus Pompeiana*).
40 von Stackelberg 2009.
41 The work of Bettina Bergmann 2014 is one of the few examples of scholarship that exclusively considers the 'neglected yet key aspect of gardens'; cf. her earlier work on boundaries and landscape, *ead.* 1991, 1992.
42 Cf. Wittgenstein's 1953 notion of 'family resemblances'. Using games as a paradigmatic example, Wittgenstein demonstrates how things that can be thought of as connected by just one essential feature may in fact be connected by a series of overlapping similarities, with no single feature common to all.
43 Scott 2013: 8.

Chapter 1

1 Plin. *Nat.* 19.49.
2 Plin. *Nat.* 19.49; 19.64. Cf. Mart. 11.18.1–2, where the author compares his window box to his large suburban estate: *Donasti, Lupe, rus sub urbe nobis; sed rus est mi maius in fenestra* (Lupus, you have given me a country estate, but I have a bigger estate in my window).
3 In this way, I follow the approach of von Stackelberg 2009, who also focuses on terminology.
4 For *hortus* as a vegetable or kitchen garden in literature, see e.g. Cato *Agr.* 1.7; Var. *R.* 1.16.3; Cic. *Fam.* 16.18.1; Virg. *G.* 4.109, 4.118; Hor. *Carm.* 4.11.2; Prop. 4.2.42; Liv. 1.54.6; Ov. *Met.* 14.624; Tac. *Ger.* 26.2.
5 Plin. *Nat.* 19.57. Cf. Lawson 1950: 98–101, who documents the gradual evolution of the *hortus* to include the cultivation of flowers.
6 Cato *Agr.* 1.7; cf. Var. *R.* 1.7.10.
7 Plin. *Nat.* 19.60.

8 Col. 5.10.1.
9 Col. 10.27–8. Despite Democritus' warning that putting up walls around a garden was 'shortsighted' and 'over the top' (see Col. 11.3.2), writers as late as the fifth century CE continued to emphasize the garden's enclosure – see Palladius, *Op. agric.* 1.34.4.
10 Col. 11.3.2–4.
11 Myers 2018: 261. Cf. Cic. *De Of.* 1.151: *Omnium autem rerum, ex quibus aliquid acquiritur, nihil est agri cultura melius* (Out of all of the occupation by which gain is secured, nothing is better than agriculture).
12 The ideal of the 'senatorial elite agriculturist' finds a forceful expression in Cato's notion of the *bonus agricola bonusque colonus* from his preface to the *De Agri cultura*. On this ideal in Cato, see Niquet 2000.
13 Marzano 2007: 82.
14 For *horti* as pleasure grounds or gardens, see e.g. Var. *R.* 2.11.12; Cic. *Dom.* 112, *Att.* 4.13; Hor. *S.* 1.9.18; Ov. *Tr.* 1.11.37; Mart. 11.34.3; Tac. *Ann.* 16.27; Juv. 10.16. Purcell 2007: 31, however, warns us that it is all too easy to accept a 'myth of a greenbelt' around Rome, arguing that the idea of the city simply becomes surrounded by a periphery of gardens is 'thoroughly misleading'.
15 On the supposed loss of the traditional *hortus*, compare Pliny (*Nat.* 19.51–2), who recalls that all citizens had their own gardens in the early days of Rome, with Juvenal's third *Satire* (3.223–31), where the speaker Umbricius states one of his reasons for leaving Rome is to be able to have a small *hortus*.
16 Plin. *Nat.* 19.50–1. Note the novelty of this concept to Rome specifically.
17 On the ownership of this type of garden, see Beard 1998: 25.
18 On early *horti* as symbols of political *withdrawal*, see Boatwright 1998: 72–4. On *horti* as symbols of political *manoeuvring*, see von Stackelberg 2009: 74–80 and Macaulay-Lewis 2013: 102.
19 Plut. *Pomp.* 44.3.
20 Plut. *Luc.* 1–3, 38.4. Lucullus' gardens were actually created two years prior to his withdrawal from politics in 58 BCE, and therefore cannot be viewed strictly as a retreat.
21 Hor. *S.* 1.9.18. Cf. D'Arms 1998: 33–44.
22 For evidence of *ollae perforatae* (potted plantings) in the city of Rome, see Messineo 1984 and Macaulay-Lewis 2006.
23 Purcell 2007: 302. On the increase of *horti* and the supposed 'abandonment' of the 'traditional' *hortus* in Late Republican Rome, see Boatwright 1998: 72–3.
24 Myers 2018: 262–3.
25 See, e.g. Hor. *Carm.* 2.15.4, 2.18.21; Sen. *Controv.* 2.1.13, 5.5; Sen. *Ep.* 86.6–7, 122–8; Plin. *Nat.* 12.6, 12.13. Note that the term *luxuria* is also used frequently in Latin to denote the immoderate growth of plants; see OLD, *sv.* '*luxuria*', '*luxurio*', '*luxuriosus*'.

26 On Tacitus' accounts in Books 11 and 12 of the *Annals*, see, for example, Boatwright 1998; Beard 1998; Pagán 2006: 65–92 and von Stackelberg 2009.
27 See e.g. Suet. *Calig.* 37.2–3; Tac. *Ann.* 13.47.2, 15.33.1, 39.1–2, 15.53.1; Suet. *Nero* 22.2. Cf. Edwards 1993: 173–206 on 'prodigal pleasures'.
28 Lawson 1950: 97.
29 Pagán 2006: 9.
30 Purcell 1987b: 203.
31 Some sites did retain the title of *horti*, such as the *Horti Maecenatis*, famously documented in Hor. *S.* 1.8. On the early *porticus* gardens of Rome, see Coarelli 1997: 515f.
32 Both Martial (2.14.10) and Propertius (2.32.12) mention the greenery of the *Porticus Pompeiana*. The *Porticus Liviae* is mentioned several times in the ancient sources as a popular resort (Ov. *Ars.* 1,72; Plin. *Nat.* 14.3.11; Strabo *Geog.* 5.3.8), but its exact location in the city is now unknown.
33 Farrar 1998: 181.
34 On the *Porticus Pompeiana* as Rome's first 'public park', see Gleason 1994.
35 von Stackelberg 2009: 89.
36 von Stackelberg 2009: 86. Note that modern English derives both 'cult' and 'cultivate' from the Latin verb *colere*, meaning both 'to worship' and 'to cultivate'; see Plin. *Nat.* 18.21 for a pun on this double meaning.
37 Neudecker 2015: 220. On plants and everyday religion, see Armstrong 2019: 21–5.
38 This intersection between sacred space and garden space will be explored more thoroughly in chapter three. It should be noted that there is no single authoritative study on sacred groves in the Roman world, although useful scholarly interpretation can be found in Stara-Tedde 1905; Grimal 1943: 53–6, 165–71; Coarelli 1993; Bodel 1994; Scheid 2003; Hunt 2016 and Carroll 2018.
39 Studies of *lararia* include Boyce 1937; Orr 1978; Froehlich 1991; Foss 1997 and Giacobello 2008.
40 See Jashemski 1979: 115 and Foss 1997: 217.
41 von Stackelberg 2009: 87. Note that Giacobello 2008 makes a distinction between *lararia* 'proper' (shrines dedicated specifically to the *Lares*) and so-called 'secondary' *lararia* (shrined dedicated to other deities who protected the house in a more general way).
42 The most up to date summary of Roman tomb gardens is Bodel 2018; cf. Graham 2018; Campbell 2008: esp. 34–9, who provides a succinct summary of the key evidence across all formats; and Brundrett 2011.
43 Bodel 2018: 199 notes one rare archaeological example from Scafati. Gregori 1987–8: 175–88, compiles a list of more than fifty inscriptions from structures in Rome dating from the Late Republican and early Imperial periods, all of which contain either the word *hortus* or *cepotaphium*. One example of a tomb featuring

garden-inspired paintings is the so-called Tomb of the Garlands at Pompeii; see Kockel 1983: 126–51.
44 *CIL* VI 10237 (*ILS* 7870).
45 *CIL* XII 5708 (*ILS* 8379).
46 *CIL* VI 9015 = 29847a (*ILS* 8120); *CIL* VI 29847; cf. Toynbee 1971: 98–9.
47 For example, *CIL* VI 13823 (*ILS* 8352); *CIL* VI 10876; *CIL* VI 10237 (*ILS* 7870).
48 However, it is important to note that, even though most Roman tomb gardens were protected by perimeter walls, not every wall around a tomb denotes the existence of a garden.
49 For example, *CIL* VI 22518 = 'this place bound by a wall with its little sacred garden (*hortulo religioso*) and its little buildings'; *CIL* VI 29961 = 'this place or garden of about five-twelfths of a *iugerum*, enclosed with a wall'; *CIL* XIV 2797 (*ILS* 8336) = 'this place as it is enclosed by a perimeter wall for the religious protection (*ad religionem*) of the tomb'.
50 Plin. *Nat.* 19.60. On the House of the Pansa (VI. 6.1), see Jashemski 1993: 127–8. The planting pattern of the rear garden is set out in a plan (pl. 42) by Charles Mazois, in the second volume of *Les ruines de Pompéi*.
51 On gardens within the *domus* across the provinces, see Morvillez 2018.
52 For an introduction to the *otium* villas of the elite, see, for example, D'Arms 1970; Ackerman 1990; Mielsche 1987; Purcell 1996; Marzano 2007 and Zarmakoupi 2014. On the ideology of villa gardens, see Hartswick 2018; and, on the archaeological examples of villa gardens around the empire, see Macaulay-Lewis 2018.
53 Jashemski 1979: 31. On the relationship between gardens of display and luxury, and those that were more 'productive', see also Jashemski 2018.
54 The term 'peristyle garden' is really a modern convention, first coined by Swoboda 1919 as *gartenperistyl*, and later refined by Grimal 1943 as *jardin-peristyle*.
55 For a diagram of the evolution of the design and placement of garden space within a 'typical' *domus*, see Farrar 1998: 16.
56 Jashemski 1979: 49–51. A short summary of fencing and boundary elements in the Roman garden can also be found in Farrar 1998: 32–5. For a discussion of the different types of raw materials used to create garden boundaries, see Bergmann 2014: 260–72.
57 An example of a garden featuring a stone wall in between columns can be found in the House of the Ship Europa (I.xv.3); see Jashemski 1993: 61.
58 Anguissola 2012 notes that there is a potential for glass to be included as fencing 'panels', but accepts that it is almost impossible to determine in most examples. Vipard 2001–2 and *id.* 2003 deals specifically with the issue of columned porticoes enclosed by glass panels.
59 As seen in the House of the Silver Wedding (V.ii.i); see Jashemski 1993: 113.
60 As seen in the large peristyle garden in the House of the Faun (VI.xiii); see Jashemski 1993: 61.

61 Gleason 2013: 16–17 provides a useful summary of the terms used by Vitruvius; cf. Landgren 2004 and von Stackelberg 2009: 16–21.
62 Vitrv. *De Arch.* 5.12.4, 6.5.2.
63 Vitrv. *De Arch.* 5.7.9, 7.5.2.
64 Vitrv. *De Arch.* 5.9.5, 6.3.10.
65 Vitrv. *De Arch.* 5.11.1.
66 Leach 2004: 34–6.
67 Zarmakoupi 2014.
68 Zarmakoupi 2014: 103–14. On Roman aspirations to emulate Greek architectural forms, cf. Wallace-Hadrill 2008: 169–80.
69 Zarmakoupi 2010: 626.
70 Leach 2004: 34; cf. Vitr. *De Arch.* 6.5.1 categorizes the peristyle among the places shared with 'outsiders' (*loca communia cum extraneis*), which even uninvited people (*invocati de populo*) have the right to enter.
71 von Stackelberg 2009: 9.
72 Cf. Purcell 1987a: esp. 189, who argues that, although the Romans had quite a sophisticated notion of different spatial areas, they did not necessarily make strict divisions or oppositions between them; for example, it would not have occurred to the Romans to say 'here is the edge of the *continentia aedificia*, the built-up area, the *rus*, countryside, begins here'.
73 von Stackelberg 2009: 48.
74 In this way, Thirdspace builds on Lefebvre's notion of the *espace vécu*. Soja 1996: 62 states that Thirdspace is 'both a space that is distinguishable from other spaces (physical and mental, or Firstspace and Secondspace) and a transcending composite of all spaces'.
75 Soja 1996: 5.
76 von Stackelberg 2009: 49.
77 von Stackelberg 2009: 49.
78 Fitzgerald and Spentzou 2018: 10 (emphasis my own).
79 Fitzgerald and Spentzou 2018: 9. The main source, in English, for the concept of 'heterotopia' is Foucault 1986 – this text is a translation of Foucault 1984, *Des espaces autres*, itself a transcript of a lecture given in 1967. Previously, Foucault had outlined the concept of heterotopia within the preface of *Les Mots et les choses*, 1966. Subsequent analysis can be found in e.g. Dehaene and De Cauter 2008; Johnson 2006 and Hetherington 1997.
80 Foucault 1986: 23.
81 Foucault 1986: 24. For Foucault, utopias also belong to this category of 'other spaces', but are fundamentally different. Like utopias, heterotopias 'relate to other sites by representing and at the same time inverting them', but, unlike utopias 'they are 'localised and real' – see Johnson 2006: 78.

82 Foucault 1986: 24–7.
83 Although each heterotopia involves all the principles to some extent, Foucault 1988: 182 suggests that some are more 'fully functioning' or 'highly heterotopic'.
84 Foucault 1986: 25–6. Roman gardens have also been viewed, conversely, as part of *utopian* discourse; see, for example, Evans 2008.
85 Pagán 2006: 15.
86 von Stackelberg 2009: 52. Cf. Johnson 2006: 81 for a response to this 'persistent association'.
87 Hetherington 1997: 41.
88 Genocchio 1995: 38. Cf. Shane 2005 on heterotopias as 'sites of exception'.
89 von Stackelberg 2009: 52.
90 Pagán 2006: 37–63.
91 Johnson 2006: 78. Cf. Defert 1997: 225, who refers to heterotopias as 'spatio-temporal units'.
92 Foucault 1986: 26.
93 The phrase 'temporal discontinuities' (*decoupages du temps*) was put forward by Foucault 1998: 182.
94 Johnson 2006: 80; cf. Foucault 1998: 179.
95 Dehaene and De Cauter 2008: 25.
96 Foucault 1986: 24. The word translated as 'site' here is the French *emplacement*, a term that has a sense of both 'space' and 'place'. Dehaene and De Cauter 2008 believe that Foucault uses the word *emplacement* to give it a technical sense, rather than use 'common' terms such as *place, lieu, endroit*, etc. Confusingly, Miskowiec's translation loses this original emphasis by using the English 'site' for *emplacement* and 'emplacement' for *la localization*.
97 Johnson 2006: 80.
98 I borrow this phrase from von Stackelberg 2009: 132.
99 This theory is set out in Hillier and Hanson 1984.
100 Grahame 1999: 54–5.
101 Fisher 2006: 184. Cf. von Stackelberg 2009: 55.
102 See, for example, Grahame 1997 and *id.* 1999. I borrow the useful one sentence summary of access analysis from Allison 2001: 198, who also provides a useful critique on the limitations of this method.
103 Anguissola 2012: 32. Cf. Anguissola 2010 and Dickmann 1997.
104 von Stackelberg 2009: 101–24, 144–9.
105 von Stackelberg 2009: 70 does note that framing is a 'key feature' of Roman gardens, 'focusing not only on the gaze, but also the imagination on a directed view'. However, unlike her use of access analysis, she does not develop the idea of framing in any thorough way.
106 Note the difference between the Oxford English Dictionary definitions: a 'boundary' is a 'line which marks the limit of an area, a *dividing* line' vs. a 'frame' can

be 'a rigid structure that surrounds something', 'a basic structure that underlies or supports a system, a concept or text', or 'an underlying *conceptual* structure' (emphases my own).

107 Platt and Squire 2017: esp. 8–84 on 'what do frames do?'. Interestingly, some scholars have stressed a connection between 'art' and 'garden space': see, for example, Jones 2016: esp. 25–74 and Kearns 2013: 151; cf. Cosgrove and Daniels 1988: 1 on landscape as 'a cultural image, a pictorial way of representing, structuring, or symbolizing surroundings'.

108 Platt and Squire 2017 12–13.

109 Platt and Squire 2017: 32.

110 Derrida 1987: esp. 15–147, responding to the Kantian notion of aesthetics, as expressed in the *Critique of Judgement*. Most notably, Kant argues that ornaments (*Zieraten*) are said to be subservient, 'parergonal' adjuncts to the central artistic *ergon*. For an introduction to Kantian aesthetics in the interpretation of ancient materials, see Platt and Squire 2017: 39, n. 71 and Squire 2018: 17–20.

111 Marriner 2002: 351.

112 Platt and Squire 2017: 49. Cf. *ibid.*: 47–59, esp. n. 89, and Squire 2018: 16, n. 36, for a summary of Derrida's approach and relevant bibliography, particularly in relation to the ancient materials.

113 Platt and Squire 2017: 38.

114 Platt and Squire 2017: 74–6.

115 However, we must be careful not to think of garden space exclusively as a 'view', even if it appears that way: see e.g. Malpas 2011 and Ingold 2000: 191. On the privileging of sight within the western sensorium, see Platts 2020: 4–5.

Chapter 2

1 An earlier version of my paratextual reading of Columella's text appeared in *Syllecta Classica* 31, 2020, 95–122. I am grateful to the journal editors for their permission to reprint this material here.

2 Virg. *G.* 116–48, transl. Gowers 2000, adapted.

3 Pagán 2006: 15.

4 Miller 1993: 40.

5 Toohey 1996: 10, for example, categorizes the *Georgics* as a didactic poem that is 'unashamedly and systematically technical'. Cf. Gale 2005: 101–2; Volk 2002: 2–3 and Nelis 2004: 79–80 on defining the didactic genre.

6 On the ideological associations of the *villa rustica* in the Roman agricultural sources, see Marzano 2007: 82–101.

7 Harrison 2004: 109.

8 For a summary of scholarship on the link between bees and the garden/gardener in Virgil's passage, see Clay 1981.
9 Cf. Putnam 1979: 251, who, noting the distance in time and space from the poet, describes the passage as 'an imaginative garden in itself'.
10 Clay 1981: 57.
11 Lines 116–19 are presented as a contrary-to-fact conditional, to which lines 147–8 provide the closing frame.
12 Like καὶ γάρ in the Greek. Thomas 1988: 170 points to similar usages of *namque* at *Ecl.* 6.31 (the beginning of Silenus' song); and *A.* 1.466 (the beginning of the ecphrasis on Dido's temple).
13 Thomas 1992: 44. Cf. La Penna 1984: 903, who terms the passage '*con un ricardo personale*'.
14 Thomas 1992: 45. Cf. *ibid.*: 45–51, where the author argues that the inclusion of *memini* and *memoranda* conveys a strong sense of poetic allusion. On the vocabulary of poetic memory, see Conte 1996.
15 Possible models for Virgil's passage include the section on gardening in Nicander's fragmentary *Georgica*, and a lost poem by the Hellenistic Philitas. On the relationship between the *Georgics* and the *Georgica*, see Harrison 2004; and on the potential relationship to Philitas, see Thomas 1992. Greek precedents are equally scarce: there are two gardens in the *Odyssey* (the garden of Alcinous in Book 7, and the garden of Laertes in Book 24), both of which, although fairly formal, are still represented as productive. For gardens in ancient Greece, see Gothein 1909; Carroll-Spillecke 1989, 1992a, 1992b; Carroll 2003: 1–30 and Giesecke 2007: 35–79. For gardens in Homer specifically, see Ferriolo 1989 and Giesecke 2007: 27–40.
16 Leigh 1994: 183 notes that, because the passage explicitly features an old man, we are reminded here 'of the ancient equation of a life with a voyage and death as a port'. On this metaphor, see e.g. Sen. *Ep.* 70.1–3; and Nisbet and Hubbard 1978 on Hor. *Carm.* 2.10.1.
17 For this argument, see Thibodeau 2001: 184–5 and Mynors 1990: 275.
18 OLD, *sv.* '*cursus*'.
19 Note the parallel pairings of *spatia/equis* (1.513–14) and *spatiis/equum* (2.541–2) in the final two lines of each book.
20 This, and all other short translations within the book, are adapted from the standard Loeb editions, unless otherwise stated. On Virgil's poetic *labor*, see Gale 2000: 185–93. On the image of the poet's journey in the chariot of the Muses, see e.g. Pindar *Ol.* 9.81, *Pyth.* 10.65, *Isth.* 8.62; Callim. *Aet.* fr. 1.25–8; Lucr. 6.47; Prop. 2.10.2, 3.1.9–14; Ov. *Am.* 3.15.18.
21 Cf. Feeney 2007: 207 on the 'relentless pressure of the farmer's opportunity-cost time'.
22 *Moretum*, 66–8; cf. Cato *Agr.* 1.7. On the *Moretum*, see e.g. Heinze 1960; Fitzgerald 1996; Kenney 1984 and Ross 1975.

23 Agricultural writers, in general, also stress that, even when weather is too bad for fieldwork, there is still plenty to do in the homestead: Hes. *Op.* 493–7; Cato *Agr.* 2.2.3, 37.3–4; Var. *R.* 1.36; Virg. *G.* 1.259–67.
24 For comparison, Cato *Agr.* makes no reference to any calendar; Var. *Ling.* 6.12 makes a distinction between 'divisions by nature' (*naturale discrimen*) and 'the names of the days given by the city' (*civilian vocabula dierum*); and Var. *R.* 1.26 makes it clear that anyone planning a landscaping project of any kind must know that cultivation involves knowing the seasonal/annual cycles *and* understanding teleology. On an introduction to calendrical astronomy and agriculture, see Gee 2000: 9–20.
25 Feeney 2007: 2. For an introduction to the practical and conceptual issues of time for the Romans, see *ibid.*: 7–42, 138–42. Cf. Laurence and Smith 1995–6.
26 Riggsby 2003: n. 36 states that 'task time' refers to a time scheme that is not about 'time when' but, rather, 'time to' (as in, 'time to reap').
27 It has been observed by modern historians that the Industrial Revolution altered people's general perceptions from task time to clock time – see e.g. Thompson 1967; Harrison 1986 and Landes 1987.
28 Laurence 1994.
29 Riggsby 2003.
30 On the issue of 'ritual time' as a way of defining and delineating power, see e.g. Beard 1987, further developed by Laurence and Smith 1995–6.
31 Spencer 2010: 57–61 is one exception.
32 See Spencer 2010: 57–61; cf. Laurence 1993: 80, who notes that the 'agricultural calendar was locked into the Roman conception of the past'.
33 Plin. *Nat.* 18.231.
34 Of interest here is Casey 1993: 9–13 on time as 'placial'. This approach states that everything in existence has a 'place' and the 'place-world' exists in time as perceived by humans.
35 Cf. Gowers 2000: 129 on the garden as marginal; and von Stackelberg 2009: 53, who argues that both Virgil and Columella emphasize the *hortus* as a product of restricted space and limited time.
36 Plin. Nat. 19.59 – a play on Virg. *G.* 3.289–90, which is itself a play on a well-established trope in didactic poetry, cf. Lucr. *DRN* 1.135–7, 5.97–9, 5.735.
37 The imagery of flowers as literature used here by Pliny is not unusual. The weaving of garlands is a common metaphor for the creation of poems or poetry books, with the term 'anthology' deriving directly from the Greek words for 'flower' (ἄνθος) and 'to gather' (λέγειν).
38 For a detailed discussion of the parallels between gardener and poet, see Perkell 1981.
39 The tradition of an old man in the garden can be found in both verse (e.g. Hom. *Od.* 24.205–344; M. Furius Bibaculus, fr. 1, Courtney; Petr. *Anth. Lat.* 471) and prose (e.g. Cic. *Cato* 51–5; Var. *R.* 3.16.10–11; Sen. *Ep.* 12; Longus Book 2). For a summary of scholarship on the old man, see Thibodeau 2001: n. 1.

40 Horace, *Carm.* 2.6.5–12. For other literary references to Tarentum, see Nisbet and Hubbard 1978: 94–6.
41 Armstrong 2019: 186–7 also notes the significance of the plane tree at the end of the passage, explicitly characterized as a shade tree for drinking under, therefore inviting relaxation and 'evoking an idea of well-deserved rest after labour'.
42 See Perkell 1981: 170–1 and Clay 1981: 60.
43 OLD, *sv.* '*turpi*' ('shameful to do, dishonourable, degrading' or 'guilty of disgraceful behaviour or practices').
44 Perkell 1981: 170.
45 Cato *Agr.* 2.7: *plostrum vetus, ferramenta vetera, servum senem*/ old wagon, old tools, old slave.
46 Virg. *G.* 4.127–9.
47 Cf. Thomas 1992: 56–60 on the success of the old man as deliberately situated *outside* of the bounds of the agricultural areas which form the premise of the rest of the *Georgics*.
48 As set out at *G.* 1.1–5. The three 'divisions' of agriculture – crops, cattle, vines – are regularly mentioned together in a single couplet throughout the *Georgics*; for example, 1.443–4, 2.22–3, 2.143–4, 2.516–7, 4.329–31, 4.559–60.
49 *Corp. Agrim.* T. 4.9; 6.32; 44.5ff; 70.8ff.
50 Virg. *A.* 5.755–6; 7.157–9.
51 *Corp. Agrim.* T. 73.2–5, 164.6–8, 166.11–13; cf. Cic. *De leg. ag.* 11.67.
52 *Corp. Agrim.* T. 44.5ff.
53 Thibodeau 2001: 179–82.
54 *Ibid.*: 180–2 details the author's interpretation of lines 144–6, which hinges on the belief that *etiam* (144) should be read as *et-iam*, with the *iam* signifying not 'already' but 'now', i.e. the trees were transplanted as saplings but can provide shade *now* they are mature.
55 Work extended into the evening (*lucubratio*) is commonly a sign of passion: see, e.g. Virg. *Ecl.* 8.85–8; Lucr. 1.140–2.
56 Perkell 1981: 171. Cf. Quinn 1968: 6 and 399, who uses the phrase 'implicit comment' to 'denote Virgil's curious, characteristic technique, not of understatement but of non-statement ... He leaves us to formulate, if we choose, the moral implications of the narrative.'
57 On Virgil's garden's uncommercial character, see Wilkinson 1969: 264. Grimal 1943: 413–15 comments on the miraculous nature of the particular combination of flowers described in the passage.
58 Var. *R.* 3.16.10.
59 Perkell 1981: 172–3. For a summary of the farmer's activities in the *Georgics*, and the depiction of *labor*, see Gale 2000: 158–85.
60 Armstrong 2019: 185–7.

61 Gale 2000: 181, commenting on Virg. *Ecl.* 1.46–58. Note the repeated references to old age (*fortunate senex*, 46/51) and bees (*apibus*, 54).
62 See Gale 2000: 181–3 for an Epicurean reading of the old man's isolation.
63 Armstrong 2019: 186.
64 Plin. *Nat.* 19.50; von Stackelberg 2009: 10.
65 See Var. *R.* 1.10.2.
66 Plin. *Nat.* 19.50; cf. Beard 1998: 28–9 on this passage.
67 On Virgil's 'green politics' in the *Eclogues*, see e.g. Dominek 2009; Jones 2013: 43–66; Martindale 2000; Weeda 2015: 54–84.
68 Campbell 2000: 95–8 on Augustus' formative influence on the practice of land-division and cultivation and his legislative push to establish a 'framework for ensuring fair play in rural communities, equitable assessments, [and] secure boundaries'.
69 Armstrong 2019: 185. Cf. von Stackelberg 2009: 14.
70 Mynors 1990: 273; cf. Perkell 1981: 169.
71 For a concise account of the poet's life, see Forster 1950.
72 All unattributed numbered references in the remainder of this chapter refer to Columella's *De Re Rustica*. On dating the *De Re Rustica*, see White 2013: 10.
73 Columella details the Roman literary tradition for agronomic literature at 1.1.12–14.
74 Columella also treats gardening in Book 11, as part of the broader discussion of the role of the *vilicus*. On gardening in Book 11 specifically, see Henderson 2002a.
75 Many manuscripts also preserve an index to Books 1–11 at the end of Book 11. An additional book, *De arboribus*, is also preserved within the text and is often positioned between Books 2 and 3, but it does not form part of the extant *De Re Rustica*.
76 The majority of the literary authorities noted by Columella at 1.1.12–14 – the Sasernae, C. Licinius Stolo, Cn. Tremelius Scrofa, C. Julius Hyginus, J. Atticus, A. Cornelius Celsus and J. Graecinus – have not survived. The only extant technical treatises in his list are Cato's *De agri cultura* and Varro's *De re rustica*.
77 Columella's success in this regard is demonstrated by the references to his work by subsequent writers. He is quoted by name by Pliny the Elder several times (*Nat.* 8.153; 15.66; 17.51; 17.162; 18.303; 19.68), and is widely quoted by authors such as Pelagonius, Eumelus, Vegetus, Palladius, Cassiodorus and Isidore. Forster 1950: 128 notes a 'neglect' of Columella in scholarship from the eighteenth century onwards, but interest has increased again within the last two decades as part of a growing body of scholarship on Roman technical writing: see, for example, Fögen 2005 and Doody et al. 2012.
78 The most recent commentary of Book 10 in English is White 2013, but several other editions also include commentary and textual notes, e.g. Ash 1930; Marsili 1962; Saint-Denis 1969; Fernandez-Galiano 1975 and Boldrer 1996.
79 On the extent to which we can view Virgil as an 'agriculturist', and the relationship between technical and didactic literature more broadly, see Doody 2007.

80 For a summary of approaches to Columella, see White 2013 12–19. Notable scholarship includes, but is not limited to, Baldwin 1963; Dallinges 1964; Noè 2001, 2002; Milnor 2005; Gowers 2000; Henderson 2002a; Pagán 2006: 19–36; Doody 2007 and Spencer 2010: 86–104.
81 Columella addresses Silvinus at the beginning of every book. 'Silvinus' can be translated as 'Forester' or 'Woody', which has led Henderson 2004: 33 and 51 to argue that he is a fictitious character. The name Silvinus also recalls the woodland deity Silvanus, an apt reference given the agricultural focus of the text: see, e.g. Cato *Agr.* 83; Virg. *Ecl.* 10.24, *G.* 1.20, *A.* 8.600.
82 Latin prose prefaces have been the subject of examination before (for example, in Janson 1964), but I propose that the deconstructive approach of paratextuality provides a particularly useful framework for understanding their role.
83 Genette 1997: 1.
84 See Jansen 2014: 5. 'Para' as 'beside' or 'next to' corresponds to the function of the Greek preposition with the dative, but the dative can also mean 'association with' something or someone; and, in the accusative, 'para' can be spatial (by, alongside, of, near, on), comparative or oppositional (against, contrary to). Vocabulary in *para* also forms a branch of words which employ some form of the Indo-European root *per*, the base meaning of which is 'through', but the semantics of which extend to 'in front of', 'before', 'toward', 'against', 'near', 'at' or 'around'.
85 Hillis-Miller 1979: 179.
86 Note, here, the debt to Derrida on the Kantian *parergon*; cf. n. 112, chpt. 1.
87 Maclean 1991: 274.
88 Lejeune 1975: 45.
89 Jansen 2014: 1. Once again, we must note the parallels between paratextuality and Derrida's approach, as set out by Platt and Squire 2017: 56.
90 This translation, as with all my translations of Columella Book 10, follows White 2013, with minor amendments.
91 Columella's notion of 'farmers of old' here is characteristically vague. Doody 2007: 191 notes that when Columella discusses alternative opinions, he often does not distinguish the specific opinion or source but, instead, uses broad descriptors such as *antique auctores* or *prisci* or *veteres*: e.g. 5.11.1–3; 11.3.3; 11.3.61.
92 As expressed at e.g. 1.pr.13–21.
93 Doody 2007: 190. Cf. Plin. *Nat.* 19.50 on the 'loss' of the traditional garden; and Juv. *Sat.* 3.223–31 on the need to leave Rome in order to have a small *hortus*. It is significant that in the earlier sumptuary laws of the second century BCE, agricultural products were specifically exempt in order to encourage self-sufficiency on one's own estate: see e.g. Gel. *Att.* 2.24.26 on the *Lex Fannia* of 161 BCE.
94 Silvinus' insistence on verse-writing is also noted at 9.16.2 and 11.1.2. The poeticism of Columella's garden is further reiterated in the garden poem (10.6) by

the phrase *numerosus hortus*, translated by Henderson 126 as 'garden symphony'. Numerus can be used to denote metrical verse; and, although its primary meaning is 'consisting in, or containing, many units or individuals', *numerosus* can also be translated as 'harmonious' or 'rythymical' (OLD, *sv.* '*numerus*', '*numerosus*'). Taking the references from 10.pr.3 and 10.6 together, Columella thus suggests his garden will be poetic in a technical sense, but also flourishing and abundant.

95 It is also of interest that Columella himself appears to parallel Virgil's 'old man in his garden'. At 12.59.5, he says that 'nature does not teach the grey-haired everything' (*nec tamen canis natura dedit cunctarum rerum prudentiam*), thus alluding to his own old age.

96 Boldrer 1996: 13 and Saint-Denis 1969: 8.

97 See e.g. Col. 9.8.3; 9.9.4; 9.9.6; 9.10.2; cf. White 2013: 32–3.

98 Spencer 2010: 94.

99 White 2013: 35.

100 Columella's overall synthesis with the *Georgics* is also further evidence of his view that both didactic poetry and technical prose provide literary models for his *agricolatio*; cf. his list of Roman agriculturalist authorities at 1.1.12.

101 Note that *stipulanti spoponderam* refers to the pledge of undertaking a contract and is used in a technical-legal sense at e.g. Cic. *Q. Rosc.* 13; and Var. *R.* 2.2.5–6. Gowers 2000: 146, n. 41 notes that *stipulanti* here also recalls its agricultural origins, from *stipula* ('stubble').

102 Boldrer 1996: 95. *Particula* is attested to before Columella, e.g. Cic. *De Orat.* 1.179; Hor. *S.* 2.2.79. Columella also uses it elsewhere at e.g. 1.2.1 and 11.2.39. In the pseudo-Virgilian *Moretum*, there is a similar emphasis on the smallness or meagreness of gardening through the use of terms such as *exiguus* (3, 62, 89, 112), *vilis* (5), *parvulus* (8), *pauper* (16, 63, 64), *paucus* (60), *redivivus* (61) and *contractus* (77).

103 The use of *membra* here to denote sub-sections in the *agricolatio* mirrors Columella's usage at 1.pr.21. Cf. Virgil *G.* 1.67–70 for the collocation of *tenuis* and *exigua*, used here to describe the slightness of the furrow and the meagreness of the water.

104 White 2013: 101. On *tenuis* as the equivalent of Callimachus' λεπτός, see Clausen 1987: 3 and 125, n. 6.

105 Gowers 2000: 135. Also note the reference at Col. 10.227 to the 'slender thread of verse' (*gracili . . . filo*).

106 Plin. *Nat.* 19.60. Cf. Gowers 2000: 133 'paltry and devoid of substance'.

107 For *faenus* as 'interest', see e.g. Cic. *Ver.* 3.167, *Flac.* 51, *Att.* 4.15.7; Sal. *Hist.* 1.11; Livy 32.27.3, 7.16.1; Tac. *Ger.* 26.1, *Ann.* 14.55; cf. Temin 2013: 170. For an introduction to loans and interest rates in antiquity, see Rovira-Guardiola 2013 and Gibbs 2013, respectively. On farmers and agriculture in the Roman economy, see Hollander 2019.

108 Gibbs 2013 notes that, after 51 and into the Empire, 12 per cent appears to be the typical rate of interest for private loans, whereas the rates on long-term ventures, such as investments in agricultural land, were much lower. At 3.3.7–11, Columella considers a rate of 6 per cent as typical for this sort of investment.

109 Cf. Hor. *Ep.* 2.1.224–5, who complains that the labour that goes into poetry goes unnoticed.

110 *Reliquum*, in specifically financial terms, refers to a 'sum of money left owing' or 'an amount in arrears': see e.g. Cic. *De Orat.* 2.352; Plin. *Ep.* 3.19.6.

111 The placement of Book 10, coupled with the statements at the end of Book 9 and beginning of Book 11, has led scholars to believe that it was originally conceived as the end of the entire treatise: see e.g. Milnor 2005: 258; Pagán 2006: 19 and Henderson 2002a, probably the most thorough treatment of the 'additions' of Books 11 and 12.

112 Gowers 2000: 134.

113 It is noteworthy that some legal texts declare the *hortus* as part of an estate (*Dig.* 7.8.12.1), whereas, in others, it is regarded as a separate and discrete space (*Dig.* 47.10.53 and 49.4.1.9).

114 I borrow this description of the supplement from Jansen 2014: 265. Derrida's formulation of the supplement can be found in his 1976 work *On Grammatology*. On the supplement in Derrida, see, for example, Gaston and Maclachlan 2001: 119–28; Culler 1982: 102–6, 166–70, 193–9; and Reynolds 2004: 47–8. For an annotated primary and secondary bibliography, see Schultz and Fried 1992; and for a summary of Derridean terms, see Lucy 2004 and Wortham 2010.

115 Reynolds 2004: 47.

116 See Culler 1982: 107, who notes Webster's definition of the supplement as 'something that makes an addition or completes'. Cf. the French *suppléer*, which can mean 'to add what is missing' or 'to supply a necessary surplus'. The link between supplement and substitute is evident in the two terms 'supply teacher' (UK) and 'substitute teacher' (US), both denoting the same teaching appointment.

117 Reynolds 2004: 47.

118 Derrida 1976: 144–5.

119 Culler 1982: 103.

Chapter 3

1 Strabo, *Geog.* 5.3.8.

2 Duret and Néraudau 2001: 330. Cf. Laurence 1993 on Rome's 'ritual landscape'.

3 For the development of the Campus Martius during the Late Republican and Augustan periods, see Favro 1996; Wiseman 1996; Haselberger and Romano 2002: 74–7; Jacobs and Conlin 2014; and Bodel 2018: 218–21.

4 Bodel 2018: 218–19.
5 Strabo 5.3.8. Cf. Livy 2.5.2 on the Campus as *ager publicus*.
6 Suet. *Aug.* 100.4 also comments on the surrounding greenery. On the Mausoleum and its grove, see Rehak 2006: 35–60; Hesberg and Panciera 1994: 35–6, 54–6; Bodel 2018: 220; Purcell 1987a; Wiseman 1996; and Duret and Néraudau 2001: 240, 330.
7 Rehak 2006: 39.
8 On the addition of the *nemus Caesarum*, see Tac. *Ann.* 15.15; Suet. *Aug.* 43.1; and Dio 66.25.3.
9 See Suet. *Caes.* 83.
10 von Stackelberg 2009: 76.
11 See Hor. *S.* 1.8.14–16 on the positive transformation of the city in his description of the new Gardens of Maecenas, which were previously an old graveyard.
12 Orlin 2007: 99.
13 von Stackelberg 2009: 89. Cf. Virg. *G.* 1.24–30, which casts Augustus as both a husbandman and a conqueror.
14 On the 'fall' of Roman religion in the Republic, see Cic. *N. D.* 2.9; *Leg.* 2.33; and *Rep.* 5.1.2. For an overview of religious continuity and change during the Augustan, see e.g. Zanker 1988: 102–35; Beard, North, and Prince 1998: 167–210; and Galinsky 2007.
15 For examples of such warnings, see *AP* 9.282; 9.312; 9.706; cf. Var. *L.* 5.49 on the confinement of old groves due to human greed.
16 Cf. Plin. *Nat.* 16.37 on place names as reminders of defunct or threatened groves.
17 Cf. Brundrett 2011: 58–9, who argues that Augustus' adaptation of sacral landscapes combined elements of both the aristocratic *horti* and the sacred groves of the gods to suit his own needs.
18 Augustus, and the Julio-Claudians at large, were neither the first nor the last rules of Rome to use the power of plants: see e.g. Plin. *Nat.* 12.111–13; 12.20; 19.169. On such 'botanizing rulers', and the role of trees in triumphs, see Totelin 2012; and Fox, forthcoming.
19 Although the ancients knew the site as '*ad Gallinas*', it is now referred to as the Villa at Prima Porta. The villa's ownership is commonly referred to as Livia's on the basis of the omen alone. Archaeologists tend to date the villa to between 30 and 25 BCE, although some suggest as early as 38 BCE – this dating fits nicely with the timing of the omen, since the day of the marriage of Livia and Augustus is noted in the *Fasti Verulani* (*IIt.* 13.2.160–1) as 17 January, and the year – 38 BCE – by Dio 48.44. For a thorough discussion of the dating of the villa, see Gabriel 1955: 2–3; and Reeder 2001: 13–34.
20 On the use of the laurel as part of a triumphal crown, see Plin. *Nat.* 15.127f.
21 Tac. *Ann.* 5.1.2; Vell. 2.95.1; Dio 48.44; Suet. *Aug.* 62.2; *Tib.* 4.3.
22 Julius Caesar was given the right to wear the laurel wreath (Dio 43.43.1); and the permanent laurel decoration on the *fasces* symbolized his perpetual right to triumph (Dio 44.44.3).

23 Suet. *Gal.* 1; Plin. *Nat.* 15.137.
24 Flory 1989: 345. On the ability of certain types of laurel to take root and regrow, see Plin. *Nat.* 17.62.
25 For the symbol of the laurel on Augustan coins, see Kent 1978: pl. 40.143; and Fullerton 1985: 478–9. The significance of the laurel and its role in Augustan ideology is well attested and need not be treated in full here; important surveys include Ogle 1910; and Flory 1995.
26 For evidence of the annual replacement of laurel boughs at the door of the house of the *flamines*, the Regia, the Curiae Veteres and the Temple of Vesta, see Ov. *Fast.* 3.135f. Excavations of Augustus' Temple of Divus Iulius reveal a series of planters around the outer walls, root samples of which prove *laurus nobilis* once grew there – see Andreae 1957: 165, figure 21.
27 Plin. *Nat.* 12.3; cf. Sen. *Ep.* 41.3; Ov. *Met.* 3.155–62; *Fast.* 3.295–6. For a comprehensive exploration of sacred trees in the Roman world, see Hunt 2016. On the extent to which the Romans perceived the divine in nature, see also Rives 2007; and Armstrong 2019: esp. 115–72.
28 The Latin term *lucus* is the most common to be applied to a sacred grove, but it is also a term particularly difficult to define; see Scheid 1993 and Coarelli 1993. For its use in literature, see e.g. Livy 24.3; Hor. *Ep.* 1.6.32; and Prop. 4.9. Servius 1.3.10 famously make a distinction between a more 'natural' *lucus* and a 'constructed' *nemus*; however, I would agree with Rüpke 2007a, who finds Servius' distinction 'too artificial.'
29 Hunt 2016: 126. Armstrong 2019: 58, however, points to a 'gap between theory and practice' in the specification of a grove as sacred.
30 Rives 2012: 165 draws a distinction between 'the sacred as defined by human authority and the sacred as more or less spontaneously perceived', with groves belonging to the latter category.
31 Bodel 2009: 26–30. Cf. Macrobius 3.3.2, who defines the sacred as 'whatever is considered to belong to the gods' (*quicquid est deorum habetur*).
32 It is noteworthy that there was a *lucus Augusti* in Spain; see Flory 1989: 354.
33 It is impossible to document the depth and breadth of scholarship on the *Ara Pacis*. Important contributions include, but are not limited to, Simon 1967; Torelli 1982: 27–61; La Rocca 1983; Zanker 1988: esp. 117–23, 172–83, 203–7; Pollini 2012: esp. 204–47, 271–308; Lamp 2013: 38–57. I would also like to thank Amy Russell for sharing a draft of unpublished work on the *Ara Pacis*, which clarified the senatorial reading of the complex for me.
34 The entire account of the 30 January ceremony can be found in Ovid's *Fasti* (1.709–24); for the ceremony on 4 July, see *IIt.* XII, 476 (July–December are not preserved in the *Fasti*).
35 There are no steps to the rear west side due to the lower elevation on the west side of the original location.

36 Elsner 1991: 55. Cf. Egelhaaf-Gaiser 2007: 206 on the difference between *templum* ('a ritually defined area') and *aedes sacra* ('a temple building', as the seat of the gods). In the Greek, note τέμενος ('a piece of land cut off'), lexically bound to the verb τέμνω ('to cut').
37 Castriota 1995: 31, n. 88, in particular points to the garlands in relief on the altar of Pergamon, dedicated to 'all gods and goddesses', as a comparison. On the Roman assimilation of the garland motif in the Late Republican and Augustan periods, see Honroth 1971: 9–22; and von Hesberg 1981: 210–45.
38 See Honroth 1971: 8; and von Hesberg 1981: 202–3.
39 These motifs (*bucrania, paterae*, garlands) also occur in friezes decorating tombs (see von Hesberg 1981: pl. 66.2 and Frischer 1982–3: pl. LXIII.1), thus, their funerary significance may also imply the eventual deification of Augustus, cf. Moretti 1948: 295. It should also be noted depictions of garlands were not limited to a religious context. They can also be found, for example, as painted decoration in the following locations contemporary with the *Ara Pacis*: the House of Livia on the Palatine (right-hand room); the House of Augustus (Room 6); and the House of P. Fannius Synister at Boscoreale (Room L). However, the function of the *Ara Pacis* does suggest the garlands on its inner walls were intended to mimic the 'real-life' counterparts as specifically altar decoration.
40 Zanker 1988: 3–4. First published in German in 1987, under the title *Augustus und die Mach der Bilder*. In this chapter, I reference the English translation.
41 Cf. Pollini 2012: 219 on the 'narrativity' of monumental structures, including the *Ara Pacis*.
42 For the *Ara Pacis* as part of Augustus' visual communication in Zanker 1988, see e.g. pp. 120–5, 158–60, 172–83, 216–17, 285–8.
43 *RG* 12.2.
44 *RG* 12.3.
45 Cornwell 2017: 159.
46 In this way, the altar acts as a replacement for the traditional military triumph (also awarded by the Senate). On the triumphal topography of the altar, see Nicolet 1991: 16–17. On rhetorics of peace and war under Augustus, see e.g. Östenberg 2009; and Raaflaub 2015. On the *Pax Augusta* and its expression through the *Ara Pacis*, see Cornwell 2017: 155–83.
47 On the similarities between the *Ara Pacis* and the Temple of Janus, see Simon 1967: 9; Torelli 1982: 32–3; and Rehak 2006: 99–100.
48 See Simon 1967: pl. 1, no. 2; and Torelli 1982: pl. II.6, pl. II.7. Similarly, a coin from the age of Domitian shows the west side of the *Ara Pacis* with the new *Janus quadrifons* of the Forum Transitorium; see Torelli 1982: pl. II.8. Interestingly, some coins depicting the *Ara Pacis* also show it with wooden doors, although the construction of these is still disputed.

49 This theory was proposed by Torelli 1982. On the limitations of and responses to Torelli's approach, see Cornwell 2017: 162, n. 16.
50 Torelli 1982: 29–32.
51 Rehak 2006: 98.
52 Dio 53.32.5–6.
53 On the reconfiguration of time during the Principate, see also Beard 1987; Newlands 1995; and Rüpke 2017.
54 Buchner 1976; cf. Elsner 1991: 52. For the most thorough response to and testing of Buchner's original theory, see Pollini 2012: 210–19.
55 Rehak 2006: 137. On the ways in which Augustus inserted himself and his family into the *fasti* more generally, see Feeney 2007: 184–90; and Gros 1976.
56 Lamp 2013: 39.
57 Again, it is impossible to cover the breadth of scholarship on the upper figural reliefs. However, the following recent contributions are useful in providing a summary of the identification debates, with appropriate bibliography: Rehak 2006: 109–38; Pollini 2012: 220–33; Lamp 2013: 42–55; and Cornwell 2017: 165–77.
58 Scholars have wanted to interpret the processional frieze as both a depiction of a real historical event (see Momgliano 1942 for a discussion of this position) and an idealized *supplicatio* (see Billows 1993). The prevalent view, however, is to interpret the processional frieze as a celebration of the imperial *domus* and a marker of dynastic succession policy (see e.g. Kleiner 1978; Torelli 1982; Rossini 2006). On the connection between the processional frieze and the sacrificial role of the altar proper, see Elsner 1991.
59 On the Aeneas vs. Numa debate, see Rehak 2001 and *id.* 2006: esp. 115–20; refuted by Pollini 2012: 221.
60 Lamp 2013: 56.
61 For a breakdown of all the plant species to be found on the *Ara Pacis*, and their location on the monument, see Caneva 2010: 42–3, Table 1. Given the fragmentary nature of the remains, we may also assume that some additional species originally depicted no longer remain.
62 Rehak 2006: 104. For forerunners of the scrollwork, see Cohon 2004.
63 Kellum 1994a: 28.
64 In 2014, in honour of the bicentennial of Augustus' death, a team of researchers displays an exhibition of the colour reconstruction of the *Ara Pacis* through the use of non-invasive light projection directly on to the monument itself. Unfortunately, there was no accompanying exhibition catalogue, but a good summary of the effects can be found in Ergin 2018. For photographs of the few fragments preserved with colour, see Caneva 2010: 131–2.
65 For example, Kraus 1953 and Petersen 1902.
66 Bianchi-Bandinelli 1970.

67 Caneva 2010.
68 Cf. Vitr. *de Arch.* 1.5, who infers that the elements of a good monument will never be simply decorative.
69 Castriota's 1995 monograph builds on previous studies by L'Orange 1962 and Büsing 1977. On the shift in perspective towards the friezes, cf. Sauron 1982 and Pollini 1993.
70 Castriota 1995: 86.
71 Castriota 1995: 28. The distinction is not quite as clear-cut as Castriota suggests, since the garlands are not devoid of an Augustan reading themselves. The number of garlands, twelve, could be viewed as alluding to the passage of the twelve *saecula*, which would mark the conclusion of the Great year and usher in a new Golden Age, the *aurea aetas* (the Augustan age) – see e.g. Holliday 1990: 545.
72 See, for examples, the articles in Dietrich and Squire's 2018 edited volume.
73 Squire 2018: 21.
74 Squire 2018: 2, 19.
75 Squire 2018: 16–17.
76 Squire 2013a: 245.
77 Squire 2013a: 270.
78 The classic response to Zanker remains Wallace-Hadrill 1989; cf. Galinsky 1996: 370–5. The essays in Hardie's 2009 edited volume also engage with this debate across a range of media and perspectives.
79 Squire 2013a: 271–2; cf. Lamp 2013: 39, who notes that even if we as scholars are supplied with 'the critical cultural knowledge necessary to 'read' the altar', we can never know how much of this knowledge was available to 'ordinary Romans'.
80 Elsner 1991: 51; cf. Elsner 1995a and Pollini 2012: 208–9 on the importance of the viewer and the multiplicity of viewer interpretations.
81 Squire 2013a: 270; cf. Platt 2009: 74.
82 For archaeological reports on the villa site, see Calci and Messineo 1984; Messineo 1992; *id.* 2001; and Zarmakoupi 2008. On the gardens of the Villa of Livia, see Klynne and Liljenstolpe 1996; *eid.* 1997–8; *eid.* 2000; and Klynne 2005.
83 On the basis of Sulze 1932: pl. 39, there appears to be no evidence of the presence of *cardines* (turning posts), nor do the jambs appear to have been cut for doors. It has, therefore, always been assumed that the archway was designed as open.
84 The basic monograph for the garden room is still Gabriel 1955, which can be supplemented by Kellum 1994b; Kuttner 1999; Reeder 2001; Spencer 2010: 155–61; and Jones 2016: 55–75.
85 For the purpose of identification moving forward, the effect of these niches is to divide the paintings into six 'panels', each with a tree at its centre. On the classification of the panels, I follow Gabriel 1955.
86 Gabriel 1955: 7–8 argued that the painted fringe was a sort of thatch. However, the ceiling is more commonly thought to suggest a grotto or cave – see, for example, Ling 1991: 150; Kuttner 1999: 27; Reeder 2001: 35–44; Spencer 2010: 160.

87 Archaeologists tend to date the villa to between 30 and 25 BCE, although some suggest as early as 38 BCE; see Reeder 2001: 13–34.
88 The division of Roman wall painting into four distinct and chronologically ordered styles comes from the work of Mau 1882, and relies heavily on Vitruvius' comments (*de Arch.* 7.5) on the development of painting styles. Useful summaries of Mau's approach and the four 'styles' can be found in Bergmann 2001; Tybout 2002; Stewart 2004: 74–92; Strocka 2007; and Lorenz 2015. Scholarly reception of Mau's system is mixed – on the need to question the conventional chronological ordering, see, for example, Bergmann 1994; and Leach 2004.
89 Kuttner 1999: 22–3.
90 On the development from the 'monochrome green fuzz' to plant specificity within Second Style garden prospects, see Kuttner 1999. The most recent overview of garden paintings is Bergmann 2018.
91 On the Auditorium, see de Vos 1983: 231–47; Haüber 1990; and Wyler 2013. The paintings date to the first century CE, during a second phase of décor.
92 For an introduction to ancient approaches to framing pictorial space, see Platt 2017: 102–16.
93 Platt and Squire 2017: 23. The Second Style predilection for illusionistic framed views can be viewed as a precursor to Alberti's concept of the picture frame as a 'window' onto a three-dimensional space that extends indefinitely beyond limits, as detailed in his 1435 treatise *De Pittura*: 'I inscribe a quadrangle of right angles, as large as I wish, which is to be considered an open window through which I see what I want to paint' – see Alberti 1966: 56.
94 On the paintings in the House of the Fruit Orchard, see Jashemski 1979: 117–19; Leach 2004: 124 and Ling 1991: 150–1.
95 In response to the lack of columns within the composition, Jones 2016: 69–71 suggests that there may have been actual columns (perhaps wooden) in the room that acted as 'illusionary support' for the ceiling above. This is a provocative suggestion, based on essentially no archaeological evidence, and it appears to be driven by the author's disbelief in an unsupported roof as an 'adventurous essay in fabulous architecture'. In the rest of his discussion, Jones clearly demonstrates that the Romans delighted in playing with boundaries, and yet does not appear willing to extend this notion of play to a full-scale immersion experiment that removes all vertical support.
96 Reeder 2001: 83.
97 Evidence indicates that the earliest examples of this style date from *c.* 40 BCE. They feature in the *atrium* of the Villa of the Mysteries at Pompeii; and the upper wall of the *cubiculum diurnum* and the rear wall of the *cubiculum* at Boscoreale. For analysis of sacral-idyllic landscapes, see e.g. Silberberg 1980; Silberberg-Peirce 1981; Leach 1974; Giesecke 2007: 120–2; and Bergmann 1992.

98 Ling 1991: 55 calls them 'the finest achievements of the early Third Style'. On the paintings in the villa, see von Blackenhagen and Alexander 1962.
99 Silberberg-Peirce 1981: 242.
100 Giesecke 2001: 21–2. On religion and rusticity in the Roman world, see North 1995.
101 Reeder 2001 is perhaps the lengthiest formation of this argument.
102 Bergmann 1992: 28.
103 Kellum 1994b: 222 suggests a 'mutually informing relationship' between the iconography and symbolism of the garden room, the actual laurel grove and the statue of Augustus from the same Prima Porta site.
104 Dio 53.16.4, transl. Cary 1917. The laurel trees mentioned in this story are the same laurel trees depicted on coins of Augustus – see n. 25 above.
105 In Virgil's *Georgics* (2.15–16), the oak is 'especially luxuriant in foliage for Jupiter' (*Iovi . . . maxima frondret aesculus*); cf. Armstrong 2019: 115–31 on the general significance of oak and its depiction in Virgil's texts. On Augustus' *corona civica*, see *Monumentum Ancyranum* 34.2. Plin. *Nat.* 16.11 notes that oak could also be used as part of a triumphal crown.
106 von Stackelberg 2009: 90.
107 On the use of myrtle in a triumphal crown, see Plin. *Nat.* 15.126–7; on the ivy, *id.* 16.9; and, on the pine, Plut. *Quaest. Conv.* 5.3.676.
108 Suet. *Aug.* 92.1–2. For a history of the palm tree, see Plin. *Nat.* 13.6–9.
109 See Pollini 1993: 197–9. Kellum 1994a: 218 notes an interesting tie between the symbolism of the Augustan palm tree on the Palatine and the cinnamon root which Livia dedicated as memorial to her deceased husband at his temple on the Palatine, since cinnamon was said to have come from the nest of the immortal Phoenix (Plin. *Nat.* 12.85–94; 10.2–5).
110 The most extensive discussion on the significance of acanthus on the *Ara Pacis* is Pollini 2012: 271–308; cf. Pollini 1993. Note that acanthus can also be seen growing at the root of both the oak and pine trees depicted in Livia's Garden Room; see Figures 9 and 10.
111 Pollini 2012: 273.
112 Caneva 2010: 108.
113 Cornwell 2017: 165 notes the similar messaging between the acanthus scrolls and the upper 'Tellus' panel.
114 Pollini 2012: 273.
115 The only sprig of laurel preserved on the frieze is to the right of the north frieze panel, whereas oak leaves and palm leaves can be found on all sides of the frieze; see Caneva 2010: 42–3, Table 1.
116 Kellum 1994a. Cf. Billows 1993: 88, who argues that the figures usually identified as Augustus and Agrippa are both holding laurel branches; and Ov. *F.* 1.711 mentions laurels being worn as part of the 30 January *dedicatio*.

117 See Pollini 2012: 291–3.
118 Kellum 1994a: 33; cf. Carettoni 1966–7.
119 Grapevines feature on all sides of the frieze and ivy can be found on the north and south walls; see Caneva 2010: 42–3, Table 1.
120 See Wyler 2013 on the Augustan approach to Dionysus; and Scapini 2015, who argues for the vitality of Dionysism during the Augustan age.
121 In contrast, Galinsky 2007: 76 notes that the simplistic schema of Apollo vs. Dionysus is just another dichotomy that 'simply does not comfortably work in an Augustan context'.
122 Sauron 1982.
123 Caneva 2010: 206.
124 Castriota 1995; Pollini 2012.
125 See Pollini 2012: 278–9, where the author also notes the bifurcation of Apolline laurel and Dionysiac ivy from the same acanthoid vine on the north wall. On Augustus and Liber/Pater, see e.g. Hor. *Ep.* 2.1.5–6; Serv. on Virg. *A.* 3.93, Virg. *G.* 1.5 and Virg. *Ecl.* 5.66; Plut. *De Is. Et Os.* 35, *De E apud Delphos* 9.
126 Plin. *Nat.* 14.11.
127 It should be noted, however, that the *Porticus* was not dedicated until 7 BCE, after the *Ara Pacis*, and so the connection drawn by Kellum could not have been something the designers of the altar complex foresaw, even if viewers did ultimately pick up on the mutual associations.
128 Platt 2009. On Vitruvian 'realism' in Book 7 of *de Architectura*, see Elsner 1995a: 51–62. The bibliography on this Vitruvian book is vast, but see, for example, Ehrhardt 1991; Sauron 1990; Clarke 1991: 49–53; Yerkes 2000; and Stewart 2004: 80–1.
129 Cf. Pollini 2012: 275 on the 'constant play between reality and illusion' in the composition.
130 Virg. *Ecl.* 2.45–55; Armstrong 2019: 241 calls this the 'most concentrated instance' of flowers appearing spontaneously as part of un-farmed landscape. See also Virg. *Ecl.* 4.18–20, where acanthus is specifically mentioned as one of the plants that Tellus brings forth without the need for cultivation.
131 On the quince, see Plut. *Mor.* 279f.; on poppies, see Ov. *F.* 4.151–4; and on rose and myrtle, see Paus. 6.24.7.
132 Tally-Schumacher and Niemeier 2016: 62, figure 2, identify twenty-four plant types in the Garden Room, nine of which (38 per cent) inspired stories involving transformation; cf. Kellum 1994a: 221.
133 On the transformation of Daphne, see Ov. *Met.* 1.548f.; on the pine and cypress, see *ibid.* 10.103f. Other plants involving a metamorphosis include acanthus (Ant. Lib. *Met.* 7); myrtle (Ov. *Met.* 10.476f.); poppy (Serv. in Virg. *Ecl.* 2.47); pomegranate (Apollod. *Bibl.* 1.25); oak (Ov. *Met.* 8.633f.); and the rose (as an agent of transformation – Apul. *Met.* 4.2.8). Kellum 1994b: 34–8 details how the animals on display also feed in to this narrative of transformation.

134 Platt 2009: 72.
135 Cf. Evans 2008: 23 on landscapes of hyperfertility allowing nature to transgress its own laws.
136 On the ritual calendar and its associated events as a means of delineating and defining power by evoking events from different chronological periods of the Roman past and arranging them into a meaningful sequence, see Beard 1987; and Laurence 1993; cf. Laurence and Smith 1995–6 and Newlands 1995: 22–4.
137 The whole account of the 30 January event can be found in Ov. *F.* 1.709–24; quoted here is 1.719–22. On different concepts of time in Ovid, see Newlands 1995: esp. 27–50.
138 Cf. Orlin 2007: 86 on how Augustus reconfigured time through the rebuilding of temples, since restored temples were re-dedicated, and the *dies natalis* moved to a new day.
139 Holliday 1990: 544.
140 Holliday 1990: 556. Cf. Elsner 1991: 55 on the play of time in the depiction of sacrifice; and Laurence 1993: 80, who argues that, in the performance of ritual, past and present become merged together to create a conception of time that is both enduring and static.
141 Foucault 1986: 25–6.
142 Cf. Foucault 1998: 175–85, who uses the phrase 'temporal discontinuities' (*decoupages du temps*) to describe how heterotopias function as 'heterochronias'.
143 Lord 2006: 3–4.
144 Cf. Orlin 2007: esp. 83 on Roman temples as both '*loci* for ritual activity' and also 'monuments in which Roman memories and Roman history resided'.
145 Cf. Hor. *Ep.* 16 on Augustus interrupting the laws of cosmic cycles.
146 See Evans 2003, repeated in Evans 2008: 21–4.
147 Evans 2008: 22.
148 On the 'ordering' of the frieze, see e.g. Caneva 2010: 153–8 (esp. figure 71); and Pollini 2012: 275.
149 Evans 2008: 22.
150 On defining the wild, see Armstrong 2019: 233–63.
151 Cf. Jones 2016: 59 on the tension between 'formal patterning and the naturalism of the local effects and textures, between aesthetic pleasure and reality effect' within the Garden Room.
152 Gleason 2019. Cf. Cofer 2015, who argues that both the *Ara Pacis* and Livia's Garden Room need not be understand as mythical at all, but as representations of real plants cultivated through grafting; although I believe Cofer pushes the idea of 'realism' too far here, his exhaustive documentation of potential signs of grafting within the compositions is useful.

153 Gleason 2019; cf. Plin. *Nat.* 12.13: *primus C. Matius ex equestri ordine, divi Augusti amicus, invenit nemora tonsilia intra hos lxxx annos/* Clipped arbours were invented within the last eighty years by a member of the Equestrian order named Gaius Matius, a friend of his late Majesty Augustus.

154 Tib. 1.3.42–4: *non domus ulla fores habuit, non fixus in agris/ qui regeret certis finibus arva, lapis.* Cf. Lee-Stecum 1998: 115; Evans 2008: 21; and Virg. *A.* 1.257–96 on Rome's 'power without limits' (*imperium sine fine*).

155 The *lex Iulia de maritandis ordinibus* was introduced in 18 BCE, and later supplemented by the *lex Papia Poppaea* in 9 CE. The two enactments are usually distinguished in the sense that the first encouraged marriage; the second, bearing children. On the statutes of these two laws, see McGinn 1998: 70–85. Dio (54.16; 56.1–10) offers accounts of the two enactments; cf. Kemezis 2007.

156 Kemezis 2007: 274.

157 Hor. *Carm.* 3.6.17: *fecunda culpae saecula*. On the Golden Age and sin, see Wallace-Hadrill 1982.

158 Evans 2008: 22–3. Cf. Favro 1996: 167f., on the 'ordering' of urban ensembles in Augustan Rome.

159 Cf. Armstrong 2019: 174–6 on Roman ideas and ideals of harmonious co-operation between humans and nature.

160 Hor. *Saec.* 10. Cf. Augustus' own claim at *RG* 34 that he exceeded all in *auctoritas* but none in *potestas*, i.e. he was *primus inter pares*.

161 Platt 2009: 45.

162 Giesecke 2007: 123.

163 Compare the perimeters of the Garden Room with, for example, the House of the Fruit Orchard; cf. n. 94 above.

164 Cf. Plin. *Nat.* 20.204 on a 'third category' *between* the wild and tame. On the delineation between wild and tame, or uncultivated and cultivated, see Armstrong 2019: 234–40.

165 Platt 2009: 45.

166 Platt 2009: 58. The full analysis of *monstra* in Horace and Vitruvius can be found at pp. 51–8.

167 Vitr. *de Arch.* 7.5.3–4, transl. Platt 2009: *Neque enim picturae probari debent, quae non sunt similes veritati, nec, si factae sunt elegantes ab arte, ideo de his statim debet 'recte' iudicari, nisi, argumentationes certas rationes habuerint sine offensionibus explicates/* For paintings that do not resemble reality should not be endorsed, nor, if artistic skill has made them elegant, should they be accordingly judged as 'correct', unless they conform to the specific requirements of their subject, executed without violation.

168 Platt 2009: 56. *Monstra* are also in violation of some of the Vitruvian principles of architecture as set out in *de Arch.* 1.2, namely order (*ordinatio*), arrangement (*dispositio*) and propriety (*decor*).

169 Platt 2009: 62.
170 Platt 2009: 65.
171 Platt 2009: 74.
172 Platt and Squire 2017: 74. Cf. Bal 2002: 133–73 on 'framing' as an alternative to mere 'context'.
173 Plin. *Nat.* 12.3; cf. n. 28 above.
174 See Levi and Levi 1967: 154–8, pl. 9; Wroth 1899: no. 29, pl. 16.13; and *ibid.*: no. 46, pl. 16.14.
175 On the Sanctuary of Venus, see Carroll 2011; on the Temple of Dionysus, see Jashemski 1979: 157–8; and on the Temple of Apollo, see Carroll and Godden 2000.
176 Brundrett 2011: 57.
177 Neudecker 2015: 220. Cf. Hughes 1994: 170.
178 Neudecker 2015: 222.
179 Reeder 2001: 75–94.
180 Kellum 1994b: 221. Cf. Flory 1989: 354–6.
181 The plantings encircling Augustus' Mausoleum, as described by Strabo, also showcase the same principle.
182 Cf. Pollini 2012: 219 on narrativity and the *Ara Pacis*.
183 Indeed, my conversations with Amy Russell have alerted me to the fact that perhaps the primary intended audience for the *Ara Pacis* was only Augustus himself – since the altar complex was an honour awarded to him, *from* the Senate.

Chapter 4

1 On the House of the Golden Bracelet *triclinium-nymphaeum* complex, see Bergmann 2008: 58–9; *ead.* 2018: 291–2; and Guzzo 2003: 402–3. For a multi-sensory approach, see Platts 2020: 181–4.
2 The rectangular pool features twenty-eight water jets; see *PPM* 6, 337.
3 Bergmann 2018: 292.
4 On the garden paintings, see Settis 2002.
5 Bergmann 2018: 295.
6 On the archaeology of the villa site and its outdoor garden spaces, cf. n. 82, chpt. 3.
7 Bergmann 2002: 87.
8 For a brief comparison of the general features of the villas located near Villa A, see Gazda 2017: 36–44. For a general assessment of the villas of the area, see Dobbins and Foss 2007: 435–54. Zarmakoupi 2014 provides a detailed comparative analysis of porticoed gardens in the Villa of the Papyri, Villa A at Oplontis, Villa Arianna A, Villa Arianna B and Villa San Marco.
9 On the Peutinger Table, see Levi and Levi 1967; and Talbert 2010.

10 de Franciscis 1979 first put forward the theory of Poppaea's ownership. For a review of the evidence, see Beard 2008: 46-7. For an appendix of the literary references to villa owners, see D'Arms 1970: 171-232.
11 For treatments of the villa, see e.g. Alessio 1965; Bracco 1975; de Franciscis 1973; *id.* 1975 *id.* 1982; Tybout 1979; D'Ambrosio et al. 2003; Clarke and Muntasser 2014; and Gazda and Clarke 2017. It should be noted that there is also a second complex at Oplontis, located 300 m to the east of Villa A, often referred to as 'Villa B'. On the Oplontis 'B' commercial site, see van der Graaff 2017: 69-71; Thomas 2017b; Muslin 2017; and Ward 2017.
12 For the geoarchaeology of the ancient Oplontis coastline, see di Maio 2014; and Muntasser and di Maio 2017.
13 Oettel 1996 dates this pattern to the third centuriation of 42 BCE, following an earlier second one in 80 BCE.
14 Cato, *Agr.* 1.3.
15 Var. *R.* 1.7.1-4; 1.16.1-3. The 'ideal villa' was also visually represented from the first century CE, when miniaturist landscape paintings seem to reflect contemporary villa architecture – see Rostovtzeff 1904; Bergmann 1991; and Lafon 1991.
16 For a summary of the renovation phases, see Zarmakoupi 2014: 48-52. For an overview of the various stages of excavation, see de Franciscis 1973 and *id.* 1975; and van der Graaf 2017.
17 Compare this with the fifty-four skeletons discovered in room 10 at the Oplontis 'B' site, suggesting that this complex was very much in 'active use' at the time of the eruption – see Thomas 2017b: 161-2.
18 Jashemski's excavation of the gardens at Oplontis began in 1974, and they are documented in Jashemski 1993: 292-301. Reconstruction drawings of select gardens can also be found in Förtsch 1993: pl. 13.2.3.
19 Villa A is one of only two grand villas – along with Villa Arianna at Stabiae – along the Bay of Naples (and outside of Pompeii) that preserve evidence of extensive formal gardens. For an overview of the four porticoed gardens at Villa A, see Zarmakoupi 2014: 249-54.
20 Gleason 2014: para. 955.
21 On the wall paintings at Oplontis, see e.g. de Franciscis 1975; Barbet 1985; Clarke 1996; and Gee 2014; *ead.* 2017; *ead.* forthcoming.
22 Traces of illusionistic garden paintings survive in two main areas of the villa – the unroofed garden room 20, and a series of garden courtyards in the east wing (68-87) – and there are also other partial painted garden on the low wall of the service courtyard (32) and the exterior walls of room 78. On the garden paintings in particular, see Jashemski 1979: 290-2; *ead.* 1993: 375-6; and Bergmann 2017; *ead.* forthcoming.
23 The Fourth Style decoration appears to be split between two phases either side of the 62 CE earthquake – see de Caro 1987: 85-6.

24 Gee 2017: 86. The combination rooms include room 5 (Second and Fourth Style); 8 (Third and Fourth); 11 (Second and Third); 14 (Second and Third); and 22 (Second, Third and Fourth).
25 Bergmann 2002: 95.
26 Bergmann 2002: 92. Cf. *ead.* 2017: 96.
27 See Bergmann 2002 (developed in Bergmann 2017) and Zarmakoupi 2014: esp. 122–39. Cf. Bergmann 1991 and 1992 on the ways in which Campanian villa architecture frames, and is framed by, the surrounding landscape.
28 For the property on the Esquiline, see Plin. *Ep.* 3.21.5. Pliny owned major estates in at least three locations in Italy; see *Ep.* 4.1, cf. Duncan-Jones 1974: 19–23.
29 There have been many attempts to 'locate' Pliny's villas among the ancient remains along the Bay of Naples. For a summary of the investigations, see Gibson and Morello 2012: 228–33.
30 On the basic similarities between the two letters, see Gibson and Morello 2012: 213.
31 Myers 2005: 104, 115; repeated in *ead.* 2018: 273.
32 Drummer 1993 seems to mark the shift in focus away from the villas' archaeological realism.
33 Heffernan 1993: 3. Etymologically, the word refers to an act of 'speaking out' (*ek-phrazein*).
34 On the 'invention' of the modern understanding, see Webb 2009: 7–9; and Becker 1995.
It is almost impossible to capture the breadth and impact of scholarship on ekphrasis. However, important contributions include, but are not limited to, Heffernan 1991; *id.* 1993; Mitchell 1994; Spitzer 1955; Wagner 1996; Webb 1999; *ead.* 2009. On ekphrasis specifically in Greek and Roman texts, see, for example, Friedländer 1912; Elsner 2002; Squire 2009; *id.* 2011: esp. 303–36; *id.* 2013b; and Zeitlin 2013.
35 The precise age of and relationship between each of each of the treatises is debated, with scholars dating them anywhere between the first and the fifth centuries CE; see Heath 2002–3.
36 The relevant sections of the *Progymnasmata* can be found in Patillon and Bolognesi 1997: 66–9; Rabe 1913: 22–3; Rabe 1926: 36–41; and Felten 1913: 67–71. For translations of these passages, see Webb 2009: 197–211.
37 Squire 2015; cf. *id.* 2011, 327–8. The four authors describe ekphrasis in remarkably similar terms: Theon, *Prog.* 118.7, calls it 'a descriptive speech which vividly brings the subject before the eyes' (ἔκφρασίς ἐστι λόγος περιηγηματικὸς ἐναργῶς ὑπ' ὄψιν ἄγων τὸ δηλούμενον); and these words are quoted verbatim by Hermogenes and Aphthonius, and then closely echoed by Nikolaus. In fact, Herm. *Prog.* 10.47 adds the phrase 'as they say' (ὡς φασίν), as if acknowledging a formulaic definition.
38 Squire 2015.

39 Nik. *Prog.* [Felten 1913: 70]: ὑπ' ὄψιν ἡμῖν ἄγοντα ταῦτα, περὶ ὧν εἰσιν οἱ λόγοι, καὶ μόνον οὐ θεατὰς εἶναι παρασκευάζοντα.
All four authors of the *Progymnasmata* use the adverb *enargôs* (translated as 'with visual vividness' to describe the process of 'bringing before the eyes'. Hermog. *Prog.* 10.48 argues that *enargeia* should also be coupled with *saphêneia* ('clarity').

40 Note that Nikolaus uses the qualification 'almost' (μόνον οὐ) in his description of the effect of ekphrasis. Cf. Goldhill 2007: 3, who notes that this qualification is important because 'rhetorical theory knows well that descriptive power is a technique of illusion, semblance, of making to appear'.

41 Cf. Philostratus, *Life of Apollonius of Tyana* VI. 19, who wrote that *phantasia* is 'wiser than *mimesis*. For imitation will represent that which can be seen with the eyes while *phantasia* will represent that which cannot, for the latter proceeds with reality as its basis' – on this passage, see Bermelin 1933; Elsner 1995a: 26; Schweitzer 1934; and Pollitt 1974: 52–4, 201–5.

42 Newlands 2002: 42–3.

43 Squire 2011: 354. See also, Cic. *Or.* 139, on the speaker who 'will put the matter before the eyes through speech' (*rem dicendo subiciet oculis*); and Quint. *Inst.* 9.2.40, on the art of 'placing before the eyes' (*illa . . . sub oculus subiecto*).

44 'Wonder' introduces and/or frames the ekphrases on the shields of Achilles (Hom. *Il.* 18.467), Heracles (Hes. *Shield* 150, 224, 318) and Aeneas (Virg. *A.* 8.619, 8.730); as well as those detailing Europa's basket (Mochus 2.38), the Ariadne tapestry (Cat. 64.51) and the Temple of Carthage (Virg. *A.* 1.456, 1.494).

45 Whitton 2013: 223.

46 This has not, of course, stopped people from trying: for example, Tanzer 1924; Van Buren 1948; and Pember's 3-D model in Spencer 2010: 11, figure 8. The tradition of reconstruction is summarized in Du Prey 1994.

47 Cf. Spencer 2010: 127–8, who argues that Pliny promotes a direct correlation between acts of viewing, reading and perceiving the villa phenomenologically; and von Stackelberg 2009: 126, who calls the letters a 'play between real and fictive space'.

48 Myers 2005: 11. Cf. Bergmann 1995: 420. More generally, Edwards 1993 notes that 'Roman descriptions of buildings (much to the frustration of modern scholars) generally work not so much to give a picture of a building's physical appearance, as to evoke certain emotional responses'.

49 See Leach 1990, with the response of Riggsby 1997. Henderson 2002b: 12–13 and *id.* 2003: 120–4 argues that the villas, and the letters that describe them, are enactments of self-modelling on Pliny's part. On the daily life of *otium* in the villas, see, for example, Laidlaw 1968: 42–52; and Leach 2003: 147–65.

50 Young 2015: 111.

51 Chinn 2007: 266.

52 Myers 2005: 104. Cf. Hales 2003: 20–3 on the connection between villas and ostentatious lifestyles.

53 Zarmakoupi 2014: 18. Cf. Hoffer 1999: 29–44, who terms the villas 'factories of letters'. Myers 2005 terms this literary-focused *otium* '*docta otia*' ('learned leisure').
54 Myers 2005: 123.
55 For such a reading, see Gamberini 1983: 141–3. Following this emphasis on rhetorical theory, Chinn 2007 deals specifically with *Ep.* 5.6 in relation to the practice and theory of ekphrasis.
56 Purcell 1996: 135. Cf. Myers 2005: 117. A number of excavated villas have revealed the same concern with displaying productivity – see Purcell 1995 and Jashemski 1987.
57 Whitton 2013: 241 notes that the prominent position of the *hortus* physically in the estate is mirrored by the central placement of the word *hortus* at 2.17.5 (it is the 537th word out of a 1,082-word letter).
58 Compare to Var. *R.* intr.2, who complains about the proliferation of 'Greekisms' in relation to villas. On the application of Pliny's terminology to archaeological finds, see Leach 1997; cf. Allison 1993 and *ead.* 2001.
59 Whitton 2013: 230. Although my focus is on sight, Platts 2020: 25–8 rightly notes the proliferation of olfactory and haptic references also found within Pliny's descriptions, with the multi-sensory experience evoked only adding to the ekphrastic experience.
60 Bergmann 1991: 66. Although the author here is discussing Statius, her point is also relevant to Pliny's descriptions. Drerup 1959 was the first to theorize on the importance of the 'framed view' in Roman domestic architecture.
61 2.17.2: *praeterea cenatio quae latissimum mare longissiumum litus villas amoenissimas possidet*. Cf. Whitton 2013: 238 on the legal term *servitutes* ('easements'), which included the right of a house not to have its views blocked.
62 Spencer 2010: 128. Cf. Stat. *Silv.* 2.2.15–19, where he recognizes the beauty of the natural landscape *and* its beauty *after* being shaped by '*ars*'.
63 Cf. Nevett 2010 on how changes in time and season impact the use of rooms in Pompeian houses.
64 Chinn 2007: 271.
65 Young 2015: 119. Note that *cernere* also introduces Statius' ekphrastic villa description in *Silv.* 2.2.
66 Cf. Stat. *Silv.* 2.2.72–5. On this passage, see Newlands 2002: 172–5.
67 It is important to note that, in this context, we are referring to a specifically elite and male series of cultural Roman values.
68 Proponents of this so-called 'empty house' model have emphasized the importance of the vista from the front door of a house through the *tablinum* and into the garden/peristyle beyond: see, for example, Wallace-Hadrill 1994: 44; Drerup 1959; Bek 1980: 185–6; Watts 1987: 187–9; Clarke 1991: 4–6; Wallace-Hadrill 1994: 44; Elsner 1995a: 76. For a reconsideration of the empty house model, see Platts 2020: 89–104.

69 Cf. Whitton 2013: 230, who argues that the accumulation of nouns at 2.17.5 (*a tergo ... respicit montes*), where Pliny 'looks back' at the rooms he has 'visited' so far, is designed to mimic such a long axial perspective.
70 These frescoes are now faded almost entirely beyond recognition, but were fortunately recorded by photos in 1967. Reconstructions by Paulo Baronio can be found in Bergmann 2017: figure 9.1.
71 Bergmann 2017: 97 also notes that, although the east and west walls appear to be mirror compositions, they actually feature many small variations (e.g. style of fountains). This, of course, reminds us of Pliny's delight in the variation of views in his triple vistas.
72 On the impact of 'permeable boundaries', Lauritsen 2012; cf. Platts 2020: 89–104 on 'leaky houses'.
73 Young 2015: 133.
74 Bergmann 2017: 108; cf. Thomas 2017a: 81–2, figure 7.5 (reconstruction of room 69's roof and *fastiguum*) and figure 7.6 (reconstruction of marble floor).
75 Bergmann 2017: 100; cf. Jashemski 1993: 298–300 on the root cavity excavations.
76 Bergmann 2017: 108 notes that the convoluted indoor-outdoor spaces of this series are extremely rare, although they do find parallel at the contemporary Villa San Marco.
77 Young 2015: 133.
78 On the impact of 'light wells' on domestic space, see Platts 2020: 152–4.
79 I borrow this phrasing from Platt and Squire 2017: 47, in their discussion of 'what do frames do?'.
80 5.6.16–18. Leach 2004: 34 provides a useful summary of the connotations of *xystus*.
81 Cic. *Q. Fr.* 3.1.5; Col. 5.6.7; cf. *Anth. Pal.* 9.23, in which a plane tree thanks a vine for covering its dead trunk with leaves.
82 Compare Figures 22 and 25, taken originally after the excavation, with Figure 18, where the motif is barely visible.
83 See de Caro 1976: figs. 32–9, for photographs of the marble fragments of these columns.
84 Bergmann 2017: 100; cf. Jashemski 1993: 294–5.
85 Young 2015: 128.
86 Cf. Spencer 2010: 131, whose translation of this section emphasizes the 'artfulness' of the garden even more: 'in the midst of this urbane work of art, a mock rural scene unfolds'.
87 Spencer 2010: 129.
88 Cf. Riggsby 2003: 169–70 on why the villa letters might be hard to follow: rooms are only generally given an orientation *relative to one another*, and so, instead of direction, Pliny merely notes adjacency – no left, right, forward, etc., but simply adverbs such as *hinc, inde, mox, deinde*, or verbs such as *asneciture, adhaeret, adiacet, adplicitum est*.

89 Spencer 2010: 130.
90 I borrow this phrasing from Young 2015: 109. Although she uses it to describe the effect of the framed view from room 21 through the window into garden 20 at Oplontis, the same principles clearly apply here.
91 This type of 'indoor' courtyard garden space seemed unlikely in reality to early commentators of Pliny, but the findings of Jashemski 1979: 52–3 confirmed many large root cavities in Pompeian courtyard gardens.
92 Spencer 2010: 132.
93 Young 2015: 314.
94 Young 2015: 134.
95 Platt and Squire 2017: 23.
96 The use of the vine motif within the borders here may also remind us of the reconfiguration of categories of 'figure' and 'ornament', as discussed in chapter three (see pp. 74); as well as Vitruvius' condemnation of vegetal motifs as structural *monstra* (see p. 97).
97 Cf. Platt 2017: 112–13 on similar framing games in *cubiculum* M at the Villa of P. Fannius Synistor at Boscoreale.
98 Platt and Squire 2017: 66. On the window or niche as a 'hiatus' or 'embrasure' in the wall, see Stoichita 1997: esp. 49, where he discusses the Dutch painting genre of *doorkijkje*, in which concentric doorways are used as perceptual framing devices.
99 These murals also find a mirror image at the northern end of the swimming pool, on the exterior walls of rooms 94 and 97, but these spaces are only partially excavated.
100 For a reconstruction of the interior of room 78, see Barker 2017.

Conclusion

1 Grahame 1999: 54–5.
2 von Stackelberg 2009: 49.
3 Johnson 2006: 80.
4 Johnson 2006: 78.
5 On this passage, see e.g. Faber 2007; Schiesaro 2003; Segal 2008; Smolenaars 1998; Tarrant 1985; Unruh 2014. On ekphrasis in Seneca more generally, see Aygon 2004.
6 See Faber 2007: 427–8, for a summary of past approaches.
7 Schiesaro 2003: 14; 64.
8 Schiesaro 2003: 4.
9 Schiesaro 2003: 64.
10 Segal 2008: 148–9; cf. Tarrant 1985: 45, who notes that the *Thyestes* is unusual for the prominence Seneca gives to setting; and Newlands 2002: 42–3.
11 On the destabilizing effect of Seneca's approach to time, see Schiesaro 2003: 177–89.

12 Sen. *Thyestes* 641–9. I borrow the term 'predatory palace' from Unruh 2014.
13 Unruh 2014: 250, notes that height is frequently associated with menace and *hubris* throughout the *Thyestes*.
14 On boundary violation and the landscape of the self in Seneca, see Segal 2008, who argues that Seneca's new vision of tragedy concerns the 'unbearable suffering possible in a world of *uninhibited* violence' (emphasis my own); cf. Seneca's earlier references to the *violentae domus* (32) and the *impia . . . domo* (46).
15 Sen. *Thyestes* 650–82.
16 The grove has previously been categorized as an example of the literary motif of the *locus horridus* (typically a gloomy forest within a nightmare world). For the motif of enclosure in the *locus horridus*, see Mugellesi 1973: 63, who comments on Seneca's 'new pictorial-visual sensitivity' (*la nuova sensibilità pittorico-visiva di Seneca*).
17 Faber 2007: 434, likens the domination of the oak over the grove to that of the tyrant over the city.
18 Smolenaars 1998, in particular, details the connection between this grove and imagery of the underworld, and argues that Seneca's description here is carefully phrased in order to recall Virgil's katabasis in the *Aeneid*.
19 Similarly, the very first words uttered in the choral ode following the messenger's description (789ff.) concerns the inversion of the natural order and the disappearance of the sun.
20 Unruh 2014: 254.
21 Cf. Virg. *A.* 10.421–3, where an oak is used as a votive tree and trophy. On this connection between the oak and spoils, see Armstrong 2019: 128–31.
22 Note that Schiesaro 2003: 189, sees regression as 'the single most relevant operating principle' within the *Thyestes*; cf. *ibid.*: 63, where the author comments on the 'mechanism of regress *ad infinitum*' within the play: 'Frames, multiplied in a sequence of horrors, become the signposts – and harbingers – of the trouncing of order.'
23 Myers 2018: 277.

Bibliography

Abbe, E. (1965) *The Plants of Virgil's Georgics*. Ithaca, NY.
Ackerman, J. S. (1990) *The Villa. Form and Ideology of Country Houses*. London.
Alberti, L. B. (1966) *On Painting*. New Haven and London.
Alessio, G. (1965) 'Oplontis', *Studi Etrusci* 33: 699–724.
Allison, P. M. (1993) 'How Do We Identify the use of Space in Roman Housing?', in E. Moorman (ed.) *Functional and Spatial Analysis of Wall Painting: Proceedings of the Fifth International Congress on Ancient Wall Painting*. Leiden: 1–8.
Allison, P. M. (2001) 'Using the Material and Written Sources: Turn of the Millennium Approaches to Roman Domestic Space', *AJA* 105.2: 181–208.
Andreae, B. (1957) 'Archäologische Funder und Grabungen im Bereich der Soprintendenzen von Rom 1949–1956/7', *Archäologischer Anzeiger* 1957: 119–358.
Anguissola, A. (2010) *Intimità a Pompei: riservatezza, condivisione e prestigio negli ambienti ad alcova di Pompeii*. Berlin and New York, NY.
Anguissola, A. (ed.) (2012) *Private Luxuria – Towards an Archaeology of Intimacy: Pompeii and Beyond*. Munich.
Armstrong, R. (2019) *Vergil's Green Thoughts. Plants, Humans, and the Divine*. Oxford.
Ash, H. B. (ed.) (1930) *L. Iuni Moderati Columella Rei Rusticae Liber Decimus: De Cultu Hortorum. Text, critical apparatus, translation, and commentary*. Philadelphia, PA.
Augé, M. (1995) *Non Places. Introduction to an Anthropology of Supermodernity*. London.
Aygon, J-P. (2004) *Pictor in Fabula. L'Ecphrasis – Descriptio dans les Tragédies de Sénèque*. Brussels.
Bal, M. (2002) *Traveling Concepts in the Humanities: A Rough Guide*. Toronto.
Baldwin, B. (1963) 'Columella's Sources and How He Used Them', *Latomus* 22: 785–91.
Ballester, X. (1990) 'La titulación de las obras en la literature Romana', *CFC(L)* 24: 135–56.
Bannon, C. J. (2009) *Gardens and Neighbours: Private Water Rights in Roman Italy*. Ann Arbor, MI.
Barbet, A. (1985) *La peinture murale romaine*. Paris.
Barker, S. J. (2017) 'Marble Floors and Paneled Walls in the East Wing Of Villa A', in E. K. Gazda and J. R. Clarke (eds). Ann Arbor, MI: 119–25.
Baroin, C. (1998) 'La maison romaine comme image et lieu de mémoire', in C. Auvray-Assayas (ed.) *Images Romaines*. Paris: 177–92.
Beard, M. (1987) 'A Complex of Times: No More Sheep on Romulus' Birthday', *PCPhS* 33: 1–15.

Beard, M. (1998) 'Imaginary *Horti*: Or Up the Garden Path', in M. Cima and E. La Rocca (eds). Rome: 23–32.
Beard, M. (2008) *The Fires of Vesuvius: Pompeii Lost and Found*. London.
Becker, A. S. (1995) *The Shield of Achilles and the Poetics of Ekphrasis*. Lanham, MD.
Beekes, R. (2010) *Etymological Dictionary of Greek*. Leiden.
Bek, L. (1980) *Towards Paradise on Earth. Modern Space Conception in Architecture – A Creation of Renaissance Humanism*. Analecta Romana Instituti Danici 9. Odense.
Bender, B. (2006) 'Place and Landscape', in C. Tilley et al. (eds) *Handbook of Material Culture*. London: 303–13.
Benjamin, W. (1985) *One Way Street and other Writings*. London.
Bergmann, B. (1991) 'Painted Perspectives of a Villa Visit: Landscape as Status and Metaphor', in E. K. Gazda (ed.) *Roman Art in the Private Sphere: New Perspectives on the Architecture and Décor of the Domus, Villa, and Insula*. Ann Arbor, MI: 49–70.
Bergmann, B. (1992) 'Exploring the Grove: Pastoral Space on Roman Walls', in J. D. Hunt (ed.) *The Pastoral Landscape, Studies in the History of Art 36*. Hanover and London: 21–46.
Bergmann, B. (1995) 'Visualizing Pliny's Villas', *JRA* 8: 406–20.
Bergmann, B. (2001) 'House of Cards', *JRA* 15: 346–8.
Bergmann, B. (2002) 'Art and Nature in the Villa at Oplontis', in T. A. J. McGinn (ed.) *Pompeian Brothels, Pompeii's Mirrors and Mysteries, Art and Nature at Oplontis, and the Herculaneum 'Basilica', JRA suppl. 47*. Ann Arbor, MI: 87–120.
Bergmann, B. (2008) 'Staging the Supernatural: Interior Gardens of Pompeian Houses', in C. Mattusch (ed.) *Pompeii and the Roman Villa: Art and Culture Around the Bay of Naples*. Los Angeles, CA: 53–69.
Bergmann, B. (2014) 'The Concept of the Boundary in the Roman Garden', in K. Coleman (ed.). Vandoeuvres: 245–99.
Bergmann, B. (2017) 'The Gardens and Garden Paintings of Villa A', in E. K. Gazda and J. R. Clarke (eds). Ann Arbor, MI: 96–110.
Bergmann, B. (2018) 'Frescoes in Gardens', in W. F. Jashemski et al. (eds). Cambridge: 278–316.
Bergmann, B. (forthcoming) 'Reading the Garden Painting', in J. R. Clarke and N. K. Muntasser (eds). New York, NY.
Berleant, A. and A. Carlson (eds) (2007) *The Aesthetics of Human Environments*. Peterborough, ON.
Bermelin, E. (1933) 'Die kunsttheorischen Gedanken in Philostrats Apollonios', *Philologus* 68: 392–414.
Bianchi-Bandinelli, R. (1970) *Rome: The Center of Power, 500 BC to AD 200*. London.
Billows, R. (1993) 'The Religious Procession of the Ara Pacis Augustae: Augustus' Supplicato in 13B.C.', *JRA* 6: 80–92.
Black, J., E. Robson, G. Cunningham, G. Zólyomi et al. (1998–2006) *The Electronic Text Corpus of Sumerian Literature* http://etcsl.orinst.ox.ac.uk.

Boatwright, M. T. (1998) 'Luxuriant Gardens and Extravagant Women: The *Horti* of Rome between Republic and Empire', in M. Cima and E. La Rocca (eds). Rome: 71–82.
Bodel, J. (1994) 'Graveyards and Groves: A Study of the Lex Lucerina', *AJAH* 11. Cambridge, MA.
Bodel, J. (2009) '"Sacred dedications": a problem of definitions', in J. P. Bodel and M. Kajava (eds) *Dediche sacre nel mondo greco-romano. Diffusione, funzioni, tipologie*. Rome: 17–30.
Bodel, J. (2018) 'Tomb Gardens', in W. F. Jashemski et al. (eds). Cambridge: 199–244.
Boldrer, F. (1996) *L. Iuni Moderati Columellae Rei Rusticae Liber Decimus*. Pisa.
Borg, B. (ed.) (2015) *A Companion to Roman Art*. Malden, MA.
Bowe, P. (2004) *Gardens of the Roman World*. Los Angeles, CA.
Boyce, G. K. (1937) *Corpus of the Lararia of Pompeii*, MAAR 14.
Bracco, V. (1975) 'Oplonti Pompeios milia trias', *Vita Latina* 58: 35–7.
Brown, F., S. Driver and C. Briggs (1996) *The Brown-Driver-Briggs Hebrew and English Lexicon*. Peabody, MA.
Brundrett, N. (2011) 'Roman Tomb Gardens: The Construction of Sacred Commemorative Landscapes', *The Brock Review* 11.2: 51–69.
Buchheit, V. (1962) *Studien zum Corpus Priapeorum*. Munich.
Buchner, E. (1976) 'Solarium Augusti und Ara Pacis', *Römische Mitteilungen* 83: 319–65.
Büsing, A. (1977) 'Ranke und Figur an der Ara Pacis Augustae', *Archäologischer Anzeiger* 247–57.
Calci, C. and G. Messineo (1984) *La villa di Livia a Prima Porta*, LSA 2. Rome.
Campbell, B. (2000) *The Writings of the Roman Land Surveyors: Introduction, Text, Translation, and Commentary*. London.
Campbell, V. (2008) 'Stopping to Smell the Roses: Garden Tombs in Roman Italy', *Arethusa* 42: 31–42.
Caneva, G. (2010) *Il codice botanico di Augusto*. Rome.
Caneva, G. and L. Bohuny (2003) 'Botanic Analysis of Livia's Villa Painted Flora (Prima Porta, Rome), *Journal of Cultural Heritage* 4: 149–55.
Carettoni, G. (1966–7) 'I problemi della zona augustea del Palatino alla luce dei recenti scavi', *Rend. Pont. Acc*. 39: 55–68.
Carroll, M. (2003) *Earthly Paradises: Ancient Gardens in History and Archaeology*. London.
Carroll, M. (2011) 'Exploring the sanctuary of Venus and its sacred grove: politics, cult, and identity in Roman Pompeii', in *Papers of the British School at Rome* 78: 63–106.
Carroll, M. (2015) 'Contextualising Roman Art and Nature', in B. Borg (ed.). Malden, MA: 231–47.
Carroll, M. (2018) 'Temple Gardens and Groves', in W. F. Jashemski et al. (eds). Cambridge: 152–64.
Carroll, M. and D. Godden (2000) 'The Sanctuary of Apollo at Pompeii: Reconsidering chronologies and excavation history', *AJA* 104: 743–54.
Carroll-Spillecke, M. (1989) ΚΗΠΟΣ: *Der antike griechische Garten*. Munich.

Carroll-Spillecke, M. (1992a) 'The Gardens of Greece from Homeric to Roman Times', *Journal of Garden History* 12: 84–101.

Carroll-Spillecke, M. (1992b) 'Grieschische Gärten', in M. Carroll-Spillecke (ed.) *Der Garten von der Antike bis zum Mittelalter. Kulturgeschichte der antiken Welt* 57. Mainz: 153–76.

Casey, E. (1993) *Getting Back Into Place: Toward a Renewed Understanding of the Place-World*. Bloomington, IN.

Castriota, D. (1995) *The Ara Pacis Augustae and the Imagery of Abundance in Later Greek and Early Roman Imperial Art*. Princeton, NJ.

Champlin, E. (2001) 'Pliny's Other Country', *JRA* 43: 121–8.

Chinn, C. M. (2007) 'Before Your Very Eyes: Pliny *Epistulae* 5.6 and the Ancient Theory of Ekphrasis', *CP* 102: 265–80.

Cima, M. and E. La Rocca (eds) (1998) *Horti Romani: atti del convegno internazionale Roma, 4–6 maggio 1995*. Rome.

Clarke, J. (1991) *The Houses of Roman Italy, 100 B.C. – A.D. 250: Ritual, Space, and Decoration*. Berkeley, CA, and Oxford.

Clarke, J. (1996) 'Landscape Paintings in the Villa of Oplontis', *JRA* 9: 81–107.

Clarke, J. (1998) *Looking at Lovemaking: Constructions of Sexuality in Roman Art, 100 B.C.–A.D. 250*. Berkeley, CA.

Clarke, J. (2003) *Art in the Lives of Ordinary Romans: Visual Representation and Non-elite Viewers in Italy, 100 B.C.–A.D. 315*. Berkeley, CA.

Clarke, J. R. and N. K. Muntasser (eds) (2014) *Oplontis: Villa A ('Of Poppaea') at Torre Annuziata, Vol. 1. The Ancient Setting and Discovery*. New York, NY: ACLS E-Book. https://hdl.handle.net/2027/fulcrum.wd375x14s.

Clarke, J. R. and N. K. Muntasser (forthcoming) *Vol. 2. Decorative Ensembles: Painting, Stucco, Pavements, Sculptures*. New York, NY: ALCS E-Book.

Clausen, W. V. (1987) *Virgil's Aeneid and the Tradition of Hellenistic Poetry*. Berkeley, CA.

Clay, J. (1981) 'The Old Man in the Garden: Georgic 4.116–148', *Arethusa* 14: 57–65.

Coarelli, F. (1993) 'I luci del Lazio: la documentazione archeologica', in O. de Cazanove and J. Scheid (eds). Naples: 367–77.

Coarelli, F. (1997) *Il Campo Marzio. Dalle origini alla fine della Repubblica*. Rome.

Cofer, C. (2015) *The Ara Pacis Augustae and the Augustan Understanding of Grafting*. PhD dissertation, Bryn Mawr College.

Cohon, R. (2004) 'Forerunners of the scrollwork of the Ara Pacis Augustae made by a Western Asiatic workshop', *JRA* 17: 83–106.

Coleman, K. (ed.) (2014) *Le jardin dans l'antiquité: Entretiens sur L'Antiquité e Classique* 60. Vandoeuvres, Fondation Hardt.

Conte, G. B. (1996) *The Rhetoric of Imitation: Genre and Poetic Memory in Virgil and Other Latin Poets*. Ithaca, NY.

Cooper, D. E. (2006) *A Philosophy of Gardens*. Oxford.

Cornwell, H. (2017) *Pax and the Politics of Peace: Republic to Principate*. Oxford.

Cosgrove, D. and S. Daniels (eds) (1988) *The Iconography of the Landscape: Essays on the Symbolic Representation, Design, and Use of Past Environments*. Cambridge.

Culler, J. (1982) *On deconstruction. Theory and criticism after structuralism.* Ithaca, NY.
Cunliffe (1971) *Fishbourne: A Roman Palace and Its Garden.* Baltimore, MA.
Dallinges, L. (1964) 'Science et poésie chez Columelle', *Études de lettres* 7: 137–54.
D'Ambrosio, A., P. G. Guzzo and M. Mastroroberto (eds) (2003) *Storie da un'eruzione: Pompei, Ercolano, Oplontis. Exhibition Catalogue, Museo Archaeologie Nazionale di Napoli: Musées royaux d'art et d'histoire (Belgium).* Milan.
D'Arms, J. (1970) *Romans on the Bay of Naples: A Social and Cultural Study of the Villas and Their Owners from 150 B.C. to A.D. 400.* Cambridge, MA.
D'Arms, J. (1998) 'Between Public and Private: the Epulum Publicum and Caesar's Horti trans Tiberim', in M. Cima and E. La Rocca (eds). Rome: 33–41.
de Alārcao, J. and R. Etienne (1981) 'Les Jardins à Conimbriga Portugal', in E. B. MacDougall and W. Jashemski (eds). Washington, DC: 67–80.
de Alārcao, J. and R. Etienne (1986) 'Archéologie et idéologie impériale à Conimbriga (Portugal)', *Comptes rendus des séances de l'Académie des Inscriptions et Belles-Lettres* 130: 120–32.
de Caro, S. (1976) 'Sculture dalla villa di Poppaea ad Oplontis', *CronPomp* 2: 184–225.
de Caro, S. (1987) 'The Sculptures of the Villa of Poppaea at Oplontis. A Preliminary Report', in E. B. MacDougall (ed.). Washington, DC: 77–103.
de Cazanove, O. and J. Scheid (eds) (1993) *Les bois sacres. Actes du colloque International de Naples. Collection du Centre Jean Bérard 10.* Naples.
de Certeau, M. (1984) *The Practice of Everyday Life.* Berkeley, CA.
Defert, D. (1997) 'Foucault, Space, and the Architects', in C. David and J-F. Chevrir (eds) *Politics/Poetics: Documenta X – The Book.* Ostfildern: 274–83.
de Franciscis, A. (1973) 'La Villa romana di Oplontis', *La Parola del Passato* 153: 453–66.
de Franciscis, A. (1975) 'Die römische Villa von Oplontis', *Antike Welt* 6: 33–6.
de Franciscis, A. (1979) 'Beryllos e la villa di Poppea ad Oplontis', in G. Kopcke and M. B. Moore (eds) *Studies in Classical Art and Archaeology. A Tribute to P. H. von Blanckenhagen.* Locust Valley, NY: 231–4.
de Franciscis, A. (1982) 'Oplontis', in *La regione sotterata dal Vesuvio Studi e prospettive. Atti del Convegno internazionale 11–15 novembre 1979.* Naples: 907–25.
Dehaene, M. and L. De Cauter (eds) (2008) *Heterotopia and Social Ordering.* London.
Derrida, J. (1976) *Of Grammatology,* trans. by G. C. Spivak. London and Baltimore, MD.
Derrida, J. (1987) *The Truth in Painting,* trans. by G. Bennington and I. McLeod. London and Chicago, IL.
De Vos, M. (1983) 'Funzione e decorazione dell' Auditorium di Maecenate', in G. P. Sartorio and L. Quilici (eds) *Roma capitali 1870–1911. L'archaeologia in Roma tra sterro e scavo.* Rome: 231–47.
Dickmann, J. A. (1997) 'The Peristyle and the Transformations of Domestic Space in Hellenistic Pompeii', in R. Laurence and A. Wallace-Hadrill (eds). *JRA* suppl. 22: 121–36.
Dietrich, N. and M. Squire (eds) (2018) *Ornament and Figure in Graeco-Roman Art and Archaeology. Rethinking Visual Ontologies in Classical Antiquity.* Berlin.

di Maio, G. (2014) 'The Geoarchaeology of the Oplontis Coastline', in J. R. Clarke and N. K. Muntasser (eds). New York, NY: 662–92.

Dobbins, J. J. and P. W. Foss (eds) (2007) *The World of Pompeii*. New York, NY.

Dominek, W. J. (2009) 'Vergil's Geopolitics', in W. J. Dominek, J. Garthwaite, and P. A. Roche (eds) *Writing Politics in Imperial Rome*. Leiden: 111–32.

Doody, A. (2007) 'Virgil the Farmer? Critiques of the *Georgics* in Columella and Pliny', *CP* 102: 180–97.

Doody, A., S. Föllinger and L. Taub (eds) (2012) 'Structures and Strategies in ancient Greek and Roman technical writing', *Studies in History and Philosophy Part A* 43.2.

Drerup, H. (1959) 'Bildraum und Realraum in der römischen Architektur', *RM* 66: 145–74.

Drummer, A. (1993) *Villa: Untersuchungen zum Bedeutungswandel eines Motivs in römischer Bildkunst und Literatur*. PhD dissertation, Munich.

Duncan-Jones, R. (1974) *The Economy of the Roman Empire: Quantitative Studies*. New York, NY.

Du Prey, P. (1994) *The Villas of Pliny from Antiquity to Posterity*. London and Chicago, IL.

Duret, L. and J. Néraudau (2001) *Urbanisme et métamorphoses de la Rome antique*. Paris.

Edwards, C. (1993) *The Politics of Immorality in Ancient Rome*. Cambridge.

Edwards, C. (1996) *Writing Rome: Textual Approaches to the City*. Cambridge.

Edwards, C. and G. Woolf (eds) (2003) *Rome the Cosmopolis*. Cambridge.

Egelhaaf-Gaiser, U. (2007) 'Roman Cult Sites: A Pragmatic Approach', in J. Rüpke (ed.). Oxford: 205–21.

Ehrhardt, W. (1991) 'Vitruv und die zeitgenössische Wandmalerei', *KJ* 39: 92–111.

Elkins, J. (1993) 'On the Conceptual Analysis of Gardens', *Journal of Garden History* 13.4: 189–98.

Elomaa, H. (2015) *The Poetics of the Carmina Priapea*. Unpublished dissertation, University of Pennsylvania.

Elsner, J. (1991) 'Cult and Sculpture: Sacrifice in the Ara Pacis Augustae', *JRS* 81: 50–61.

Elsner, J. (1995a) *Art and The Roman Viewer. The Transformation of Art from the Pagan World to Christianity*. Cambridge.

Elsner, J. (1995b) 'Review of Castriota (1995)', *BMCR* 95.09.05.

Elsner, J. (2002) 'Introduction: The Genres of Ekphrasis', *Ramus* 31: 1–18.

Ergin, G. (2018) 'The Colours of the Ara Pacis', *Acta Classica Mediterranea* 1: 9–24.

Ernout, A. and A. Meillet (1959) *Dictionnaire étymologique de la langue latine. Histoire des mots*. Paris.

Evans, R. (2003) 'Searching for Paradise: Landscape, Utopia, and Rome', *Arethusa* 36: 285–307.

Evans, R. (2008) *Utopia Antiqua: Readings of the Golden Age and Decline at Rome*. London and New York, NY.

Faber, R. A. (2007) 'The Description of the Palace in Seneca's "Thyestes" 641–82 and the Literary Unity of the Play', *Mnemosyne* 60: 427–42.

Farrar, L. (1998) *Ancient Roman Gardens*. Stroud.
Farrar, L. (2016) *Gardens and the Gardeners of the Ancient World: History, Myth, and Archaeology*. Oxford and Philadelphia, PA.
Favro, D. (1996) *The Urban Image of Augustan Rome*. Cambridge.
Feeney, D. (2007) *Caesar's Calendar: Ancient Time and the Beginnings of History*. Berkeley, CA.
Felten, J. (ed.) (1913) *Nicolaus, Progymnasmata*. Leipzig.
Fernandez-Galiano, M. (ed.) (1975) *L.J.M. Columela. De cultu hortorum. Introducción, texto, traducción, y notas*. Madrid.
Ferriolo, M. V. (1989) 'Homer's Garden', *Journal of Garden History* 9: 86–94.
Fisher, K. D. (2006) 'Messages in stone: constructing sociopolitical inequality in Late Bronze Age Cyprus', in E. C. Robertson, J. D. Seibert, D. C. Fernandez and M. U. Zender (eds) *Space and Spatial Analysis in Archaeology*. Calgary, AB: 123–32.
Fisher, K. D. (2009) 'Placing social interaction: an integrative approach to analyzing past built environments', *Journal of Anthropological Archaeology* 28: 439–57.
Fitzgerald, W. (1996) 'Labor and Laborer in Latin Poetry: The Case of the Moretum', *Arethusa* 29: 389–418.
Fitzgerald, W. and E. Spentzou (eds) (2018) *The Production of Space in Latin Literature*. Oxford.
Flory, M. (1989) 'Octavian and the Omen of the *Gallina Alba*', *CJ* 84: 343–56.
Flory, M. (1995) 'The Symbolism of the Laurel in Cameo Portraits of Livia', *Memoirs of the American Academy in Rome* 40: 43–68.
Flower, H. I. (1996) *Ancestor Masks and Aristocratic Power in Roman Culture*. Oxford.
Fögen, Th. (ed.) (2005) *Antike Fachtexte Ancient Technical Texts*. Berlin.
Forster, E. S. (1950) 'Columella and his Latin Treatise on Agriculture', *Greece and Rome* 19: 123–8.
Förtsch, R. (1993) *Archäologischer Kommentar zu den Villenbriefen des jüngeren Plinius*. Mainz am Rhein.
Foss, P. (1997) 'Watchful Lares: Household Organization and the Rituals of Cooking and Eating', in R. Laurence and A. Wallace-Hadrill (eds). *JRA* suppl. 22: 197–218.
Foucault, M. (1986) 'Of Other Spaces', trans. by J. Miskowiec, *Diacritics* 16: 22–7.
Foucault, M. (1988) 'Different Spaces', in J. D. Faubion (ed.) *Aesthetics, Method and Epistemology: Essential Works of Foucault Volume 2*. London: 175–85.
Francis, M. and R. T. Hester (eds) (1990) *The Meaning of Gardens: Idea, Place, and Action*. London and Cambridge, MA.
Friedländer, P. (1912) *Johannes von Gaza und Paulus Silentarius. Kunstbeschreibungen Justinianischer Zeit*. Leipzig.
Frischer, B. (1982–3) '*Monumenta et Arae Honoris Virtutisque Causa*: Evidence of Memorials for Roman Civic Heroes', *Bulletino della commissione archeologic communale di Roma* 88: 51–86.
Froehlich, T. (1991) *Lararien und Fassadenbilder in den vesuvstäden. Untersuchungen zur 'volkstümlichen' pomejanischen Malerei*. Mainz.

Fullerton, M. D. (1985) 'The Domus Augusti in Imperial Iconography of 13–12 BC', *AJA* 89: 473–73.

Gabriel, M. (1955) *Livia's Garden Room at Prima Porta*. New York, NY.

Gale, M. (2000) *Virgil on the Nature of Things: The Georgics, Lucretius and the Didactic Tradition*. Cambridge.

Gale, M. (ed.) (2004) *Latin Epic and Didactic Poetry: Genre, Tradition, and Individuality*. Swansea.

Gale, M. (2005) 'Didactic Epic', in S. Harrison (ed.) *A Companion to Latin Literature*. London: 101–15.

Galinsky, K. (1996) *Augustan Culture: An Interpretive Introduction*. Princeton, NJ.

Galinsky, K. (2007) 'Continuity and Change: Religion in the Augustan Semi-Century', in J. Rüpke (ed.). Oxford: 71–82.

Gamberini, F. (1983) *Stylistic Theory and Practice in the Younger Pliny*. Hildesheim.

Gaston, S. and I. Maclachlan (eds) (2001) *Reading Derrida's Of Grammatology*. London.

Gazda, E. K. (2017) 'Villa on the Bay of Naples: The Ancient Setting of Oplontis', in E. K. Gazda and J. R. Clarke (eds). Ann Arbor, MI: 30–47.

Gazda, E. K. and J. R. Clarke (eds) (2017) *Leisure and Luxury in the Age of Nero: The Villas at Oplontis near Pompeii*. Ann Arbor, MI.

Gee, E. (2000) *Ovid, Aratus and Augustus: Astronomy in Ovid's Fasti*. Cambridge.

Gee, R. (2014) 'Fourth Style "Responses" to Period Rooms of the Second and Third Styles at Villa A ("of Poppaea") at Oplontis', in N. Zimmerman (ed.) *Antike Malerei zwischen Lokalstil und Zeitstil. Akten des XI Internationalem Kolloquiums der AIPMA, Association Internationale pour la Peinture Murale Antique, 13–17 September 2010 in Ephesos*. Vienna: 89–96.

Gee, R. (2015) 'Workshops and Patterns of Movement at Villa A, Oplontis', in S. Lepinski and S. McFadden (eds) *Beyond Iconography, Materials, Methods and Meaning in Ancient Surface Decoration*. Boston, MA: 115–36.

Gee, R. (2017) 'Layered Histories: The Wall Painting Styles and Painters of Villa A', in E. K. Gazda and J. R. Clarke (eds). Ann Arbor, MI: 85–95.

Gee, R. (forthcoming) 'The Wall Paintings of Villa A', in J. R. Clarke and N. K. Muntasser (eds). New York, NY.

Genette, G. (1997) *Paratexts, Thresholds of Interpretation*, translated by J. E. Lewin. Cambridge.

Genocchio, B. (1995) 'Discourse, Discontinuity, Difference: The Question of Other Spaces', in S. Watson and K. Gibson (eds) *Postmodern Cities and Spaces*. Oxford: 35–46.

Giacobello, F. (2008) *Larari pompeiari: Iconografia e cult dei Lari in ambito domestico*. Milan.

Gibbs, M. (2013) 'Interest Rates', in R. S. Bagnall et al. (eds) *Encyclopaedia of Ancient History*. Oxford: 3471–3.

Gibson, R. and R. Morello (2012) *Reading the Letters of Pliny the Younger: An Introduction*. Cambridge and New York, NY.

Giesecke, A. (2001) 'Beyond the Gardens of Epicurus: The Utopics of the Ideal Roman Villa', *Utopian Studies* 12: 13–32.

Giesecke (2007) *The Epic City. Urbanism, Utopia, and the Garden in Ancient Greece and Rome*. Cambridge, MA.

Gleason, K. (1994) 'Porticus Pompeiana: A New Perspective on the First Public Park of Ancient Rome', *Journal of Garden History* 14: 13–27.

Gleason, K. (2010) 'Constructing Nature: The Built Garden. With Notice of a New Monumental Garden at the Villa Arianna, Stabiae', *Proceedings of the International Congress of Classical Archaeology*. http://bollettinodiarcheologiaonline.beniculturali.it.

Gleason, K. (ed.) (2013) *A Cultural History of Gardens in Antiquity*. London.

Gleason, K. (2014) 'The Landscape Palaces of Herod the Great', *Near Eastern Archaeology* 77: 76–97.

Gleason, K. (2019) 'The lost dimension: pruned plants in Roman gardens', *Vegetation History and Archaeobotany*.

Goldhill, S. (2007) 'What is Ekphrasis For?', *CP* 102: 1–19.

Gordon, R. L. (1990) 'The Veil of Power: Emperors, Sacrificers, and Benefactors', in M. Beard and J. North (eds) *Pagan Priests. Religion and Power in the Ancient World*. London: 199–231.

Gothein, M. (1909) 'Der griechische Garten', *Mitteilungen des kaiserlich deutschen archäologischen Instituts, athenische Abteiluing* 34: 100–44.

Gowers, E. (2000) 'Vegetable Love: Columella and Garden Poetry', *Ramus* 29.2: 127–48.

Graham, E-J. (2018) 'There buds the laurel: Nature, temporality, and the making of place in the cemeteries of Roman Italy', *TRAJ* 1.3: 1–16.

Grahame, M. (1997) 'Public and Private in the Roman House: Investigating the Social Order of the *Casa del Fauno*', in R. Laurence and A. Wallace-Hadrill (eds). *JRA* suppl. 22: 137–64.

Grahame, M. (1999) 'Reading the Roman House: The Social Interpretation of Spatial Order', *Theoretical Roman Archaeology and Architecture: The Third Conference Proceedings*: 48–74.

Gregori, G. L. (1987–8) 'Horti sepulcrales e cepotaphia nelle iscrizione urbane', *BCAR* 92: 175–88.

Grimal, P. (1943) *Les Jardins Romains*. Paris.

Gros, P. (1976) *Aurea Templa. Resherches sure l'architecture réligeuse de Rome a l'epoque d'Auguste*. Rome.

Guzzo, P. G. (2003) *Storie da un'eruzione: Pompei, Ercolano, Oplontis: Guida alla mostra*. Naples and Milan.

Hales, S. (2003) *The Roman House and Social Identity*. Cambridge.

Halloran, J. (2006) *Sumerian Lexicon: A Dictionary Guide to the Ancient Sumerian Language*. Los Angeles, CA.

Halpern, L. C. (1992) 'The uses of paintings in garden history', in J. D. Hunt (ed.). Cambridge, MA: 183–202.

Hardie, P. (ed.) (2009) *Paradox and the Marvellous in Augustan Literature*. Oxford.

Harrison, M. (1986) 'The ordering of the urban environment: time, work, and the occurrence of crowds 1790–1835', *Past & Present* 110: 134–68.

Harrison, S. (2004) 'Virgil's Corycius Senex and Nicander's Georgica: Georgics 4.116–48', in M. Gale (ed.). Swansea: 109–23.

Hartswick, K. (2018) 'The Roman Villa', in W. F. Jashemski et al. (eds). Cambridge: 72–86.

Haselberger, L. (ed.) (2014) *The Horologium of Augustus: Debate and Context.* Portsmouth, RI.

Haselberger, L. and D. G. Romano (2002) 'Mapping Augustan Rome', *JRA* suppl. 50. Portsmouth, RI.

Haüber, C. (1990) 'Zur Topographie der Horti Maecenatis und der Horti Lamiani auf dem Esquilin in Rom', *KJ* 23: 11–107.

Haüber, C. (1998) 'The Esquiline Horti: New Research', in A. Frazer (ed.) *The Roman Villa, Villa Urbana.* Philadelphia, PA: 55–64.

Heath, M. (2002–3) 'Theon and the History of the Progymnasmata', *Greek, Roman, and Byzantine Studies* 43: 129–60.

Heffernan, J. (1991) 'Ekphrasis and Representation', *New Literary History* 22.2: 297–316.

Heffernan, J. (1993) *The Museum of Words: The Poetics of Ekphrasis from Homer to Ashbery.* Chicago, IL.

Heinze, R. (1960) 'Das Kraeuterkaesgericht (Moretum)', *Vom Geist des Roemertums.* Stuttgart.

Henderson, J. (2002a) 'Columella's Living Hedge: The Roman Gardening Book', *JRS* 92: 110–33.

Henderson, J. (2002b) *Pliny's Statue. The Letters, Self-Portraiture, and Classical Art.* Exeter.

Henderson, J. (2003) 'Portrait of the Artist as a Figure of Style: P.L.I.N.Y.'s Letters', *Arethusa* 36: 115–25.

Henderson, J. (2004) *The Roman Book of Gardening.* London.

Herter, H. (1932) *De Priapo.* Giessen.

Hesberg, H. and S. Panciera (1994) *Das Mausoleum des Augustus: der Bau und seine Inschriften, AbhMünch* 108. Munich.

Hetherington, K. (1997) *The Badlands of Modernity. Heterotopia and Social Ordering.* London and New York, NY.

Hillier, B. and J. Hanson (1984) *The Social Logic of Space.* Cambridge.

Hillis-Miller, J. (1979) 'The Critic as Host', in H. Bloom (ed.) *Deconstruction and Criticism.* London and New York, NY: 177–207.

Hinds, S. (1998) *Allusion and Intertext: Dynamics of Appropriation in Roman Poetry.* Cambridge.

Hoffer, S. (1999) *The Anxieties of Pliny the Younger.* Atlanta, GA.

Hollander, D. (2019) *Farmers and Agriculture in the Roman Economy.* London and New York, NY.

Holliday, P. J. (1990) 'Time, History and Ritual on the Ara Pacis Augustae', *Art Bulletin* 72.4: 542–57.

Honroth, M. (1971) *Stadtrömische Girlanden: Ein Versuch zur Entwicklungsgeschichte römische Ornamentik*. Vienna.
Horsfall (1981) 'Some problems of titulature in Roman literary history', *BICS* 28: 103–14.
Hughes, J. D. (1994) *Pan's Travail: Environmental Problems of the Ancient Greeks and Romans*. Baltimore, MD.
Hunt, A. (2016) *Reviving Roman Religion: Sacred Trees in the Roman World*. Cambridge.
Hunt, J. D. (1992) *Gardens and the Picturesque: studies in the history of landscape architecture*. Cambridge, MA.
Hunt, J. D. (2000) *Greater Perfections. The Practice of Garden Theory*. Philadelphia.
Ingold, T. (2000) *Perception of the Environment: Essays on livelihood, dwelling, and skill*. London and New York, NY.
Jacobs, P. W. and D. A. Conlin (2014) *Campus Martius. The Field of Mars in the Life of Ancient Rome*. Cambridge.
Jansen, L. (ed.) (2014) *The Roman Paratext: Frames, Texts, and Readers*. Cambridge.
Janson, T. (1964) *Latin Prose prefaces: studies in literary conventions*. Stockholm.
Jashemski, W. F. (1979) *The Gardens of Pompeii, Herculaneum and the Villas Destroyed by Vesuvius*, Vol. 1. New Rochelle, NY.
Jashemski, W. F. (1993) *The Gardens of Pompeii, Herculaneum and the Villas Destroyed by Vesuvius: Appendices*, Vol. 2. New Rochelle, NY.
Jashemski, W. F. (2018) 'Produce Gardens', in W. F. Jashemski et al. (eds). Cambridge: 121–51.
Jashemski, W. F. and F. G. Meyer (eds) (2002) *A Natural History of Pompeii*. Cambridge.
Jashemski, W F., K. Gleason, K. Hartswick and A. Malek (eds) (2018) *Gardens of the Roman Empire*. Cambridge.
Johnson, P. (2006) 'Unravelling Foucault's Different Spaces', *History of the Human Sciences* 19: 75–90.
Jones, F. (2013) *Virgil's Garden: The Nature of Bucolic Space*. London.
Jones, F. (2016) *The Boundaries of Art and Social Space: The Caged Bird and Other Art Forms*. London and New York, NY.
Kearns, C. (2013) 'Visual Representations of gardens: diachronic perspectives on the art of landscape', in K. Gleason (ed.). London: 151–76.
Kellum, B. (1994a) 'What we see and what we don't see. Narrative structure and the Ara Pacis Augustae', *Art History* 17.1: 26–45.
Kellum, B. (1994b) 'The Construction of Landscape in Augustan Rome: The Garden Room at the Villa *ad Gallinas*', *Art Bulletin* 76.2: 211–24.
Kemezis, A. M. (2007) 'Augustus and the Ironic Paradigm: Cassius Dio's Portrayal of the Lex Julia and Lex Papia Poppaea', *Phoenix* 61: 270–85.
Kenney, E. J. (1984) *The Ploughman's Lunch: Moretum*. Bristol.
Kent, J. P. C. (1978) *Roman Coins*. London.
Kleiner, D. E. E. (1978) 'The Great Friezes of the *Ara Pacis Augustae*. Greek Sources Roman Derivatives and Augustan Social Policy', *Mélanges de l'École française de Rome; Antiquité* 90: 753–85.

Klinger, F. (1967) *Virgil. Bucolica. Georgica. Aeneis*. Zurich.

Klynne, A. (2005) 'The Laurel Grove of the Caesars: Looking in and Looking Out', in B. Santillo Frizell and A. Klynne (eds) *Roman Villas around the Urbs: Interaction with Landscape and Environment*. Rome: 1–9.

Klynne, A. and P. Liljenstolpe (1996) 'The Villa of Livia at Prima Porta: A Report on the Excavation of Room 45', *OpRom* 21: 89–100.

Klynne, A. and P. Liljenstolpe (1997–8) 'The Imperial Gardens of the Villa of Livia at Prima Porta: A Preliminary Report on the 1997 Campaign', *OpRom* 22–3: 127–47.

Klynne, A. and P. Liljenstolpe (2000) 'Investigating the Gardens of the Villa of Livia', *JRA* 13: 223–33.

Kockel, V. (1983) *Die Grabbauten vor dem Herkulaner Tor Pompeji*. Mainz.

Kraus, T. (1953) *Die Ranken der Ara Pacis*. Berlin.

Kreiger, M. (1967) 'The Ekphrastic Principle and the Still Movement of Poetry; or Lakoön Revisited', in P. W. McDowell (ed.) *Poet as Critic*. Evanston, IL: 2–36.

Kuttner, A. (1999) 'Looking outside inside: ancient Roman garden rooms', *Studies in the History of Gardens & Designed Landscapes* 19.1: 7–35.

Lafon, X. (1991) 'Les bains privés dans l'Italie romaine au IIe siècle av. J-C', *Collection de l'Ecole française de Rome* 142: 97–114.

Laidlaw, W. A. (1968) 'Otium', *Greece and Rome* 15: 42–52.

Lamp, K. S. (2013) *A City of Marble: The Rhetoric of Augustan Rome*. Columbia, SC.

Landes, D. S. (1987) 'The ordering of the urban environment: time, work, and the occurrence of crowds 1790–1835', *Past & Present* 116: 192–8.

Landgren, L. (2004) *Lauro myrto et buxo frequenta: A Study of the Roman Garden through Its Plants*. PhD dissertation, Lund University.

Lane Fox, R. (2014) 'Early Christians and the garden: image and reality', in K. Coleman (ed.). Vandoeuvres: 363–95.

La Penna, A. (1984) *La Letteratura Latina Del Primo Periodo Augusteo (42–15 A.C.)*. Rome.

Larmour, D. and D. Spencer (eds) (2007) *The Sites of Rome: Time, Space, Memory*. Oxford.

La Rocca, E. (1983) *Ara Pacis Augustae. In occasione del restauro della front orientale*. Rome.

Latte, K. (1970) *Römische Religiongeschichte*. Munchen.

Laurence, R. (1993) 'Emperors, nature and the city: Rome's ritual landscape', *Accordia Research Papers* 4: 79–87.

Laurence, R. (1994) *Roman Pompeii: Space and Society*. London.

Laurence, R. (1996) 'Ritual, Landscape, and the Destruction of Place in the Roman Imagination', in J. Wilkins (ed.) *Approaches to the Study of Ritual*. London: 111–21.

Laurence, R. and C. Smith (1995–6) 'Ritual, Time and Power in Ancient Rome', *Accordia Research Papers* 6: 133–51.

Laurence, R. and A. Wallace-Hadrill (eds) (1997) *Domestic Space in the Roman World: Pompeii and Beyond*. JRA suppl. 22.

Lauritsen, M. T. (2012) 'The Form and Function of Boundaries in the Campanian House', in A. Anguissola (ed.). Munich: 95–114.
Lawson, J. (1950) 'The Roman Garden', *Greece & Rome* 19: 97–105.
Leach, E. W. (1974) 'Sacral-Idyllic Landscape Painting and the Poems of Tibullus' First Book', *Latomus* 39: 47–69.
Leach, E. W. (1988) *The Rhetoric of Space: Literary and Artistic Representations of Landscape in Republican and Augustan Rome*. Princeton, NJ.
Leach, E. W. (1990) 'The Politics of Self-Presentation: Pliny's letters and Roman Portrait Sculpture', *Classical Antiquity* 9: 19–39.
Leach, E. W. (1997) 'Oecus on Ibycus: Investigating the Vocabulary of the Roman House', in R. Jones and S. Bon (eds) *Space and Sequence in Ancient Pompeii*. Oxford: 50–71.
Leach, E. W. (2003) 'Otium as Luxuria in the Status Economy of Pliny's Letters', *Arethusa* 36: 147–66.
Leach, E. W. (2004) *The Social Life of Painting in Ancient Rome and on the Bay of Naples*. Cambridge and New York, NY.
Lee-Stecum, P. (1998) *Powerplay in Tibullus: Reading Elegies Book One*. Cambridge.
Lefebvre, H. (1974) *The Production of Space*. Oxford.
Leigh, M. (1994) 'Servius on Vergil's Senex Corycius : New Evidence', *MD* 33: 181–95.
Lejeune, P. (1975) *La Pacte autobiographique*. Paris.
Levi, A. and M, Levi (1967) *Itineraria picta. Contributo allo studio della Tabula Peutingeriaria*. Rome.
Ling, R. (1991) *Roman Painting*. Cambridge.
Littlewood, A. R. (1987) 'Ancient Literary Evidence for the Pleasure Gardens of Roman Country Villas', in E. B. MacDougall (ed.). Washington, DC: 7–30.
L'Orange, H. P. (1962) *Ara Pacis Augustae: la zona floreale*. Rome.
Lord, B. (2006) 'Foucault's Museum: Difference, Representation and Genealogy', *Museum and Society* 4: 1–14.
Lorenz, K. (2015) 'Wall Painting', in B. Borg (ed.). Malden, MA: 252–67.
Lucy, N. (2004) *A Derrida Dictionary*. Oxford.
Macaulay-Lewis, E. (2006) 'The role of ollae perforate in understanding horticulture, planting techniques, and plant trade in the Roman world', in J. P. Marcel et al. (eds) *The Archaeology of Crop Fields and Gardens*. Puglia: 207–20.
Macaulay-Lewis, E. (2013) 'Use and Reception', in K. Gleason (ed.). London: 99–118.
Macaulay-Lewis, E. (2018) 'The Archaeology of Gardens in the Roman Villa', in W. F. Jashemski et al. (eds). Cambridge: 121–51.
MacDougall, E. B. (ed.) (1987) *Ancient Roman Villa Gardens*. Washington, DC.
MacDougall, E. B. and W. Jashemski (eds) (1981) *Ancient Roman Gardens*. Washington, DC.
Maclean, M. (1991) 'Pretexts and Paratexts: The Art of the Peripheral', *New Literary History* 22.2: 273–9.
Maggiuli, G. (1995) *Incipiant silvae cum primum surgere: Mondo Vegetale e Nomenclatura della Flora di Virgilio*. Rome.

Malek, A. (ed.) (2013) *A Sourcebook for Garden Archaeology: Methods, Techniques, Interpretations and Field Examples*. Paris.

Malpas, J. (ed.) (2011) *The Place of Landscape: Concepts, Contexts, Studies*. Cambridge, MA.

Marriner, R. (2002) 'Derrida and the Parergon', in P. Smith and C. Wilde (eds) *A Companion to Art Theory*. Oxford: 349–59.

Marsili, A. (1962) *L. Iuni Moderati Columellae Rei Rusticae Cepericus De Cultu Hortorum Liber Decimus*. Pisa.

Martindale, C. A. (2000) 'Green Politics: The Eclogues', in C. A. Martindale (ed.) *The Cambridge Companion to Virgil*. Cambridge: 107–24.

Marzano, A. (2007) *Roman Villas in Central Italy: A Social and Economic History*. Leiden and Boston, MA.

Mau, A. (1882) *Pompeii, its Life and Art*. New York, NY.

Mayer, E. (2012) *The Ancient Middle Classes. Urban Life and Aesthetics in the Roman Empire, 100 BCE – 250 CE*. Cambridge, MA, and London, UK.

McGinn, T. A. J. (1998) *Prostitution, Sexuality, and the Law in Ancient Rome*. Oxford and New York, NY.

McIntyre, J. (2008) *Written into the Landscape: Latin Epic and the Landmarks of Literary Reception*. PhD dissertation, University of St. Andrews.

Messineo, G. (1984) 'Ollae Perforatae', *Xenia* 8: 65–84.

Messineo, G. (1992) 'La Villa di Livia a Prima Porta a dieci anni dalla ripressa dello Scavo', *Atti della Pontificia Accademia Romana di Archeologia. Rendiconti* 65: 11–21.

Messineo, G. (ed.) (2001) *Ad gallinas albas: Villa di Livia*. Rome.

Mielsche, H. (1987) *Die römische Villa. Architektur und Lebensform*. Munich.

Miller, J. H. (1979) 'The Critic as Host', in H. Bloom et al. (eds) *Deconstruction and Criticism*. London and New York, NY: 217–54.

Miller, M. (1993) *The Garden as an Art*. New York, NY.

Milnor, K. (2005) *Gender, Domesticity, and the Age of Augustus. Inventing Private Life*. Oxford.

Mitchell, W. J. T. (1994) *Picture Theory: Essays on Verbal and Visual Representation*. Chicago, IL.

Momgliano, A. (1942) 'The Peace of the Ara Pacis', *Journal of the Warburg and Courtauld Institutes* 5: 228–31.

Moretti, G. (1948) *Ara Pacis Augustae*. Rome.

Morvillez, E. (2018) 'The Garden in the Domus', in W. F. Jashemski et al. (eds). Cambridge: 17–71.

Moynihan, E. (1979) *Paradise as a Garden in Persia and Mughal India*. New York, NY.

Mugellesi, R. (1973) 'Il senso della natura in Seneca tragico', in *Argentea Aetas In Memoriam E.V. Marmorale*. Genoa.

Muntasser, N. and G. di Maio (2017) 'The Geological Landscape of Oplontis and the Eruption of Mount Vesuvius', in E. K. Gazda and J. R. Clarke (eds). Ann Arbor, MI: 48–56.

Muslin, J. (2017) 'Working and Living in Oplontis B: Material Perspectives on Trade and Consumption', in E. K. Gazda and J. R. Clarke (eds). Ann Arbor, MI: 166-70.

Myers, K. S. (2005) 'Docta Otia: Garden Ownership and Configurations of Leisure in Statius and Pliny the Younger', *Arethusa* 38: 103-29.

Myers, K. S. (2018) 'Representations of Gardens in Roman Literature', in W. F. Jashemski et al. (eds). Cambridge: 278-316.

Mynors, R. A. B. (1990) *Virgil: Georgics*. Oxford.

Nelis, D. (2004) 'From Didactic to Epic: *Georgics* 2.458-3.48', in M. Gale (ed.). Swansea: 73-107.

Neudecker, R. (2015) 'Gardens', in R. Raja and J. Rüpke (eds) *A Companion to the Archaeology of Religion in the Ancient World*. Chichester: 220-34.

Nevett, L. C. (2010) *Domestic Space in Classical Antiquity*. Cambridge.

Newlands, C. (1995) *Playing with Time: Ovid and the Fasti. Cornell Studies in Classical Philology 55*. Ithaca, NY.

Newlands, C. (2002) *Statius' Silvae and the Poetics of Empire*. Cambridge.

Nicolet, C. (1991) *Space, Geography, and Politics in the Early Roman Empire*. Ann Arbor, RI.

Nielsen, I. (2013) 'Types of Gardens', in K. Gleason (ed.). London: 41-74.

Niquet, H. (2000) 'The Senatorial Elite Agriculturalist', in K. Pollman (ed.) *Double Standards in the Ancient and Medieval World*. Göttingham: 121-33.

Nisbet, R. G. M. and M. Hubbard (1978) *A Commentary on Horace Odes Book II*. Oxford.

Noè, E. (2001) 'La memoria dell' antico in Columella: Continuità, distanza, conoscenza', *Athenaeum* 89: 319-43.

Noè, E. (2002) *Il Progetto di Columella: Profito Sociale, Economico, Culturale*. Como.

North, J. A. (1995) 'Religion and Rusticity', in T. J. Cornell and K. Lomas (eds) *Urban Society in Roman Italy*. London: 135-50.

O'Connor, E. M. (1989) *Symbolum salacitatis: A Study of the God Priapus as a Literary Character*. New York, NY.

Oettel, A. (1996) *Fundkontexte römischer Vesuvvillen im Gebiet um Pompeji*. Cambridge.

Ogle, M. B. (1910) 'Laurel in Ancient Religion and Folklore', *AJP* 31: 287-311.

Orlin, E. (2007) 'Augustan Religion and the Reshaping of Roman Memory', *Arethusa* 40: 73-92.

Orr, D. (1978) 'Roman Domestic Religion: A Study of the Roman Household Deities and their Shrines at Pompeii an Herculaneum', *Aufstieg und Niedergang der römischen Welt*, II.16.2. New York, NY.

Östenberg, I. (2009) 'From conquest to *pax Romana*. The *signa recepta* and the end of the Triumphal Fasti in 19 BC', in O. Hekster, S. Schmidt-Hofner and C. Witschel (eds) *Ritual Dynamics and Religious Change in the Roman Empire*. Leiden: 53-75.

Pagán, V. E. (2006) *Rome and the Literature of Gardens*. London.

Patillon, M. and G. Bolognesi (eds) (1997) *Aelius Theón, Progymnasmata*. Paris.

Perkell, C. (1981) 'On the Corycian Gardener of Vergil's Fourth Eclogue', *TAPA* 111: 167-77.

Petersen, E. (1902) *Ara Pacis Augustae*. Wein.

Platt, V. (2009) 'Where the Wild Things Are: Locating the Marvelous in Augustan Wall Painting', in P. Hardie (ed.). Oxford: 41–74.

Platt, V. (2017) 'Introduction: Framing Pictorial Space', in V. Platt and M. Squire (eds). Cambridge: 102–16.

Platt, V. and M. Squire (eds) (2017) *The Frame in Classical Art: A Cultural History*. Cambridge.

Platts, H. (2020) *Multisensory Living in Ancient Rome. Power and Space in Roman Houses*. London and New York, NY.

Pollan, M. (1991) *Second Nature: A Gardener's Education*. New York, NY.

Pollard, E. (2009) 'Pliny's Natural History and the Flavian Templum Pacis: Botanical Imperialism in First-Century C.E. Rome', *Journal of World History* 20: 309–38.

Pollini, J. (1993) 'The Acanthus of the Ara Pacis as an Apolline and Dionysiac Symbol of *Anamorphosis, Anakyklosis,* and *Numen Mixtum*', in M. Kubelik and M. Schwartz (eds) *Von der Bauforschung zur Denkmalpflege, Festschrift für Alois Machatschek sum 65. Geburtstag*. Vienna: 181–217.

Pollini, J. (2012) *From Republic to Empire: Rhetoric, Religion, and Power in the Visual Culture of Ancient Rome*. Norman.

Pollitt, J. J. (1974) *The Ancient View of Greek Art: Criticism, History and Terminology*. Cambridge.

Pucci, P. (1978) 'Lingering on the Threshold', *Glyph* 3: 52–73.

Purcell, N. (1987a) 'Tomb and Suburb', in H. von Hesberg and P. Zanker (eds) *Römische Gräberstraßen*. Munich: 25–41.

Purcell, N. (1987b) 'Town in country and country in town', in E. B. MacDougall (ed.). Washington, DC: 185–203.

Purcell, N. (1995) 'The Roman Villa and the Landscape of Production', in T. J. Cornell and K. Lomas (eds) *Urban Society in Roman Italy*. London: 151–79.

Purcell, N. (1996) 'The Roman Garden as a Domestic Building', in I. M. Barton (ed.) *Roman Domestic Buildings*. Exeter.

Purcell, N. (2001) 'Dialectical Gardening', *JRA* 14: 546–56.

Purcell, N. (2007) 'The *horti* of Rome and the landscape of property', in A. Leone, D. Palombi and S. Walker (eds) *Res bene gestae. Riecerche di storia urbana su Roma antica in onore di Eva Margareta Steinby*. Rome: 361–78.

Putnam, M. J. (1979) *Virgil's Poem of the Earth. Studies in the Georgics*. Princeton, NJ.

Quinn, K. (1968) *Virgil's Aeneid: A Critical Description*. London and Ann Arbor, MI.

Raaflaub, K. A. (2015) 'The politics of peace cults in Greece and Rome', in T. R. Kämmerer and M. Koiv (eds) *Cultures in Comparison: Religion and Practice in Ancient Mediterranean Religions*. Münster: 103–29.

Rabe, H. (ed.) (1913) *Hermogenes Opera*. Leipzig.

Rabe, H. (ed.) (1926) *Aphthonius, Progymnasmata*. Leipzig.

Reay, B. (2005) 'Agriculture, Writing, and Cato's Aristocratic Self-Fashioning', *CA* 24.2: 331–61.

Reeder, J. C. (2001) *The Villa of Livia Ad Gallinas Albas: A Study in the Augustan Villa and Garden*. Providence, RI.

Rehak, P. (2001) 'Aeneas or Numa? Rethinking the Meaning of the Ara Pacis Augustae', *The Art Bulletin* 83: 190–208.

Rehak, P. (2006) *Imperium and Cosmos: Augustus and the Northern Campus Martius*. Madison, WI.

Repton, H. (1816) *Fragments on the Theory of Landscape Gardening, including some remarks on Grecian and Gothic Architecture*. London.

Reynolds, J. (2004) 'Decision', in J. Reynolds and J. Roffe (eds) *Understanding Derrida*. London and New York, NY: 46–53.

Richlin, A. (1992 [1983]) *The Garden of Priapus*. Oxford.

Richter, W. (ed.) (1972) *Der Liber De Arboribus und Columella*. Munich.

Riggsby, A. (1997) '"Public" and "Private" in Roman Culture: the Case of the Cubiculum', *JRA* 10: 36–56.

Riggsby, A. (2003) 'Pliny in Space (and Time)', *Arethusa* 36.2: 167–86.

Rives, J. (2007) *Religion in the Roman Empire*. Oxford.

Rives, J. (2012) 'Control of the Sacred in Roman Law', in O. Tellegen-Couperus (ed.) *Law and Religion in the Roman Republic*. Leiden: 165–80.

Ross, D. (1975) 'The *Culex* and the *Moretum* as Post-Augustan Literary Parodies', *Harvard Studies in Classical Philology* 79: 235–63.

Ross, S. (1998) *What Gardens Mean*. Chicago, IL.

Ross, S. (2007) 'Gardens, Nature, Pleasure', in A. Berleant and A. Carlson (eds). Peterborough, ON: 252–72.

Rossini, O. (2006) *Ara Pacis*. Milan.

Rostovtzeff, M. (1904) 'Pompejanische Landschaften und römische Villen', *Jahrbuch des Deutschen Archäologischen Instituts* 19: 103–26.

Rovira-Guardiola, C. (2013) 'Loan Greek and Roman', in R. S. Bagnall et al. (eds) *Encyclopaedia of Ancient History*. Oxford: 4129–31.

Rüpke, J. (2007a) *Religion of the Romans*. Malden, MA.

Rüpke, J. (ed.) (2007b) *A Companion to Roman Religion*. Oxford.

Rüpke, J. (2017) 'Doubling Religion in the Augustan Age: Shaping Time for an Empire', in J. Ben Dov and L. Doering (eds) *The Construction of Time in Antiquity: Ritual, Art, Identity*. Cambridge: 50–68.

Russell, A. (2016) *The Politics of Public Space in Republican Rome*. Cambridge.

Rykwert, J. (1982) *The Necessity of Artifice: Ideas in Architecture*. New York, NY.

Saint-Denis, E. (ed.) (1969) *Columelle De L'agriculture Livre X (De l'horticulture). Text, étabili, traduit, et commenté*. Paris.

Santoro, A. (ed.) (1946) *Il Libro X di Columella. Introduzione, Texto e Commento, Versione*. Bari.

Sargeaunt, J. (1920) *The Trees, Shrubs, and Plants of Virgil*. Oxford.

Sauron, G. (1982) 'Le message symbolique des rinceaux de l'Ara Pacis Augustae', *Comptes rendres des séances de l'Académie des Inscriptions et Belles-Lettres*, 126: 81–101.

Sauron, G. (1990) 'Les monstres au couer des conflits esthétiques à Rome au 1er siècle avant J-C', *Revue de l'art* 90: 35–45.

Scapini, M. (2015) 'Augustus and Dionysus's Triumph: A Non-Existent Paradox', *Acta Ant. Hung.* 55: 185: 209.

Scheid, J. (1984) 'La Spartizione a Roma', *Studi Storici* 4: 945–56.

Scheid, J. (1985) 'Sacrifice et banquet à Rome: quelques problèmes', *MEFRA* 97: 193–206.

Scheid, J. (1993) '*Lucus, nemus*. Qu'est-ce qu'un bois sacre?', in O. de Cazanove and J. Scheid (eds). Naples: 13–18.

Scheid, J. (2003) *An Introduction to Roman Religion*. Edinburgh.

Schiesaro, A. (2003) *The Passions in the Play: Thyestes and the Dynamics of Senecan Drama*. Cambridge.

Schröeder, B-J. (1999) *Titel und Text: zur Entwicklung lateinischer Gedichtüberschriften, mit Untersuchungen zu lateinsichen Buchtiteln, Inhaltsverzeichnissen und anderen Gliederungsmitteln*. Berlin.

Schultz, W. R. and L. L. B. Fried (eds) (1992) *Jacques Derrida: An Annotated Primary and Secondary Bibliography*. Oxon and New York, NY.

Schweitzer, B. (1934) 'Mimesis und Phantasia', *Philologus* 89: 286–300.

Scott, M. (2013) *Space and Society in the Greek and Roman Worlds*. Cambridge.

Segal, C. (2008) 'Boundary Violation and the Landscape of the Self in Senecan Tragedy', in J. Fitch (ed.) *Oxford Readings in Classical Studies: Seneca*. Oxford: 136–56.

Settis, S. (2002) *Le pareti ingannevoli: la Villa di Livia e la pittura di giardino*. Milan.

Shane, D. G. (2005) *Recombinant Urbanism: Conceptual Modeling in Architecture, Urban Design and City Theory*. Chichester.

Sherwin-White, A. N. (1966) *The Letters of Pliny: A Historical and Social Commentary*. Oxford.

Silberberg, S. (1980) *A Corpus of the Sacral-Idyllic Landscape Paintings in Roman Art*. PhD dissertation, University of California, Los Angeles.

Silberberg-Peirce, S. (1981) 'Politics and Private Imagery: The Sacral-Idyllic landscapes in Augustan art', *Art History* 3: 1–24.

Simon, E. (1967) *Ara Pacis Augustae*. London.

Smolenaars, J. (1998) 'The Vergilian background of Seneca's Thyestes 641–682', *Vergilius* 44: 51–65.

Soja, E. (1996) *Thirdspace: Journeys to Los Angeles and Other Real-And-Imagined Places*. Malden, MA.

Spencer, D. (2010) *Roman Landscape: Culture and Identity. Greece & Rome. New Surveys in the Classics, 39*. Cambridge.

Spirn, A. W. (1998) *The Landscape of Language*. New Haven, CT.

Spitzer, L. (1955) 'The "Ode on a Grecian Urn" or Content vs. Metagrammar', *Comparative Literature* 7: 203–25.

Squire, M. (2009) *Image and Text in Graeco-Roman Antiquity*. Cambridge.

Squire, M. (2011) *The Iliad in a Nutshell: Visualizing Epic on the Tabulae Iliacae*. Oxford.

Squire, M. (2013a) 'Embodied Ambiguities on the Prima Porta Augustus', *Art History* 36: 242–79.
Squire, M. (2013b) 'Ekphrasis at the Forge and the Forging of Ekphrasis: The Shield of Achilles in Graeco-Roman Word and Image', *Word & Image* 29: 157–91.
Squire, M. (2015) 'Ekphrasis: Visual and Verbal Interactions in Ancient Greek and Latin', *Oxford Handbooks Online*.
Squire, M. (2018) 'To haunt, to startle, and way-lay: Approaching ornament and figure in Graeco-Roman art', in N. Dietrich and M. Squire (eds). Berlin: 1–35.
Stara-Tedde, G. (1905) 'I boschi sacri del' antica Roma', *BC* 33: 189–232.
Stewart, P. (1997) 'Fine Art and Coarse Art: The Image of Roman Priapus', *Art History* 20(4): 575–88.
Stewart, P. (2004) *Roman Art*. Oxford.
Stoichita, V. I. (1997) *The Self-Aware Image: An Insight into Early Modern Meta-Painting*, trans. by A. M. Glasheen. Cambridge.
Stroka, V. M. (2007) 'Domestic decoration: Painting and the "Four Styles"', in J. J. Dobbins and P. W. Foss (eds) *The World of Pompeii*. London: 302–22.
Sulze, H. (1932) 'Die unterirdischen Räume der Villa der Livia in Prima Porta', *Mitteilungen des Deutschen Archäologischen Instituts, Römische Abteilung* 47: 174–97.
Swoboda, K. M. (1919) *Römische unde romanische Paläste. Eine architekturgeschictliche Untersuchung*. Vienna.
Talbert, R. (2010) *Rome's World: The Peutinger Map Reconsidered*. Cambridge.
Tally-Schumacher, K. and N. Niemeier (2016) 'Through the Picture Plane: Movement and Transformation in the Garden Room at the Villa *ad Gallinas* at Prima Porta', *Chronika* 6: 58–71.
Tanzer, H. (1924) *Villas of Pliny the Younger*. New York, NY.
Tarrant, R. J. (1985) *Seneca's Thyestes*. Atlanta, GA.
Temin, P. (2013) *The Roman Market Economy*. Princeton.
Thibodeau, P. (2001) 'The Old Man and His Garden (Verg. Georg. 4.116–148)', *MD* 47: 175–95.
Thomas, M. (2017a) 'Framing Views in Villa A: From the Late Republic to the Age of Nero', in E. K. Gazda and J. R. Clarke (eds). Ann Arbor, MI: 78–84.
Thomas, M. (2017b) 'Oplontis B and the Wine Industry in the Vesuvian Area', in E. K. Gazda and J. R. Clarke (eds). Ann Arbor, MI: 160–5.
Thomas, R. F. (1988) *Virgil: Georgics. Volumes I and II*. Cambridge.
Thomas, R. F. (1992) 'The Old Man Revisited: Memory, Reference and Genre in Virgil Georgics 4.116–148', *MD* 29: 35–70.
Thompson, E. P. (1967) 'Time, work-discipline and industrial capitalism', *Past & Present* 38: 56–97.
Thulin, C. (ed.) (1913) *Corpus Agrimensorum, Vol I*. Berlin.
Tilley, C. (1994) *A Phenomenology of Landscape: Places, Paths and Monuments*. Oxford.
Toohey, P. (1996) *Epic Lessons: An Introduction to Ancient Didactic Poetry*. New York, NY.
Torelli, M. (1982) *Typology and Structure of Roman Historical Reliefs*. Ann Arbor, MI.

Totelin, L. (2012) 'Botanizing Rulers and their Herbal Subjects: Plants and Political Power in Greek and Roman Literature', *Phoenix* 66.1/2: 122–44.
Toynbee, J. M. C. (1971) *Death and Burial in the Roman World*. London and Baltimore, MD.
Tuan, Y-F. (1979) *Space and Place. The Perspective of Experience*. Minneapolis, MN.
Tuplin, C. (1996) 'The Parks and Gardens of the Achaemenid Empire', in *id. Achaemenid Studies*. Stuttgart: 80–131.
Tybout, R. (1979) 'Oplontis', *Hermeneus* 51: 263–83.
Tybout, R. (2002) 'Response to the comments of B. Bergmann and C. H. Hallett (*JRA* 14, 56–7)', *JRA* 15: 346–8.
Uden, J. (2007) 'Impersonating Priapus', *AJP* 128: 1–26.
Uden, J. (2010) 'The Vanishing Gardens of Priapus', *HSCP* 105: 189–219.
Unruh, D. B. (2014) 'The Predatory Palace: Seneca's *Thyestes* and the Architecture of Tyranny', in A. Kemezis (ed.) *Urban Dream and Realities in Antiquity* 375: 246–77.
Valentine, G. (2001) *Social Geographies: Space and Society*. Oxon and New York, NY.
Van Buren, A. (1948) 'Pliny's Laurentine Villa', *JRS* 38: 35–6.
van der Graaff (2017) 'Ten Seasons of Excavations at Oplontis (2006–2015)', in E. K. Gazda and J. R. Clarke (eds). Ann Arbor, MI: 66–71.
van Erp-Houtepen, A. (1986) 'The etymological origin of the garden', *Journal of Garden History* 6.3: 227–31.
Vipard, P. (2001–2) 'Un aménagement méconnu: les portiques fenêtres', in R. Bedon (ed.) *Les agréments de la vie urbaine en Gaule romaine er dans les regions voisines. Hommage à Pierre Pouthier*. Limoges: 39–56.
Vipard, P. (2003) 'Les portiques fenêtrés dans les domus du haut-empire romain', *BAC* 30: 99–134.
Volk, K. (2002) *The Poetics of Latin Didactic. Lucretius, Vergil, Ovid, Manilius*. Oxford.
von Blackenhagen, P. and C. Alexander (1962) *The Paintings from Boscotrecase*. Heidelberg.
von Hesberg, H. (1981) 'Girlandenschmuck der republikanischen Zeit in Mittelitalien', in *Mitteilungen des Deutschen Archäologischen Institus Rom* 88: 201–45.
von Stackelberg, K. T. (2009) *The Roman Garden: Space, Sense and Society*. London.
von Stackelberg, K. T. (2013) 'Meaning', in K. Gleason (ed.). London: 119–34.
Wagner, P. (1996) 'Introduction', in P. Wagner (ed.) *Icons-Texts-Iconotexts: Essays on Ekphrasis and Intermediality*. Berlin: 1–40.
Wallace-Hadrill, A. (1982) 'The Golden Age and Sin in Augustan Ideology', *Past & Present* 95.1: 19–36.
Wallace-Hadrill, A. (1987) 'Time for Augustus: Ovid, Augustus, and the Fasti', in M. Whitby, P. Hardie and M. Whitby (eds) *Homo Viator. Classical Essays for John Bramble*. Bristol: 221–30.
Wallace-Hadrill, A. (1989) 'Rome's Cultural Revolution', *JRS* 79: 157–64.
Wallace-Hadrill, A. (1994) *Houses and Society in Pompeii and Herculaneum*. Princeton.
Wallace-Hadrill, A. (2008) *Rome's Cultural Revolution*. Cambridge.

Ward, C. (2017) 'Luxury, Adornment, and Identity: The Skeletons and Jewelry from Oplontis B', in E. K. Gazda and J. R. Clarke (eds). Ann Arbor, MI: 171-9.
Watts, C. M. (1987) *A Pattern Language for Houses in Pompeii, Herculaneum, and Ostia*. PhD dissertation, University of Austin Texas.
Webb, R. (1999) 'Ekphrasis Ancient and Modern: The Invention of a Genre', *Word & Image* 15: 7-18.
Webb, R. (2009) *Ekphrasis, Imagination, and Persuasion in Ancient Rhetorical Practice and Theory*. Farnham.
Weeda, L. (2015) *Vergil's Political Commentary in the Eclogues, Georgics, and Aeneid*. De Gruyter Open Poland.
White, D. J. (2013) *Columella Res Rustica 10: A Study and Commentary*. PhD dissertation, University of Florida.
Whitton, C. (2013) *Pliny the Younger: Epistles Book II*. Cambridge.
Wilkinson, L. P. (1969) *The Georgics of Virgil*. Cambridge.
Wiseman, D. J. (1983) 'Mesopotamian Gardens', *Anatolian Studies* 33: 137-44.
Wiseman, T. P. (1996) 'Campus Martius', in *LTUR* 1: 220-4. Rome.
Wissowa, G. (1912) *Relgion und Kultus der Römer*. Munchen.
Wittgenstein, L. (1953) *Philosophical Investigations (Philosophische Untersuchengen)*. Oxford.
Wortham, S. M. (2010) *The Derrida Dictionary*. London.
Wroth, W. (1899) *British Museum Catalogue of Greek Coins: Galatia, Cappadocia, and Syria*. London.
Wyler, S. (2013) 'An Augustan Trend Towards Dionysos: Around the Auditorium of Maecenas', in Bernabé et al. (eds) *Redefining Dionysos*. Berlin: 542-53.
Yerkes, S. (2000) 'Vitruvius' *monstra*', *JRA* 13: 234-51.
Young, A. (2015) *'Green Architecture': The Interplay of Art and Nature in Roman Houses and Villas*. PhD dissertation, University of California, Berkeley.
Zanker, P. (1979) 'Die Villa als Vorbild des späten pompejanischen Wohngeschmacks', *JDAI* 94: 460-523.
Zanker, P. (1988) *The Power of Images in the Age of Augustus*, translated by A. Shapiro. Ann Arbor, MI.
Zarmakoupi, M. (2008) 'Designing the landscapes of the Villa of Livia at Prima Porta', in D. Kurtz (ed.) *Essays in Classical Archaeology for Eleni Hatzivassiliou 1977-2007*. Oxford: 269-76.
Zarmakoupi, M. (2010) 'The architectural design of luxury villas around the Bay of Naples', in M. Aoyagi and C. Angelelli (eds) *AMOENITAS. Rivista di Studi Miscellanei sulla Villa Romana* 1. Rome: 33-41.
Zarmakoupi, M. (2014) *Designing for Luxury on the Bay of Naples (c. 100 BCE - 79 CE): Villas and Landscapes*. Oxford.
Zeigler, K. et al. (eds) (1979) *Der Kleine Pauly. Lexicon der Antike. Auf der Grundlage Pauly's Realencyclopädie der classischen Altertumswissenschaft*. Stuttgart.
Zeitlin, F. (2013) 'Figure: Ekphrasis', *Greece and Rome* 60: 17-31.

Index Locorum

Cato		5.6.13	116, 132
Agr. 1.7	12, 32	5.6.16–18	124–5
Agr. 2.4	35	5.6.20–2	129, 131
Col.		5.6.32	125
1.pr.21	47, 56	5.6.35	127–8
1.pr.21–8	56	5.6.36	125
1.1.12	48	5.6.37–40	130–1
1.1.17	47	5.6.41	112
2.21.1	36	5.6.43	112
2.21.4	36	Plin. *Nat.* 1.137	65
3.3.7–11	56	12.13	14
5.10.1	12	12.3	66, 99
9.2.2–3	53	12.6	14
9.4.4	53	14.7	38
9.6.17	57	18.231	37
10.pr.1–5	50–7	19.49	11
10.1–5	52–3	19.50	13, 45
10.27–8	13	19.52	38
10.30–4	6	19.57	12
10.40	55	19.59	36
10.93	55	19.60	12
10.94	55	35.116	78
10.140–3	56	Prop.	
10.230	55	3.13.47	64
11.1.1–2	56–7	Pseud. Virg.	
11.3.2–4	13	*Moretum* 66–8	35
Dio		Sen.	
53.16.4	81	*Thy.* 641–82	146–50
Dion. Hal.		Strabo	
Ant. Rom. 1.7.8	64	5.3.8	61–2
		Suet.	
Hor.		*Aug.* 91–2	83
Saec. 10	94	*Galb.* 1	65
Ov.		Tib.	
F. 1.719–22	89–90	1.3.42–4	93
Plin. *Ep.* 2.17.1	112	Var.	
2.17.5	113, 115	*L.* 5.152	64
2.17.21	115–16, 124	*R.* 1.7.10	12, 32
5.6.7	115–16		

Virg.		Vitr.	
A. 10.467–8	35	De Arch. 5.7.9	17
E. 1.46–58	43–4	5.9.5	17
2.45–55	88	5.11.1	17
G. 140	34	5.12.4	17
2.541–2	34	6.3.10	17
3.95–100	39	6.5.2	17
3.284–5	34–5	7.5.2	17
4.114–148	29–47	7.5.3–4	97
4.118	113–14		

Index

acanthus 31, 86, 125
   Ara Pacis Augustae 73–4, 83–5, 89
   Livia's Garden Room 89
agricolatio 47–8, 54, 56, 58–9
agriculture
   agronomic literary tradition 30, 32, 40, 46, 47–8
   Roman identity 13, 51–2
   temporal considerations 29, 35–6
   see also hortus
Apollo 81, 86, 88, 99
Ara Pacis Augustae
   ambiguity 67, 93–4, 97–8, 139
   cultural framing 26, 70–2, 98
   compositional characteristics 68–9, 74, 84–7, 94
   fertility 93
   figure vs. ornament 74–6, 87, 97–8
   location 71–2, 98
   lucus 68, 98–102, 142
   sacred precinct 69–70, 96
   Temple of Janus 71
   time 89–91
   transformation 85, 88–9, 150
ars
   vs. *natura* 114, 128, 131, 136, 140
ars topiara 17
Augustus
   botanical mythology 64–7, 87, 142
   honours 68, 70–1
   legislation 40, 93
   marriage to Livia 65
   political regime 72, 85
   power of images 70–2, 76, 84, 87, 101
   transformation of city of Rome 61–3, 98–100

Bay of Naples 107, 139
bees 32–3, 41, 43, 47, 52–3

Campus Martius 13, 61–7, 70–2, 74, 81, 96, 98–102
Cato the Elder, 12, 32, 35, 39, 47–8, 108

cepotaphium 15
Columella 6, 12–13, 29–30, 36, 47–8, 50–9, 125, 142
contained profusion 26, 67, 91–3, 98
cultus hortorum 50

deconstruction 9, 22, 26, 94, 143
Derrida, Jacques
   parergon 26–7, 76
   supplement 30, 57–9, 144–6
Dio 81
Dionysius of Halicarnassus 64
Dionysus 86, 99
domus 16–18
   privacy 24
   in Seneca's *Thyestes* 148–50

ekphrasis 111–13, 117, 147
enargeia, see under ekphrasis

garden boundaries 1–3
   vs. architectural boundaries 18–19, 24–5, 27, 97, 138, 140, 143
   as frames 24–7, 117–22, 130
   mediation 18–19, 124
   as a porous membrane 7, 9, 27, 106, 124, 130, 140, 143
   structural features 17
   in wall paintings 78–9, 81, 95–6, 135–6, 137–8
garden paintings
   House of the Golden Bracelet 103–6
   Pliny the Younger 131–2
   stylistic development 78–80, 95, 102–3
   tombs 16
   see also Livia's Garden Room; Villa A at Oplontis
gens Iulia 65, 81
gymnasia 15, 17, 18

fertility 14, 56, 69–70, 86, 88
   hyperfertility, 26, 67, 90–3, 98

Foucault, Michel
    heterochronia 22
    heterotopia 21–3, 25, 26, 67, 90–1, 98, 102, 142, 145
frames 25–7
    importance of the framed view, 110, 114–17, 119–20, 123–4, 130
    see also garden boundaries; wall painting
framing
    literary, *see under* ekphrasis; paratext
frameworks
    cultural and ideological 23, 26, 60, 98
    metaphorical 17, 22
    temporal 22, 26, 29, 44, 60, 67, 94
    theoretical 3–5, 9, 20–2, 75–6, 143–5

Gallina Alba omen 65–7, 76
Golden Age 64, 87, 93–4, 96
green architecture 127, 140, 144

heredium 45
Hillier and Hanson 143
    access analysis 24–5
Horace 14, 38, 93–4, 97
Horologium Augusti 89
horti 12–14, 19, 45, 64, 99
    Horti Caesarum 63, 99
    Horti Maecenatis 63, 99
    Horti Pompeiani 63
hortus
    definition 12, 14, 16–17
    literary tradition 33
    relationship to agriculture 45–6, 51, 89, 142
    Roman identity 13–14, 52
hyperfertility, *see under* fertility

intermediality 7–9, 20, 106–7

Jashemski, Wilhelmina 109, 126
Julian calendar 36–7
Julio-Claudians, *see under gens Iulia*
Julius Caesar 65, 99

Kant, Immanuel 26, 76

land confiscations 45–6
landscape 3–5
    see also sacral-idyllic; wall painting

lararia 15
laurel
    Apollo 66, 81, 88
    Ara Pacis Augustae 69, 86
    Augustus 66, 81
    Gallina Alba 65
    grove of the Caesars 65, 81
    Livia's Garden Room 81, 82
    Mausoleum of Augustus 62
    Pliny the Younger 125
    Villa A at Oplontis 105
Lefebvre, Henri
    space and society 4
    spatial turn 8
Lex Iulia 93
Livia
    marriage to Augustus 65
    villa at Prima Porta 77
Livia's Garden Room
    compositional characteristics 77–8, 81–3, 91–4
    multiple perimeters 94–6, 139
    relationship to Four Styles 78–81
    transformation 88–9
loans 56
loci relicti 39–40, 43
locus amoenus 43–4, 46
lucus 66, 68, 98–101, 148
Lugale 5

maceria 16, 125, 126
marginality 22, 37, 56, 76, 102
Mau, August, *see under* wall painting; Four Styles
Mausoleum of Augustus 62, 66
memory 4
    Virgil 30, 33, 44–6

nemora tonsilia 92
nemus 63, 148–50

oak
    Ara Pacis Augustae 85–6
    Augustus 81, 83
    Livia's Garden Room 77, 81–2
    Seneca's *Thyestes* 149
otium 37, 107, 113
Ovid 89–90

paradeisos 2

paratext 30, 48–50, 57–8, 144
parergon, *see under* Derrida
peristyle 16–18, 24–5, 108
phantasia, see under ekphrasis
pine
   Ara Pacis Augustae 69
   Livia's Garden Room 77, 82–3, 88, 92
   Villa A at Oplontis 105, 132
Pliny the Elder
   Gallina Alba 65
   on gardens 11
   on the *hortus* 12–13, 38, 45
   on *horti* 13
   on trees 99
Pliny the Younger 112–16, 124–32
Pompeii
   House II.8.6 15
   House VII.6.3 15
   House of Menander 35
   House of Octavius Quartio 25
   House of the Fruit Orchard 78–9
   House of the Golden Cupids 25
   House of the Golden Bracelet 103–6
   House of the Labyrinth 24
   House of the Pansa 16
   House of the Vetii 6
porticus 14–17
   Nikopolis 100
   Porticus Liviae 14, 86–7
   Porticus Pompeiana 14–15
Priapus 6
Propertius 64
Pseudo-Virgiliana 35, 43

Res Gestae 70–2
rus
   vs. *urbs* 128

sacral-idyllic 68, 80–1, 99–102, 146
Seneca the Younger 146–50
senex Corycius 38–9, 41–3
Silvinus 49–50, 52–4, 57–8
Soja, Edward
   Thirdspace 20–1, 29, 107, 144
space
   as a product of social relations 4
   theoretical approaches 20–5
Strabo 61–2, 67, 100
Suetonius 65, 83

Tarentum 30–1, 38
temple enclosures 15, 69, 99–101
   Temple of Apollo 86, 99
   Temple of Janus 70–1
   Temple of Venus Victrix 15
Tibullus 93
time
   Augustus 72
   clock time 37
   eternity 85, 90, 94
   poetic 34–5, 40, 45–7
   task time 37, 41, 42
   temporal dislocation 87–91, 98, 142, 145; *see also* Foucault; heterotopia
   seasonality 22, 32, 36–7, 41–2, 90, 116
   and space 4, 25, 29–30, 33, 37–8, 40, 44–5
trompe l-oeil 78

Varro 32, 48, 64, 108
villa 18–19
   as political metaphor 113
Villa A at Oplontis
   atrium-core room series 117–20, 126, 130–1, 135
   east-wing room series 120–4, 130–2, 136–7
   exterior wall of room 78, 137–8
   garden paintings 117–23, 126, 131–8
   history 108–10
   location 107
viewing
   multiplicity of views 114–15, 119–21
   thematics of viewing 114, 139
Vesuvian eruption 109
Virgil 29–49, 52–4, 58–9, 88, 113–14
viridia 17, 130–1
Vitruvius 17
   monstra 97

wall painting
   Four Styles 78–81, 100, 109, 136
   framing features 78–81, 95–8, 103–5
   Pliny the Younger 129, 132
   see also sacral-idyllic

xystus 17
   Pliny the Younger 114, 124–8

Zanker, Paul 70, 76, 87

www.ingramcontent.com/pod-product-compliance
Lightning Source LLC
Chambersburg PA
CBHW062224300426
44115CB00012BA/2216